AF538348

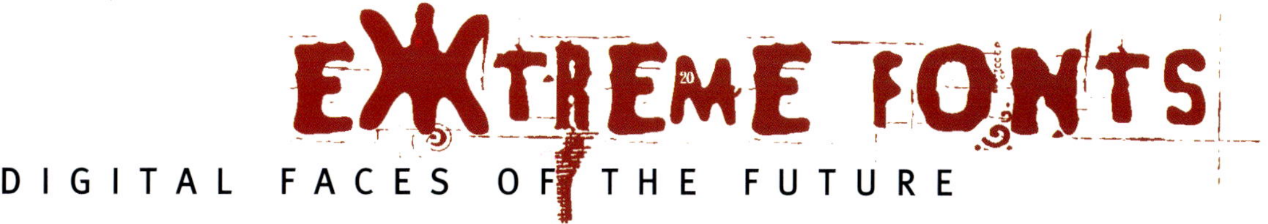

DIGITAL FACES OF THE FUTURE

by Spencer Drate and Jütka Salavetz
foreword by Pete McCracken
backword by Elliott Earls

Madison Square Press

E CD1, CD2 & MC FEATURING

BOLICAL BROTHERS, STOPPA &

PREY.

fonstiv

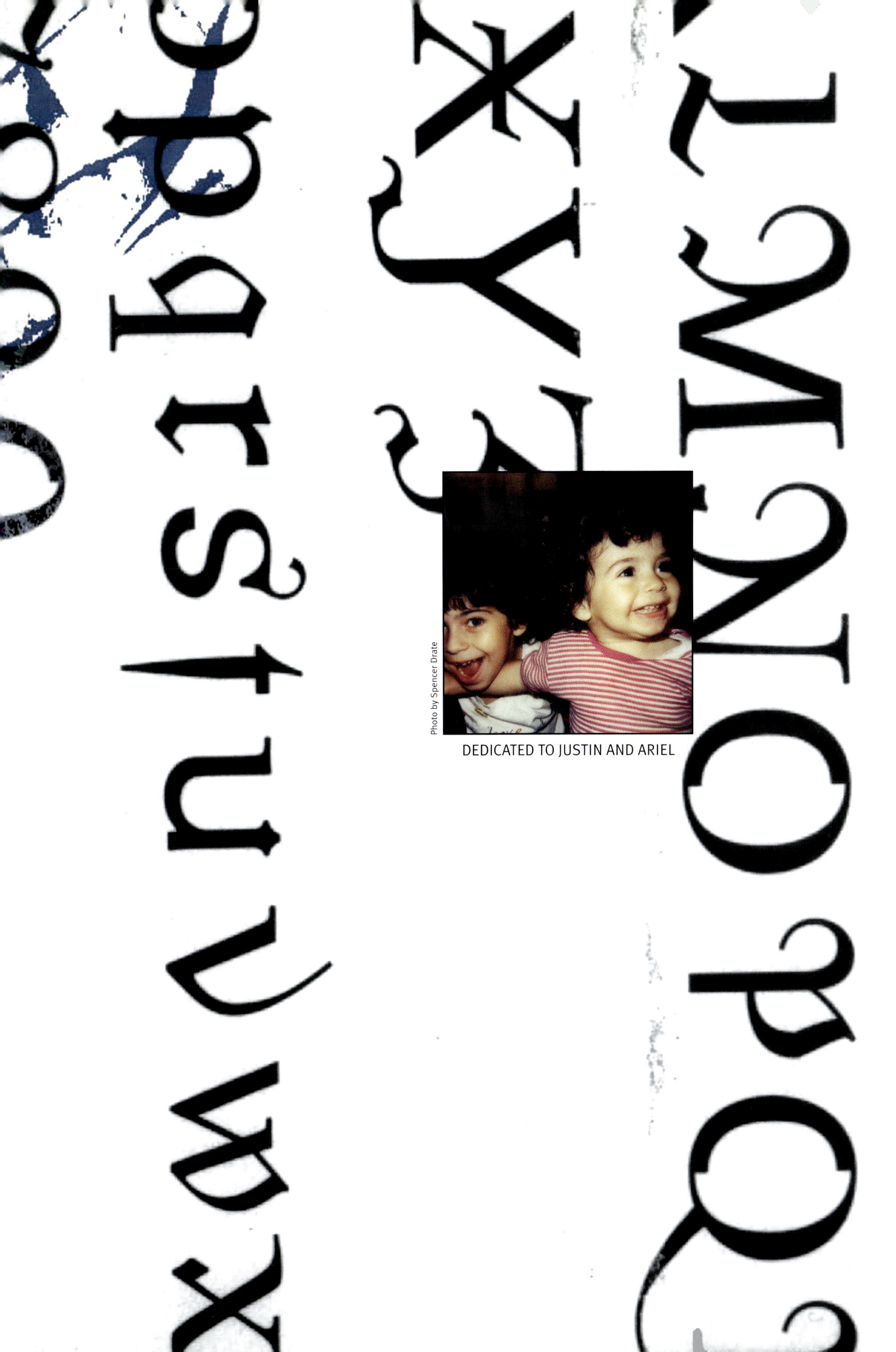

Photo by Spencer Drate

DEDICATED TO JUSTIN AND ARIEL

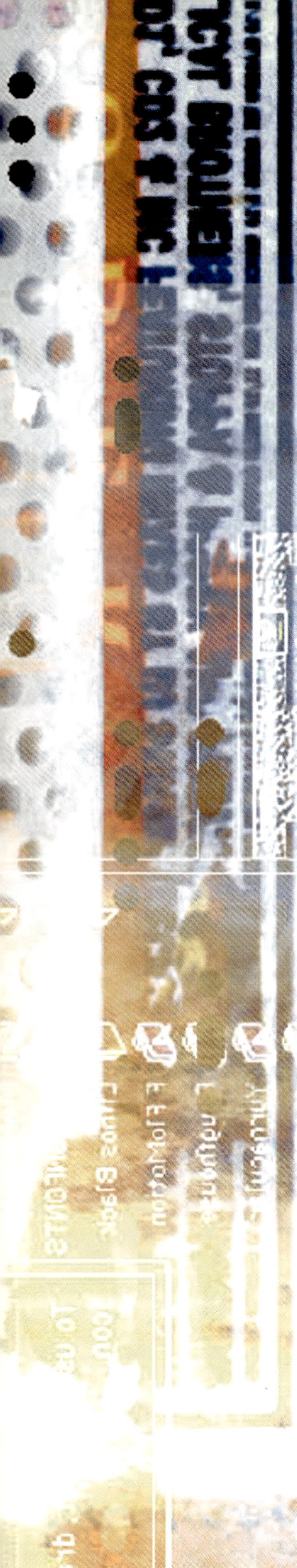

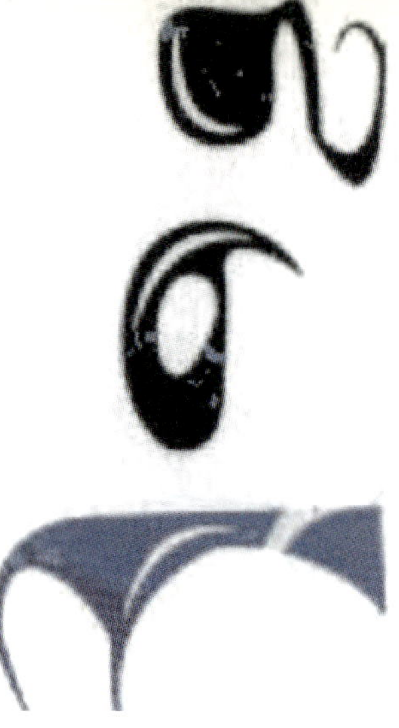

ACKNOWLEDGEMENTS:

We would like to thank Gerald McConnell and Madison Square Press for the vision. Justin and Ariel for inspiration. Ned Davis, Tom Olejar, [T-26], Growingstudio. All that contributed to this great type book. All typefaces and typeheads, and Theres Wegmann, Sean and Katie.

EXTREME FONTS

Digital Faces of the Future

ISBN 0-942604-74-1
Library of Congress Catalog Card Number 98-067524

Cover and book concept design: Sean Mosher-Smith and Slow Hearth studio inc.
Design and layout: Theres Wegmann (www.trans-form.net)

Distributed in North America to the trade and art markets by:
North Light Books
an imprint of F/W Publications, Inc.
1507 Dana Avenue
Cincinnati, Ohio 45207
1-800/289-0963

Distributed throughout the rest of the world by:
Hearst Books International
1350 Avenue of the Americas
New York, New York 10019

Published by:
Madison Square Press
10 East 23rd Street
New York, New York 10010
Fax: (212) 979-2207, Phone: (212) 505-0950

Printed in Hong Kong

Table of Contents

Key for Fonts

- ✖ Font Name
- ■ Designer
- ▲ Released by

Key for graphics

- ● Name of Piece
- ■ Designer
- ✖ Font Name
- ★ Client
- ◆ Photographer / Illustrator

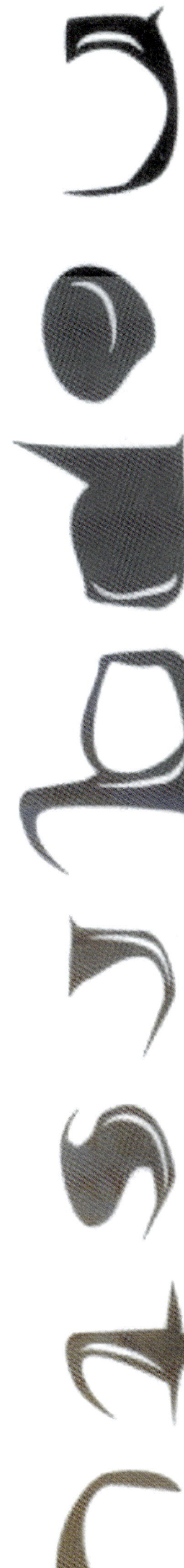

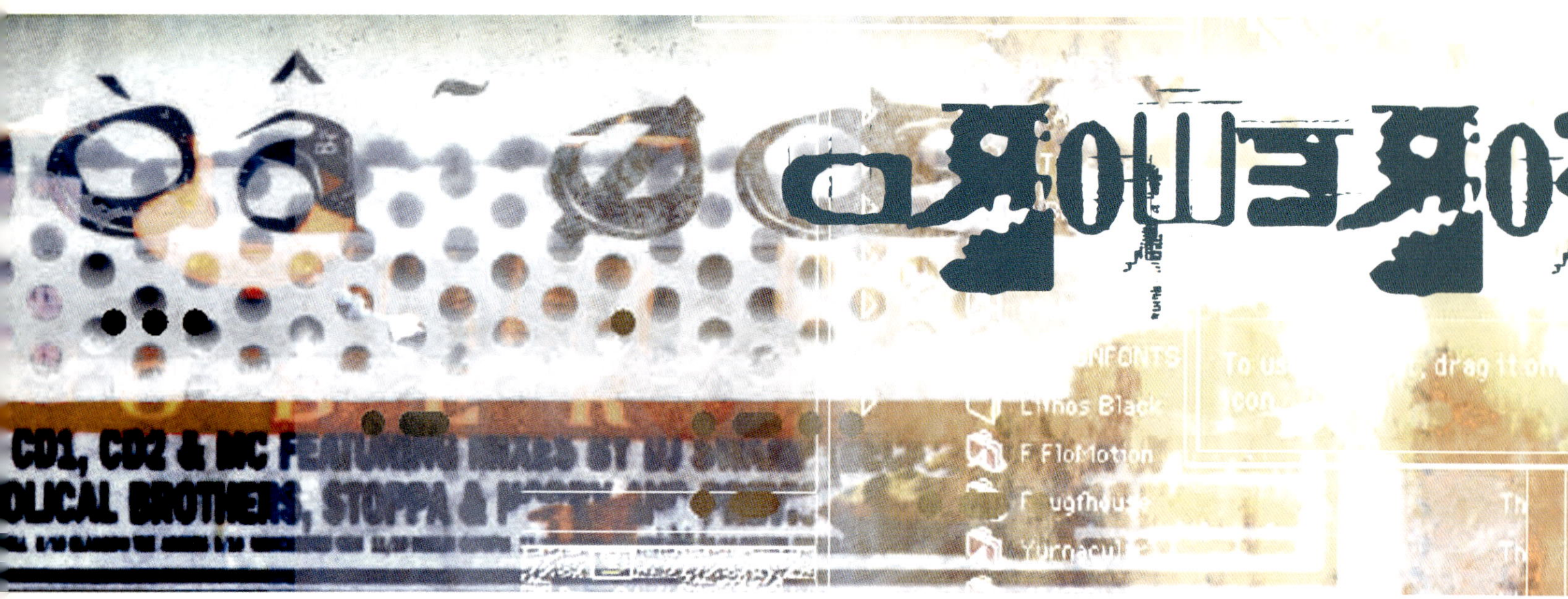
CD1, CD2 & MC
OLICAL BROTHERS, STOPPA &
Lithos Black
F FloMotion

This ain't no type polemic. And it ain't about pretty faces no more.

Type has been twisted, pulled, kicked, degraded, abused, dissolved, punched, whacked, puked, shat and regenerated. Where is the integrity in that? I have more respect for a person who can piss out their name in the snow than someone who runs filters over their words.

The amount of typejunk that's being generated all over the world is overwhelming. Advancements in technology in the last two decades have glorified a field that by its very nature should put anybody to sleep sitting around discussing it at dinner. Has this caused the industry to think it can master every artistic field with a wave of a magic hand?

What bugs most these days are not the type-enthusiasts, the type-wannabes, the typegeeks, or stereotypes--it's the pedantic type-mavens that are sitting around self-amusing themselves with home movies they're meticulously splicing together with pseudo-intellectual friends and then calling their self-indulgent shit art. (Please keep the hobbies in the garage or go back to school.)

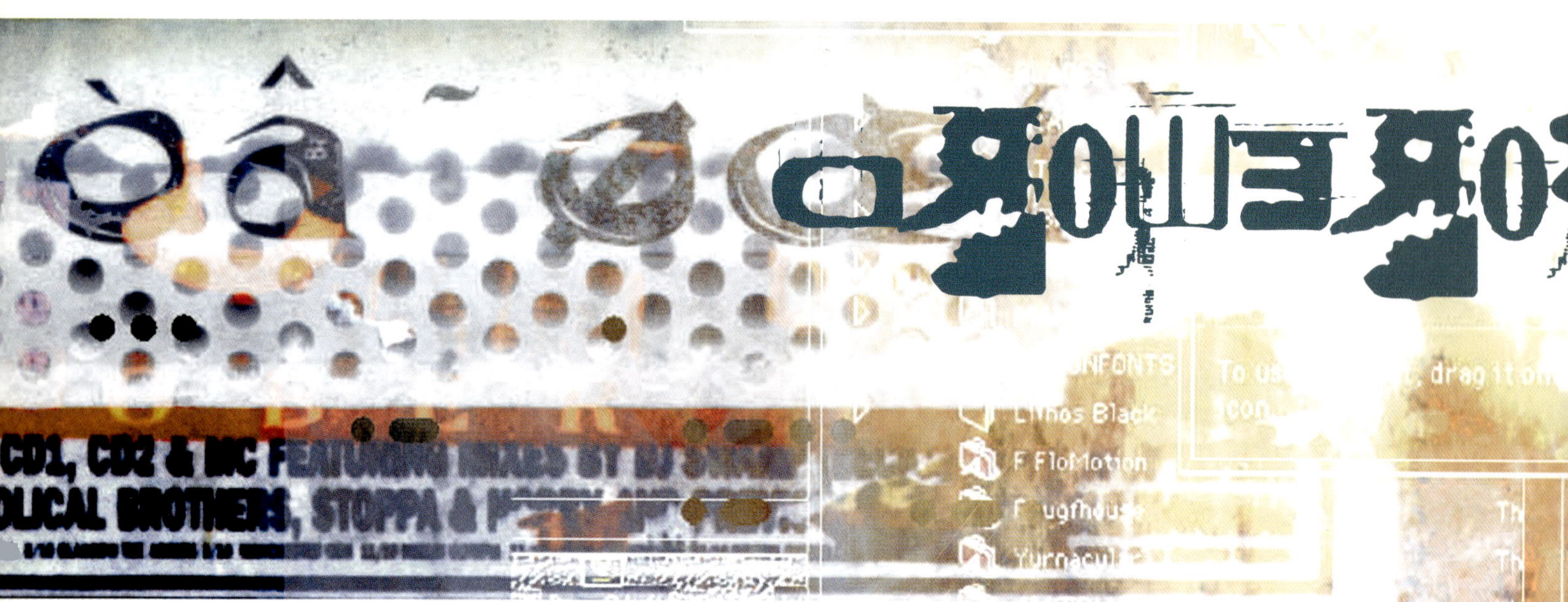
CD1, CD2 & MC FEATURING
STOPPA &
F FloMotion

The divided attention within our discipline is caused by the accelerated speed of our lives overloading our ability to tackle just one problem with a clear mind. We are catapulting ourselves into the Future, desperately trying to do more in one day then we should, or could desperately do a decade ago. The work overall within the industry suffers.

I challenge anyone calling him or herself a typographer to sit down and draw one typeface without interruption for as long as it takes and if the prodigy is ugly just start a new face.

There is a handful of typographers worldwide who have dedicated themselves, their families and their lives to cutting new faces. You'll see some of them in this book; others' work you'll never see printed. Their designs are unique and refreshing. Most of the celebrated type stars have long since exhausted their ideas and type gurus have passed away.

As a sculptor sculps, a writer writes, a philosopher philosophizes, a director directs, and a photographer photographs--a typographer should type.

Crack

1

ABCDEFGHIJK
LMNOPQRSTUVWXYZ
abcdefghijklmnopqrstuvwxyz
0123456789
{@®©¢Á*$Ñ%&?}

2

ABCDEFGHIJK
LMNOPQRSTUVWXYZ
0123456789
[Ⓐ®©¢Á*$Ñ%&?]

pablo a. medina

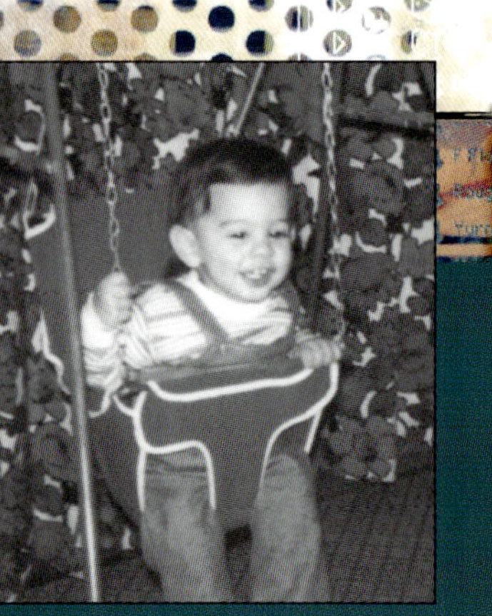

My ideas are discovered in Chinese fast food joints and used bookstores. They come from the missing "H" in "Chicken C_ow Mein" and the font used as page numbers in a 1926 book worth 50 cents. It is in these instances where humanity breathes and culture is expressed in its purest form. As a designer, culture at its most sincere is what I'm after. Without it, I am limited to using a palm tree as an image for a Cuban novel or a long windy highway to convey the Internet. My goal is to stay as far away from the "stock photography" aesthetic (with its offensively insincere imagery) as possible and to explore thoroughly the culture of the everyday in order to express it as sincerely and uniquely as possible.

Pablo A. Medina was born in Washington, D.C., of Cuban-Colombian parents. He studied fine arts and design at Pratt Institute and has been a graphic designer in New York City for the last four years. His work has appeared in a number of magazines and publications, among them *Idea* magazine, *Blue* magazine, and *Plazm*. A recent article in *How* magazine featured his work in font design. Most of his font designs are based on the unique signage he observes in the different Latin American neighborhoods of the New York area, and he has used storefront typography as a launching pad for a number of his alphabets.

1

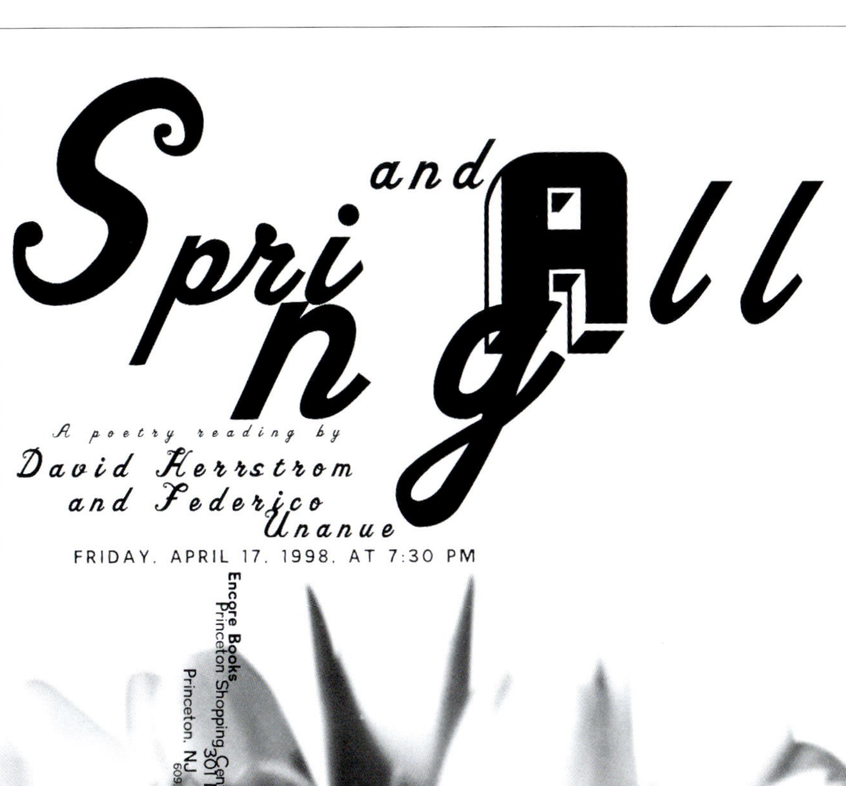

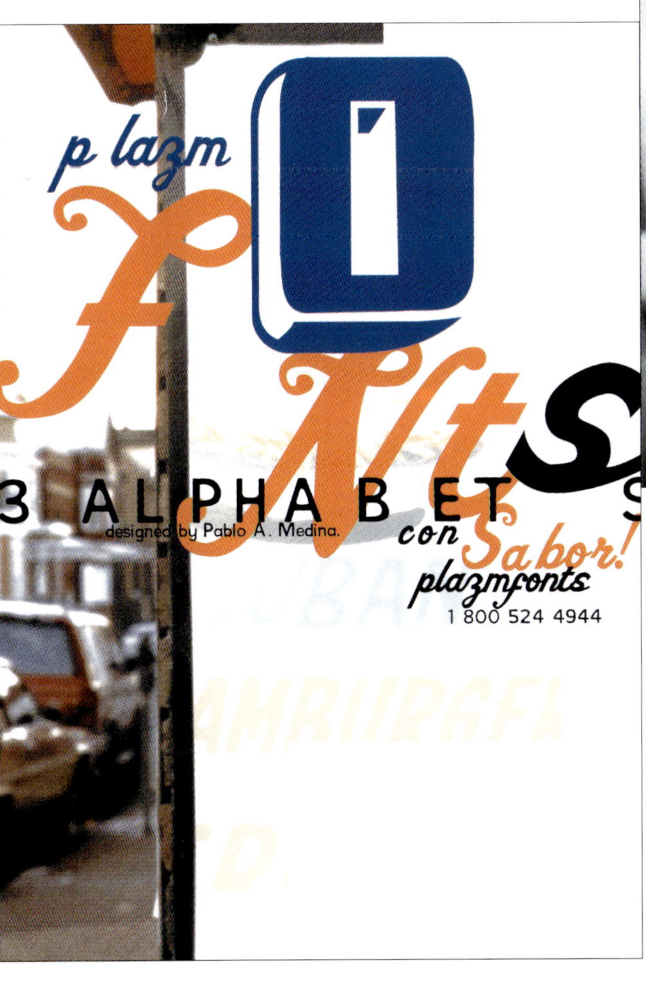

2

1 ✖ Vitrina
■ Pablo A. Medina
▲ Plazm Fonts + Pablo A. Medina

2 ✖ Cuba
■ Pablo A. Medina
▲ Plazm Fonts + Pablo A. Medina

1 ● Flyer for a poetry reading
■ Pablo A. Medina
✖ Vitrina, Cuba
◆ Katie Collins

2 ● Plazm Ad
■ Pablo A. Medina
✖ Vitrina, Cuba
★ Plazm magazine

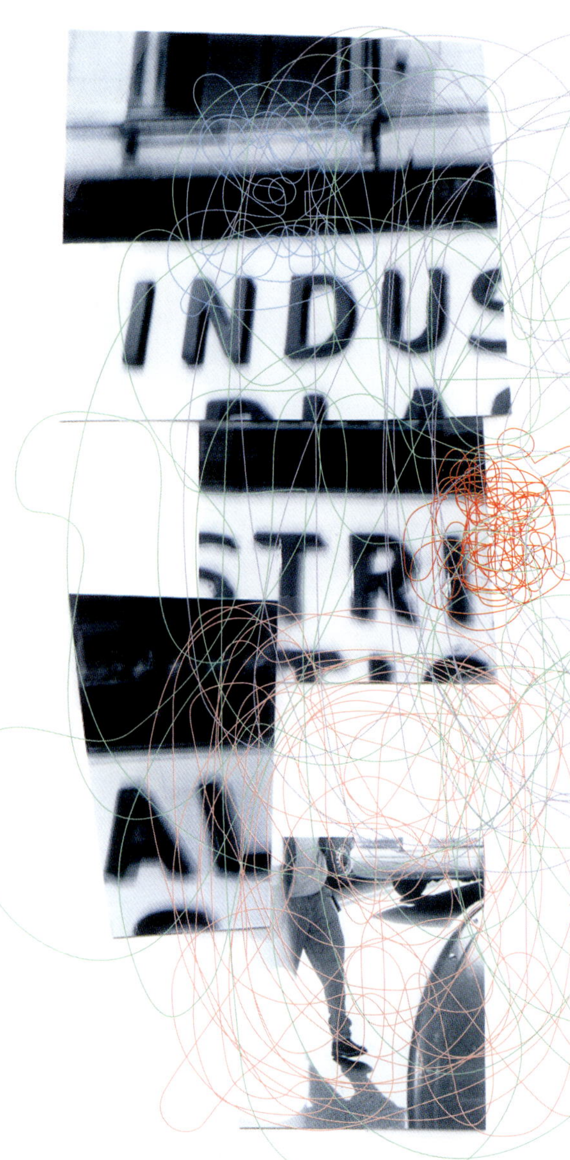

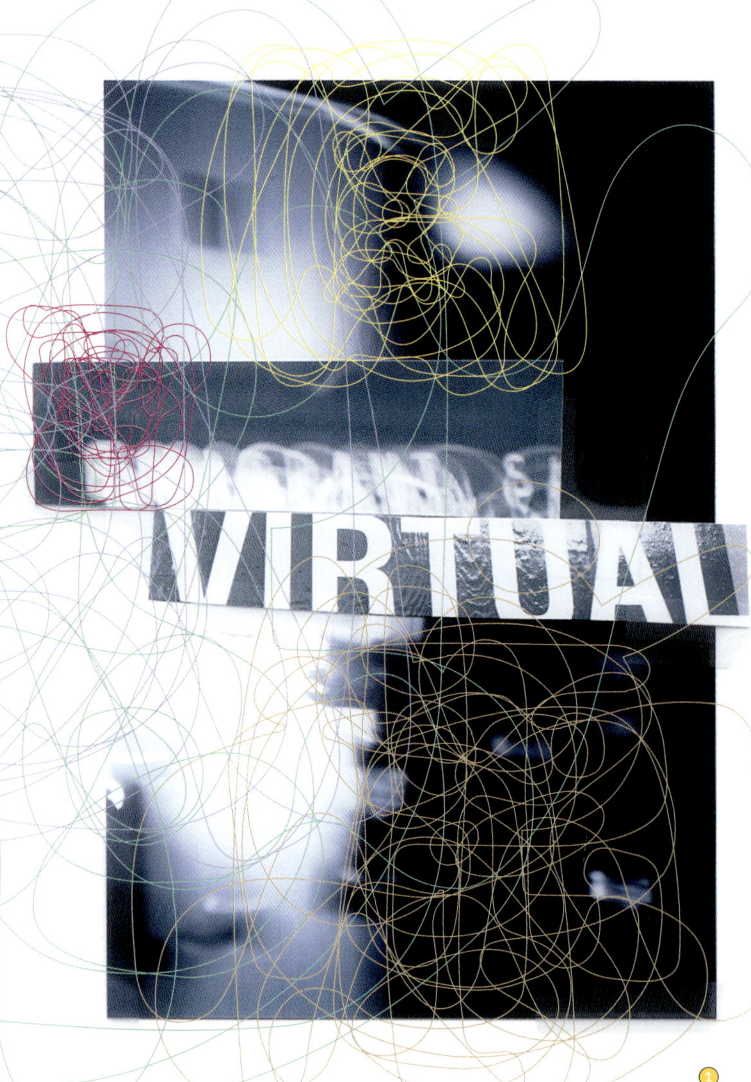

1

1

ABCDEFGHIJKLMNOPQRSTUVWXYZ
abcdefghijklmnopqrstuvwxyz
0123456789 (@¢$#✽%&)

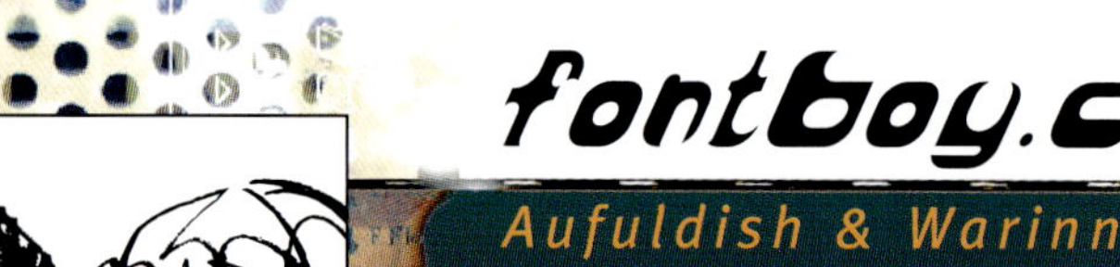

fontboy.com

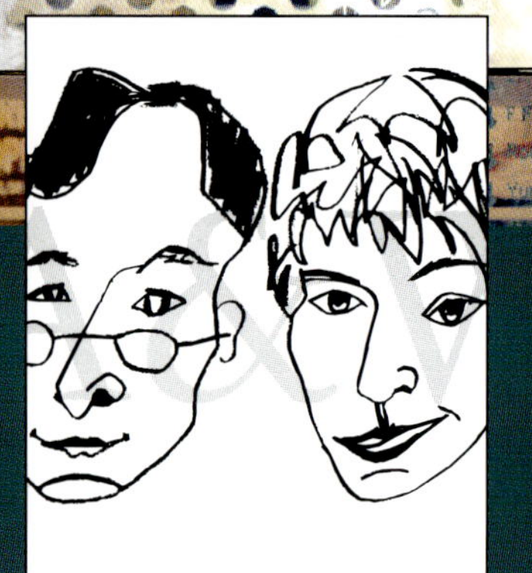

Aufuldish & Warinner

FontBoy.com was launched in the summer of 1995 to manufacture and distribute fonts designed by Bob Aufuldish and Kathy Warinner of the design office, Aufuldish & Warinner. The foundry maintains a Web site at www.fontboy.com with a secure storefront where fonts are available in Mac and Windows formats. The foundry has released fonts ranging from the quirky and handmade to the geometrically precise. The current direction of our work incorporates more classical elements into the fonts, simultaneously using process-oriented techniques to defy the designer's linear expectations. We try to stay focussed on what interests us rather than trying to chase trends. We are interested in the wide-open early 20th century modernism rather than the formulaic high modernism of the international style. Our motto is Baroque Modernism for the New Millennium.

Bob Aufuldish is a partner in Aufuldish & Warinner and an Affiliate Associate Professor at the California College of Arts and Crafts, where he teaches graphic design and typography and is Design Director of Sputnik CCAC, a student-staffed design office. He has designed and produced projects for clients such as SFMOMA, V2 Records, and Chronicle Books. He has participated in a number of exhibitions, including, Icons: Magnets of Meaning, at the San Francisco Museum of Modern Art. **Kathy Warinner** is the managing partner of Aufuldish & Warinner, where she has designed and produced projects for a wide variety of clients, including: packaging systems for The Nature Company and Smith & Hawken, advertising campaigns for Franklin Funds, corporate identity for Conari Press, and over 50 books and jacket designs for Chronicle Books, HarperCollins, Random House, and others. In addition, her illustrations have appeared on the cover of over 20 books.

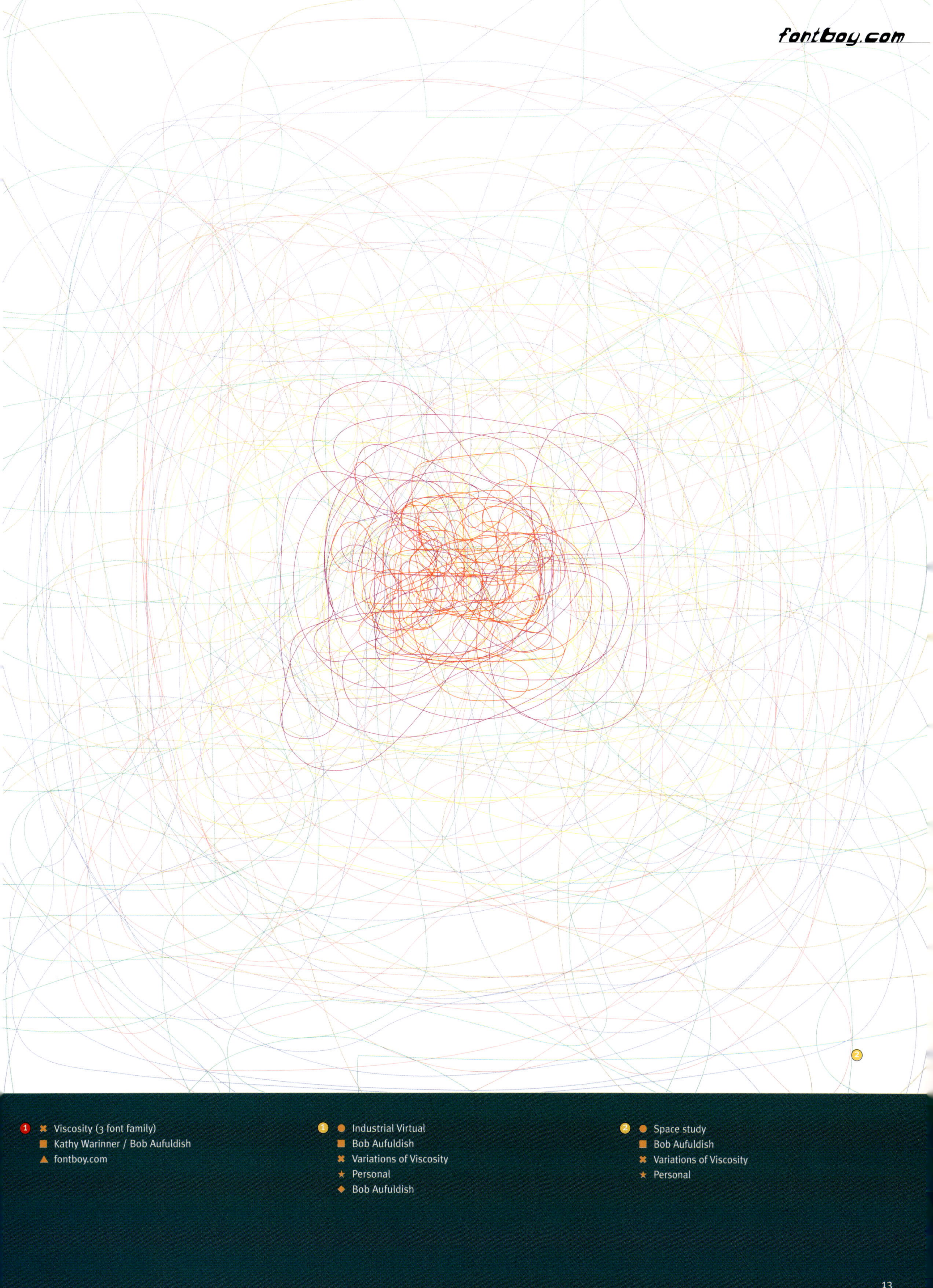

1 ✖ Viscosity (3 font family)
■ Kathy Warinner / Bob Aufuldish
▲ fontboy.com

1 ● Industrial Virtual
■ Bob Aufuldish
✖ Variations of Viscosity
★ Personal
◆ Bob Aufuldish

2 ● Space study
■ Bob Aufuldish
✖ Variations of Viscosity
★ Personal

2

ABCDEFGHIJKLMNOPQRSTUVWXYZ
abcdefghijklmnopqrstuvwxyz
0123456789
(@¢$#%&)

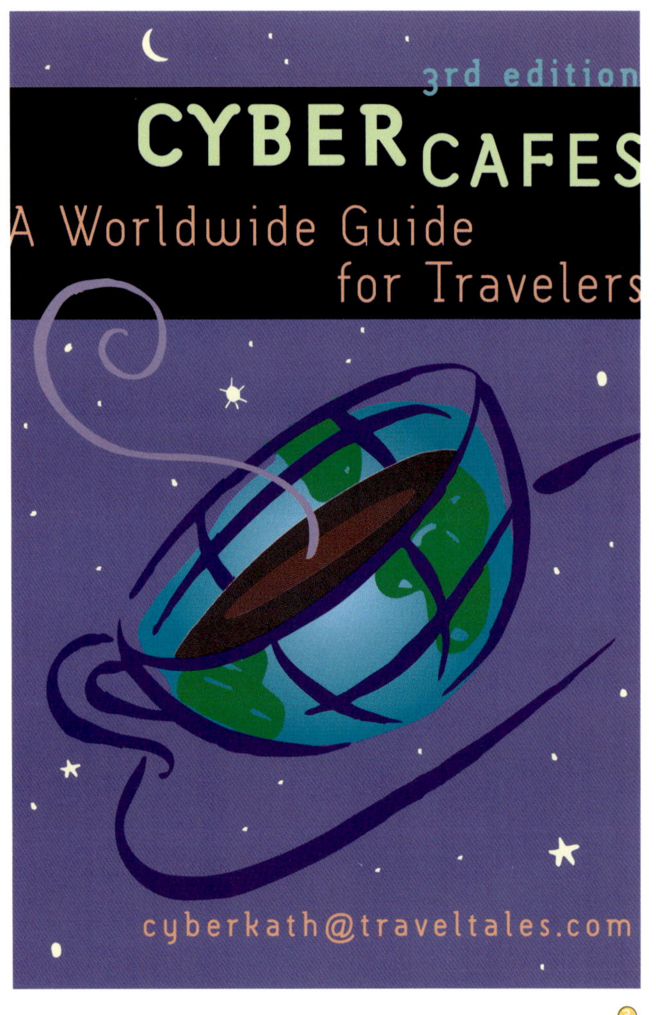

3

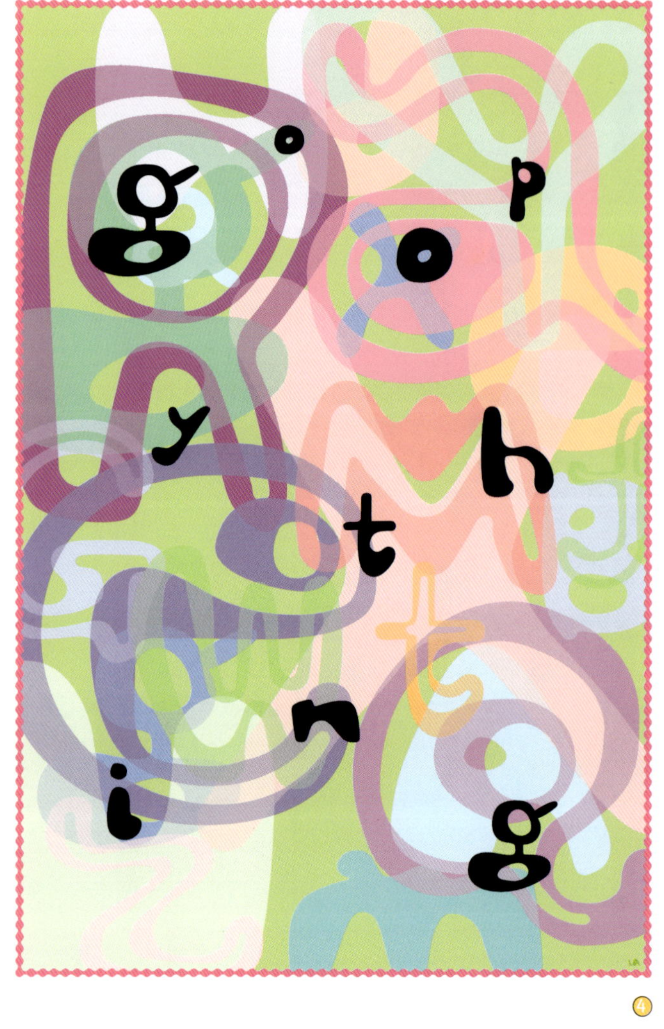

4

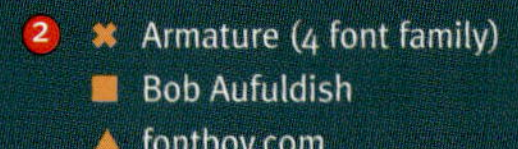
2 Armature (4 font family)
Bob Aufuldish
fontboy.com

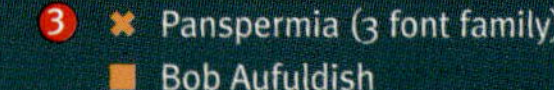
3 Panspermia (3 font family)
Bob Aufuldish
fontboy.com

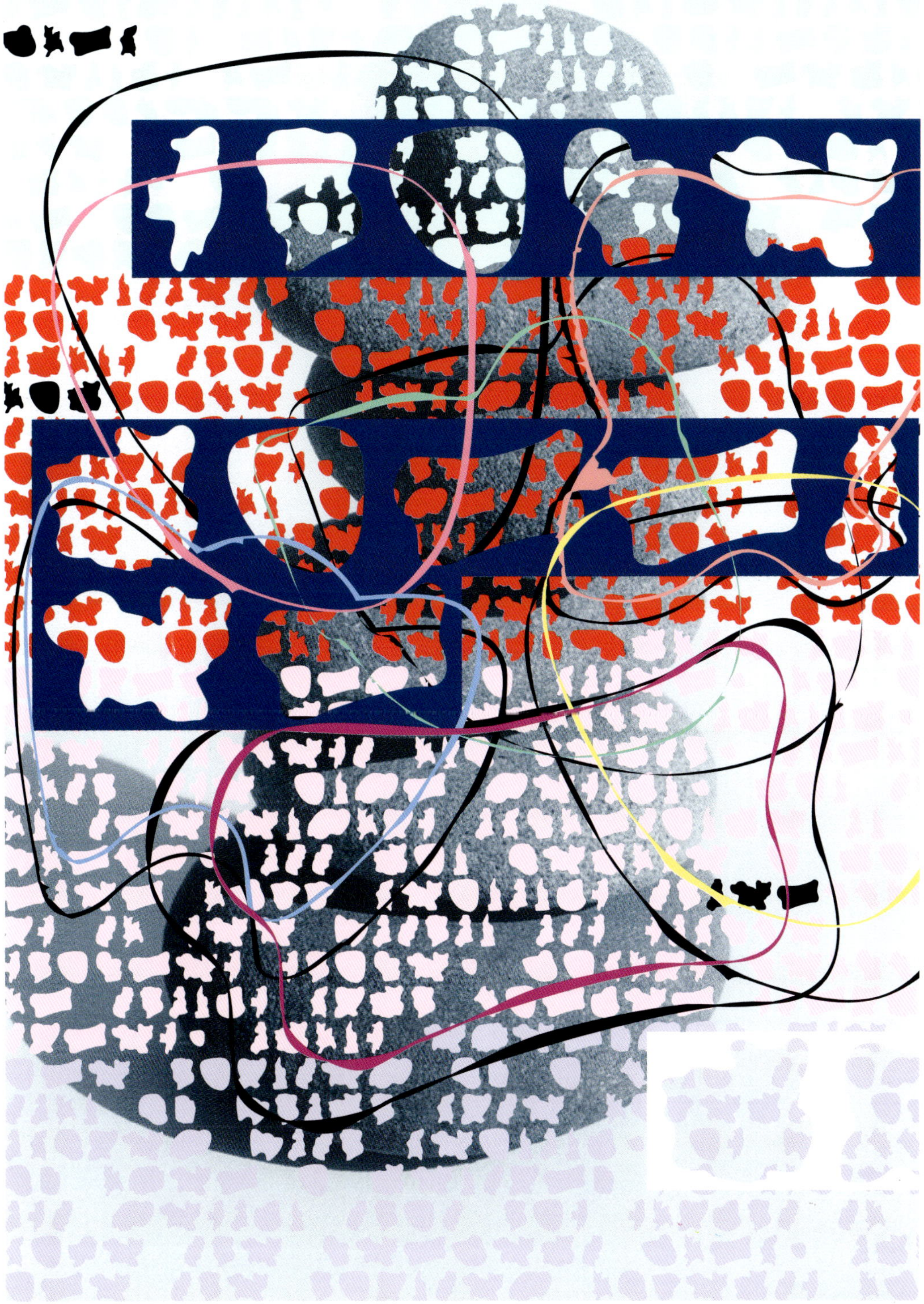

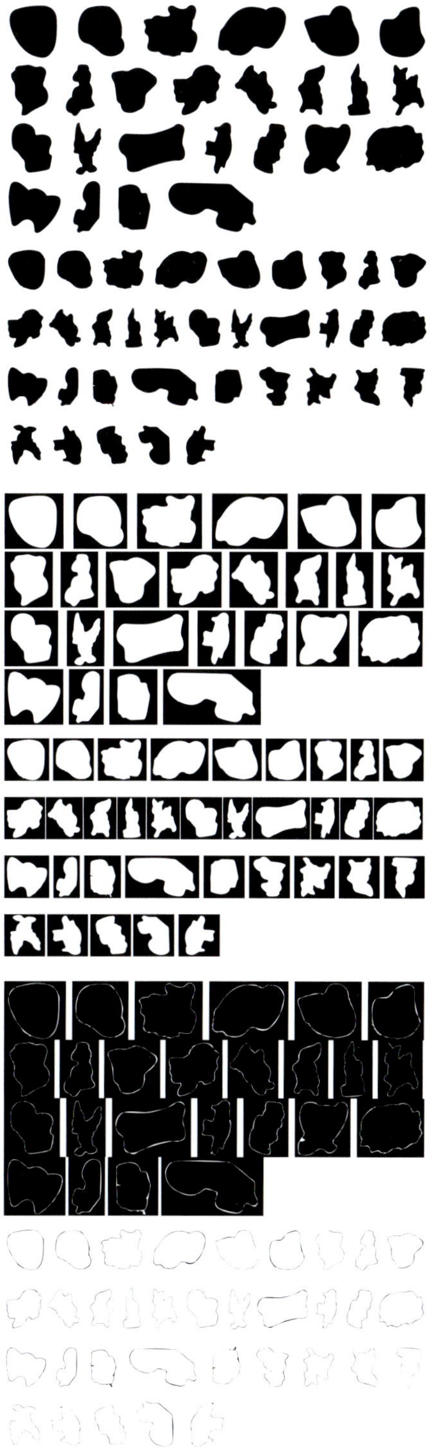

3

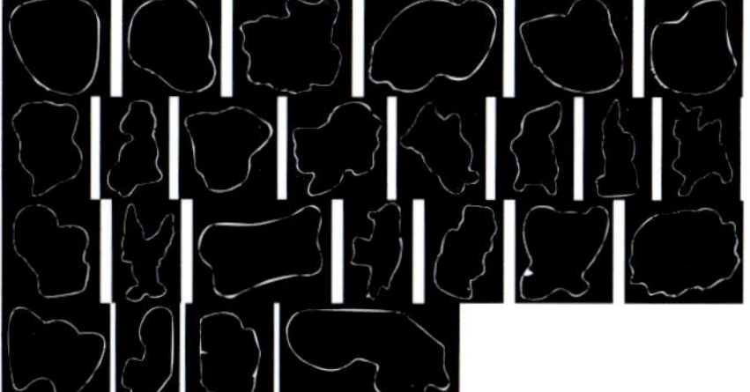

5

3
- Cybercafes book cover
- Kathy Warinner
- Variations of Armature
- 10 Speed Press
- Kathy Warinner

4
- Goopy Thing
- Bob Aufuldish
- Variations of Viscosity
- Personal

5
- Rosetta Stones
- Bob Aufuldish
- Variations of Panspermia
- Personal
- Bob Aufuldish

ABCDEFGHIJKLMNOP
QRSTUVWXYZ
abcdefghijklmnop
qrstuvwxyz
0123456789 (@¢$#%&)

4

5

ABCDEFGHIJKLMNOP
QRSTUVWXYZ
abcdefghijklmnopq
rstuvwxyz
0123456789 (@¢$#%&)

ABCDEFGHIJKLMNOP
QRSTUVWXYZ
abcdefghijklmnopq
rstuvwxyz
0123456789 (@¢$#%&)

4 Whiplash (3 font family)
Bob Aufuldish
fontboy.com

5 Punctual (6 font family)
Bob Aufuldish
fontboy.com

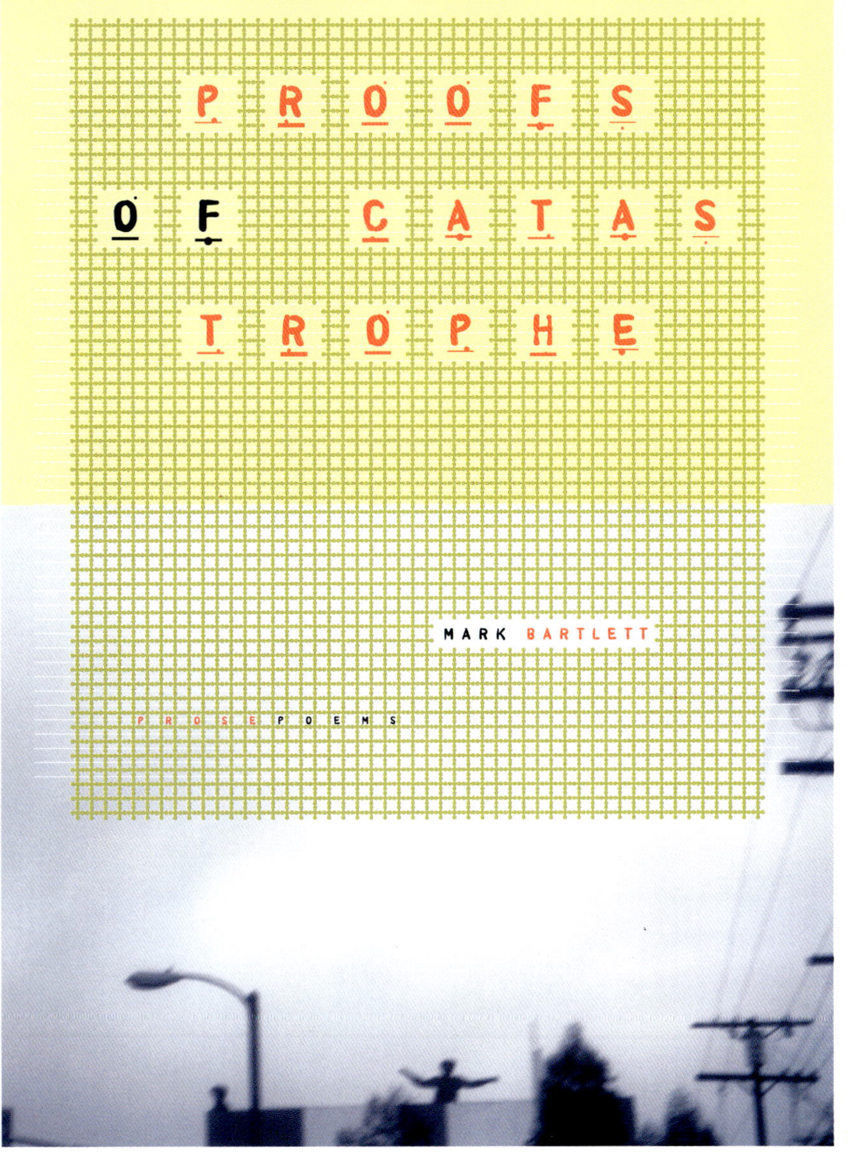

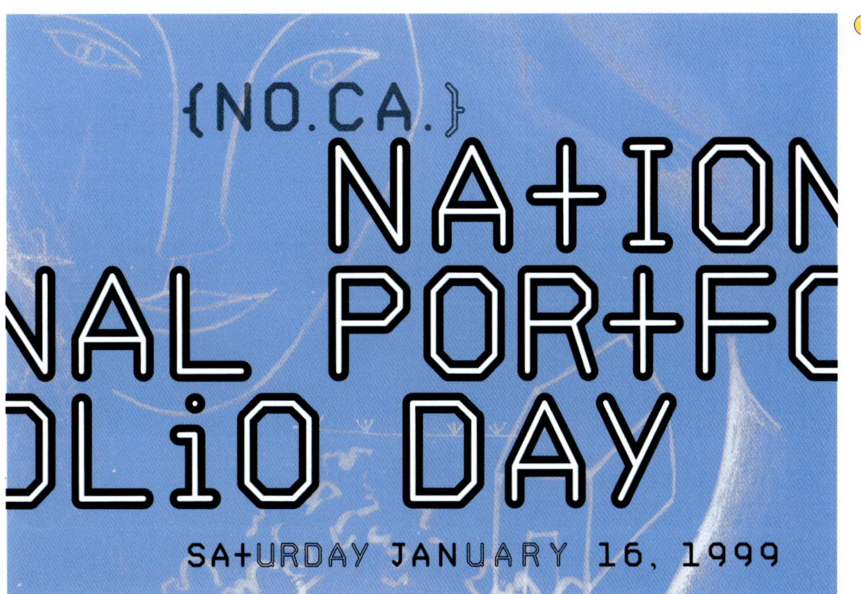

6
- ● Proofs of Catastrophe book cover
- ■ Bob Aufuldish
- ✖ Variations of Whiplash
- ★ Mark Bartlett
- ◆ Bob Aufuldish

7
- ● Portfolio Day poster (detail)
- ■ Bob Aufuldish
- ✖ Variations of Punctual
- ★ California College of Arts and Crafts Office of Enrollment Services
- ◆ Kathy Warinner

ABCDEFGHIJKLMNOPQRSTUVWXYZ
abcdefghijklmnopqrstuvwxyz
0123456789
([!@®©$£¿?%&*])

1

ABCDEFGHIJKLMNOPQRSTUVWXYZ
abcdefghijklmnopqrstuvwxyz
0123456789
({!@®©$&?&})

2

ABCDEFGHIJKLMNOPQRSTUVWXYZ
abcdefghijklmnopqrstuvwxyz
0123456789
([«!@®©$£¢?%&*»])

3

ABCDEFGHIJKLMNOPQRSTUVWXYZ
abcdefghijklmnopqrstuvwxyz
0123456789
([«!@®©$£¢?%&*»])

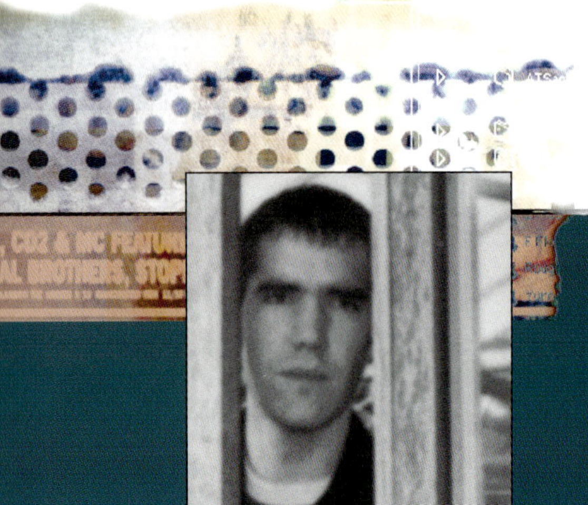

darren scott

The communication power of typography is beyond imagination; even on the level of basic text, visual language can evoke powerful emotion. This is without taking into consideration the multiple levels of connotation that can be developed by carefully selecting a typeface or creating an inspirational piece of design. If there is a philosophy, I think it should be simply consideration.

I am 23 years old and it is barely 3 years since I graduated from Salford University in Manchester with a B.A. Design Practice in 1996. A Manchester lad born and bred, I avoided the bright lights of London and opted to stay in the North. In late 1996 I was installed as Designer and Typographic Consultant at McCann-Erickson Manchester, a member of the world's largest global adverstising network. Working for such a large company gives me the opportunity to experience all aspects of the industry and the benefits of dealing with international blue chip clients. Designing fonts was something I developed as a student. I was asked to develop a typeface for FUSE 15 [Cities] which led to Berlin[er] my first digital font. The love affair with visible language developed from there. Since then I have developed several fonts which are distributed by [T-26] in Chicago. I came across [T-26] when they lectured in the UK and the relationship grew from there. I was impressed by their dedication to promotional material.

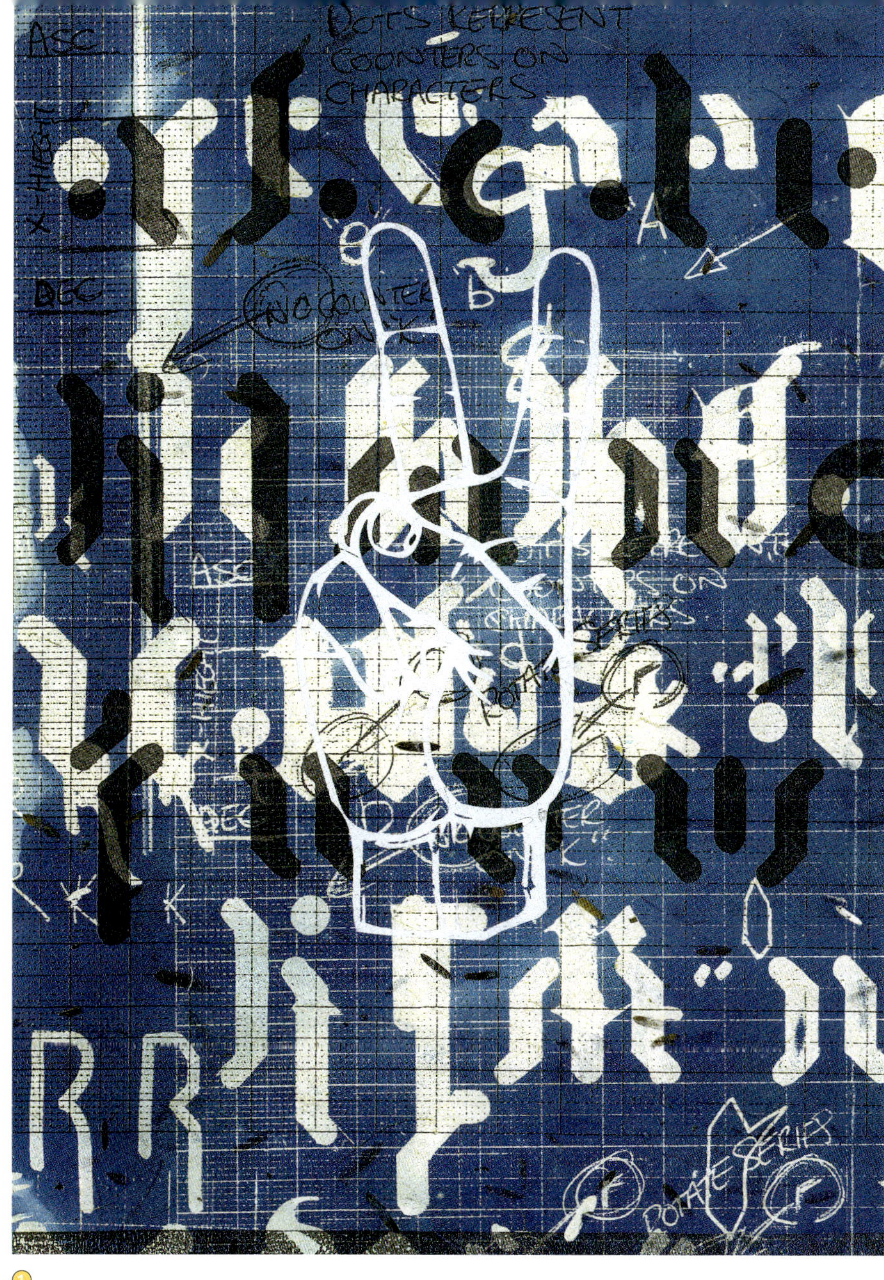

1

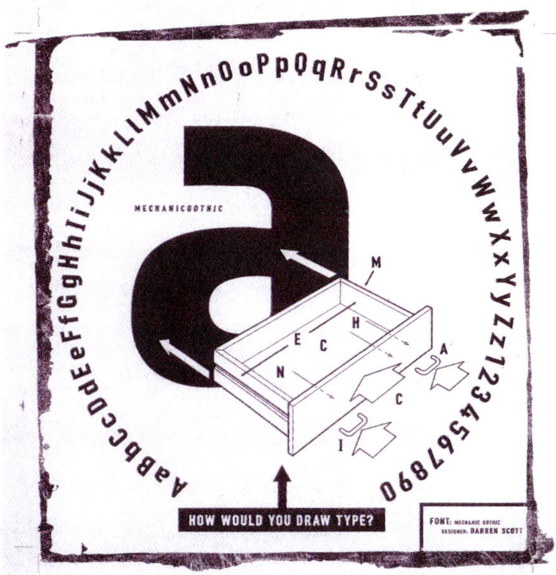

2

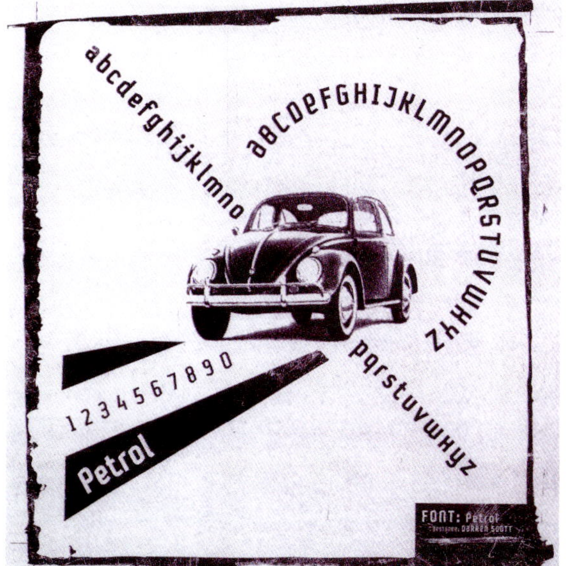

3

1 ✖ Berlin[er] Regular / Berlin[er] Gothic
■ Darren Scott
▲ [T-26] and FUSE

2 ✖ Mechanic Gothic Regular (a 2 weight family)
■ Darren Scott
▲ [T-26]

3 ✖ Petrol Medium (an 8 weight family)
■ Darren Scott
▲ [T-26]

1 ● Berlin[er] Poster
■ Darren Scott
✖ Berlin[er] and handrawn lettering
★ Darren Scott

2 ● Mechanic Gothic Exhibition Piece
■ Darren Scott
✖ Mechanic Gothic
★ ITC

3 ● Petrol Exhibition Piece
■ Darren Scott
✖ Petrol
★ ITC

4

ABCDEFGHIJKLMNOPQRSTUVWXYZ
abcdefghijklmnopqrstuvwxyz
0123456789
([«!@®©$£¢?%&*»])

ABCDEFGHIJKLMNOPQRSTUVWXYZ
abcdefghijklmnopqrstuvwxyz
0123456789
([!@$£¢?%&*])

5

ABCDEFGHIJKLMNOPQRSTUVWXYZ
abcdefghijklmnopqrstuvwxyz
0123456789
([!@$£¢?%&])

4 ✖ TSI Aggregate Regular (a 4 weight family)
■ Darren Scott
▲ unreleased

5 ✖ Rub On - Thin / Rub On - Lite (a 4 weight family)
■ Darren Scott
▲ [T-26]

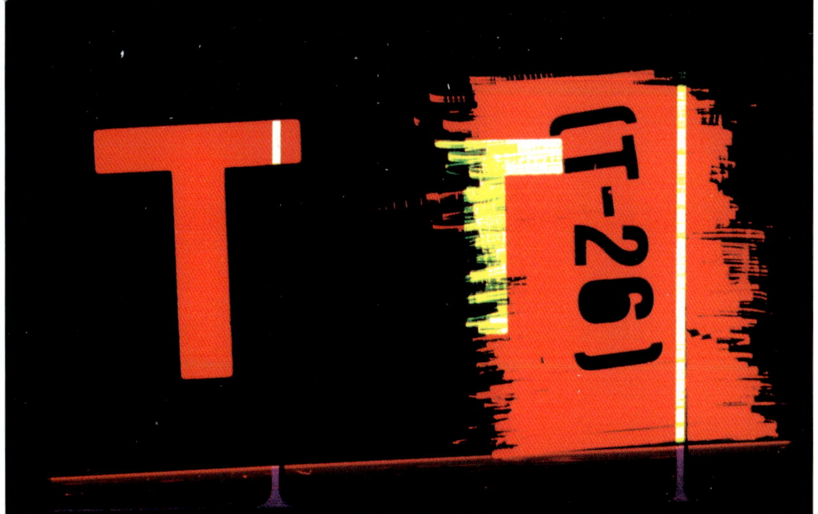

4

5

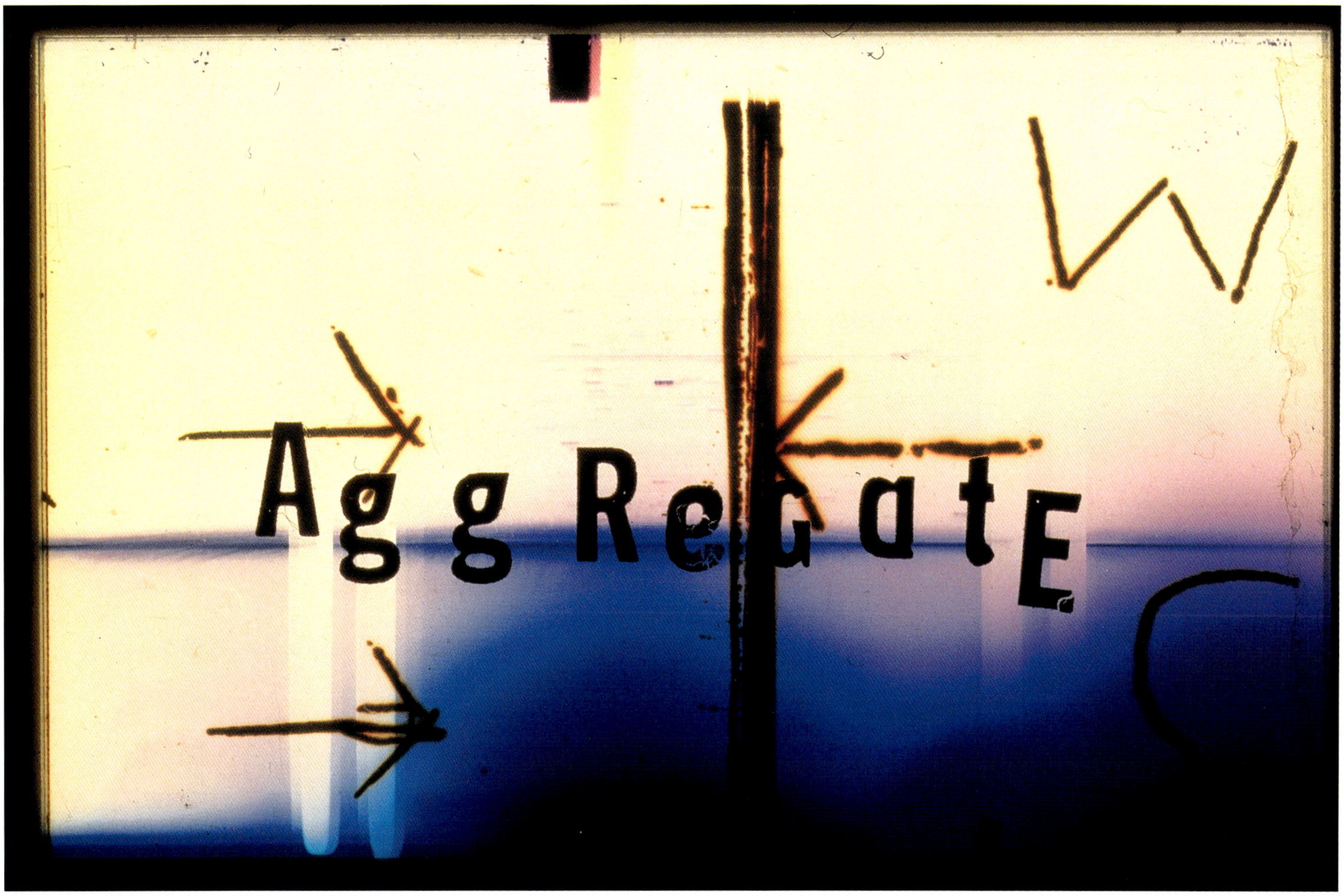

4 ● T-26 Bizcard Reverse
■ Darren Scott
✖ Rub On (T-26) and hand lettering
★ T-26

5 ● TSI Movie Still
■ Darren Scott
✖ TSI Aggregate / Rub-down manipulated
★ TSI Font Foundry

ABCDEFGHIJKLMNOPQRSTUVWXYZ
abcdefghijklmnopqrstuvwxyz
0123456789
([«!@®©$£¢?%&*»])

6

ABCDEFGHIJKLMNOPQRSTUVWXYZ
abcdefghijklmnopqrstuvwxyz
0123456789
([!@®©$£¢?%&*»])

7

ABCDEFGHIJKLM
NOPQRSTUVWXYZ
abcdefghijklm
nopqrstuvwxyz
0123456789
([!@®©$£¢?%&])

8

ABCDFGHIJKLM
NOPQRSTUVWXYZ
abcdefghijklm
nopqrstuvwxyz
0123456789
([«!@®©$£¢?%&*»])

6 ✖ Launderette-Rinse / Launderette-Wash (a 3 weight family)
■ Darren Scott
▲ [T-26]

7 ✖ Circuit
■ Darren Scott
▲ [T-26]

8 ✖ Hydrate (a 10 weight family)
■ Darren Scott
▲ unreleased

ABCDEFG
HIJKLMN
OPQRSTU
VWXYZ
0123456789
([«!@®©$£¢?%&*»])

9

ABCDEFGHIJKLMNOPQRSTUVWXYZ
ABCDEFGHIJKLMNOPQRSTUVWXYZ
Ø123456789
[!@®©$£¢?&°]

ABCDEFGHIJKLMNOPQRSTUVWXYZ
ABCDEFGHIJKLMNOPQRSTUVWXYZ
0123456789
[!@®©$£¢?&°]

10

9 Retoric Regular (a 2 weight family)
Darren Scott
[T-26]

10 Bad Angel - Sinner / Bad Angel -Saint
Darren Scott
[T-26]

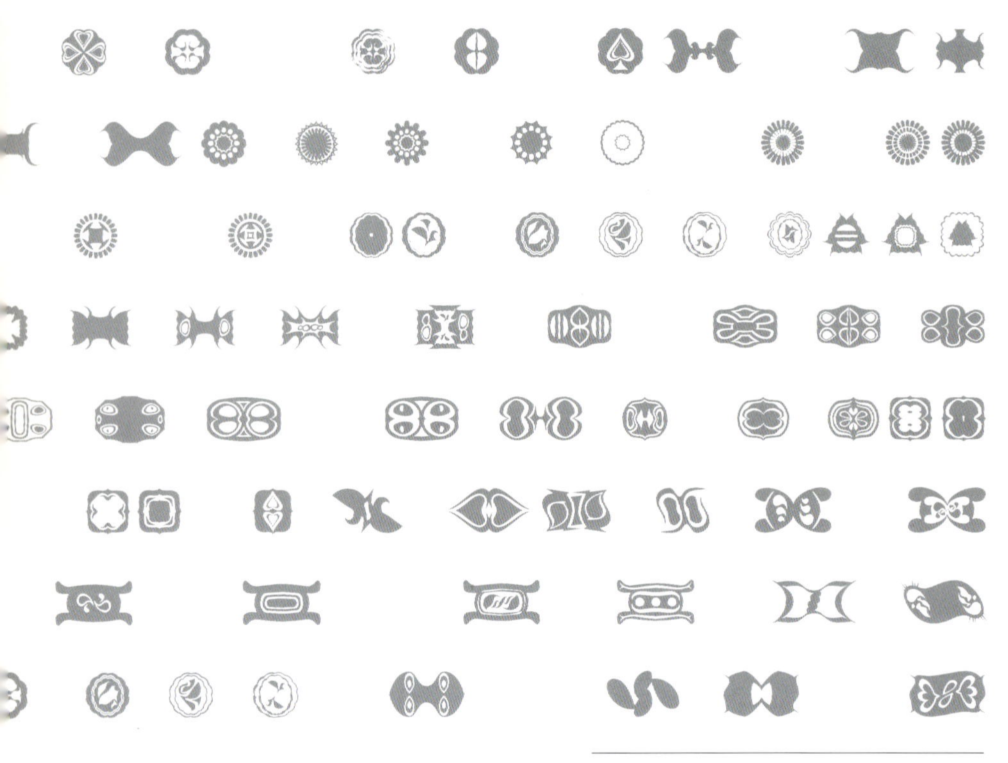

1

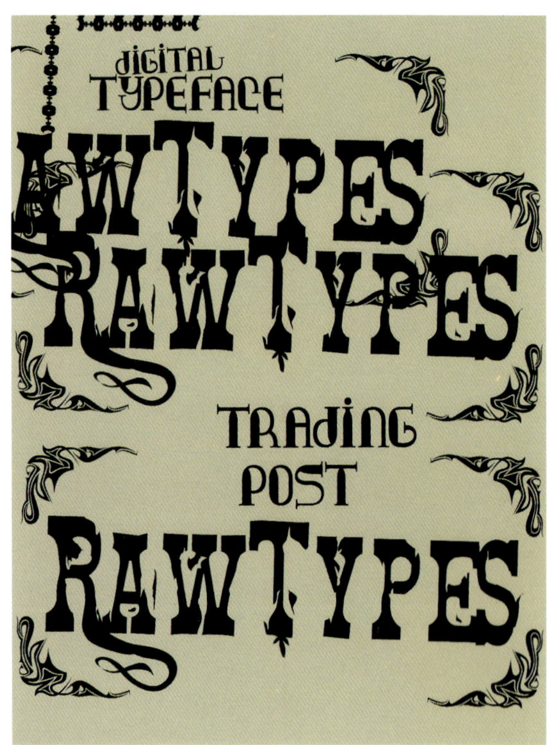

1

ABCDEFGHIJKLMNOPQRSTUVWXYZ
0123456789 (AT¢$NO.%AND)

2

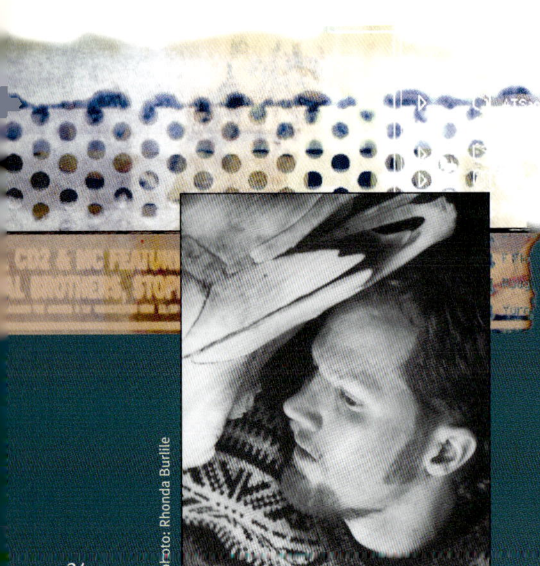

photo: Rhonda Burlile

marcus burlile

Burlile Design / Raw Types

Most of my fonts are derived from personal interests and emotions. I believe a typeface is an appendage of the designer. The type style alone should convey the theme. The type is the rendering. It should evoke an emotional response, which determines how complex, structured, or organic the font design will be.

Burlile studied art, design and typography in La Jolla, California. His pursuit of self-exploration with type and lettering have yielded over seventy digital fonts featured worldwide by such type foundries as [T-26], Fontworks UK, Fonthaus, Precision Type, AGFA, Atomic Type, Monotype, Type USA, Plazm Fonts and RawTypes. Type experiments can also be seen expressed within his fine art paintings. As a design consultant and freelance art director for a vast portfolio of clients, his work has appeared within national as well as international magazines and typography award books.

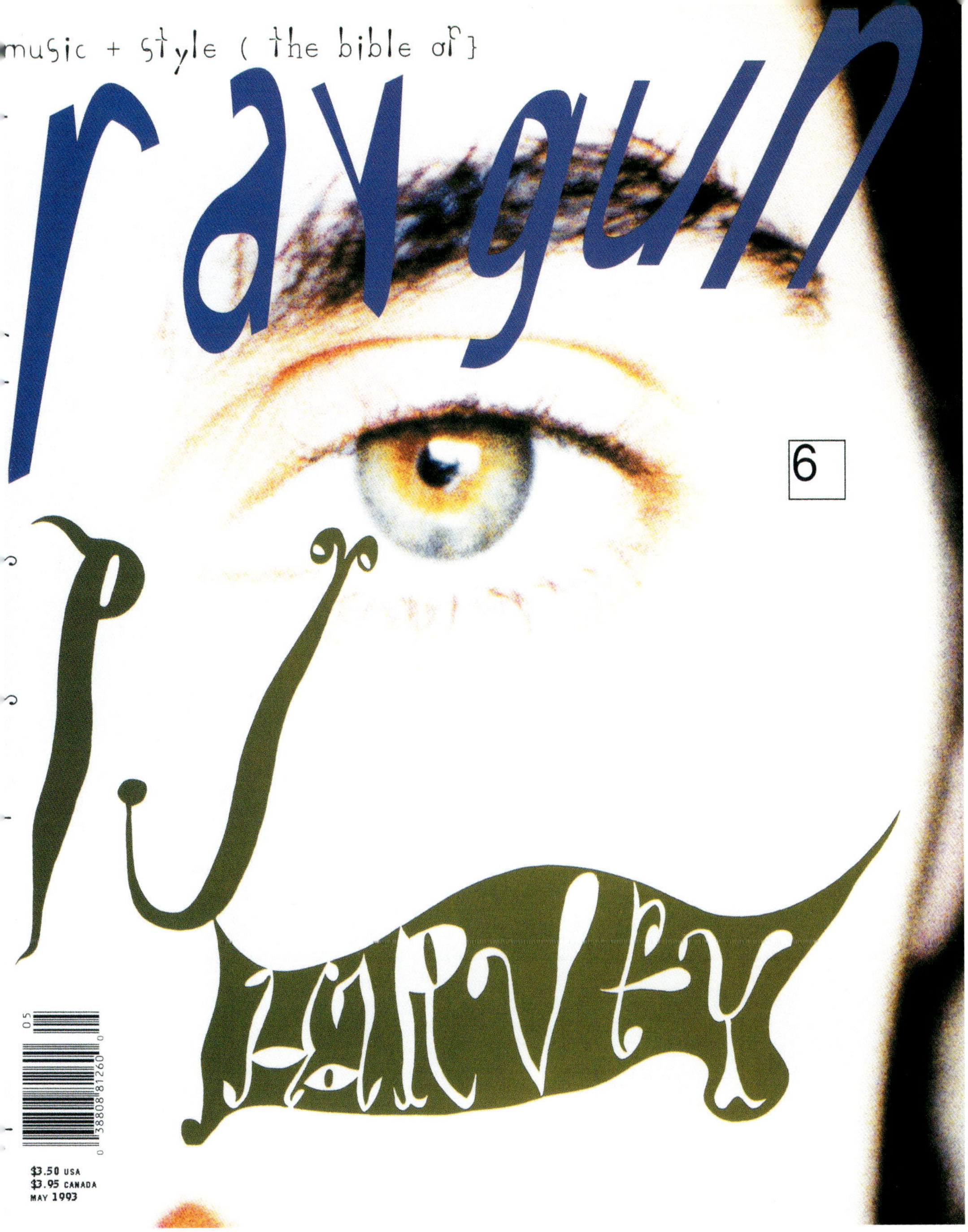

music + style (the bible of }

raygun

6

PJ Harvey

$3.50 USA
$3.95 CANADA
MAY 1993

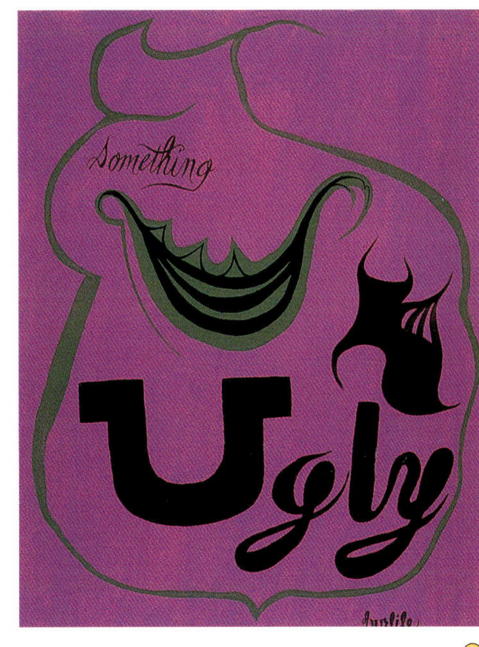

abcdefghijklmnopqrstuvwxyz
abcdefghijklmnopqrstuvwxyz
0123456789 (@¢$#⊕ and)

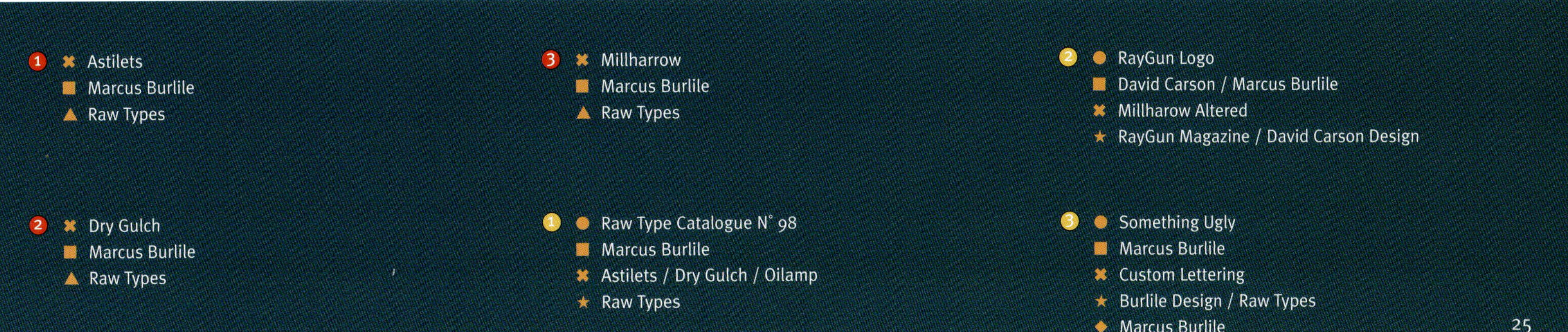

1 ✖ Astilets
■ Marcus Burlile
▲ Raw Types

2 ✖ Dry Gulch
■ Marcus Burlile
▲ Raw Types

3 ✖ Millharrow
■ Marcus Burlile
▲ Raw Types

1 ● Raw Type Catalogue N° 98
■ Marcus Burlile
✖ Astilets / Dry Gulch / Oilamp
★ Raw Types

2 ● RayGun Logo
■ David Carson / Marcus Burlile
✖ Millharow Altered
★ RayGun Magazine / David Carson Design

3 ● Something Ugly
■ Marcus Burlile
✖ Custom Lettering
★ Burlile Design / Raw Types
◆ Marcus Burlile

4

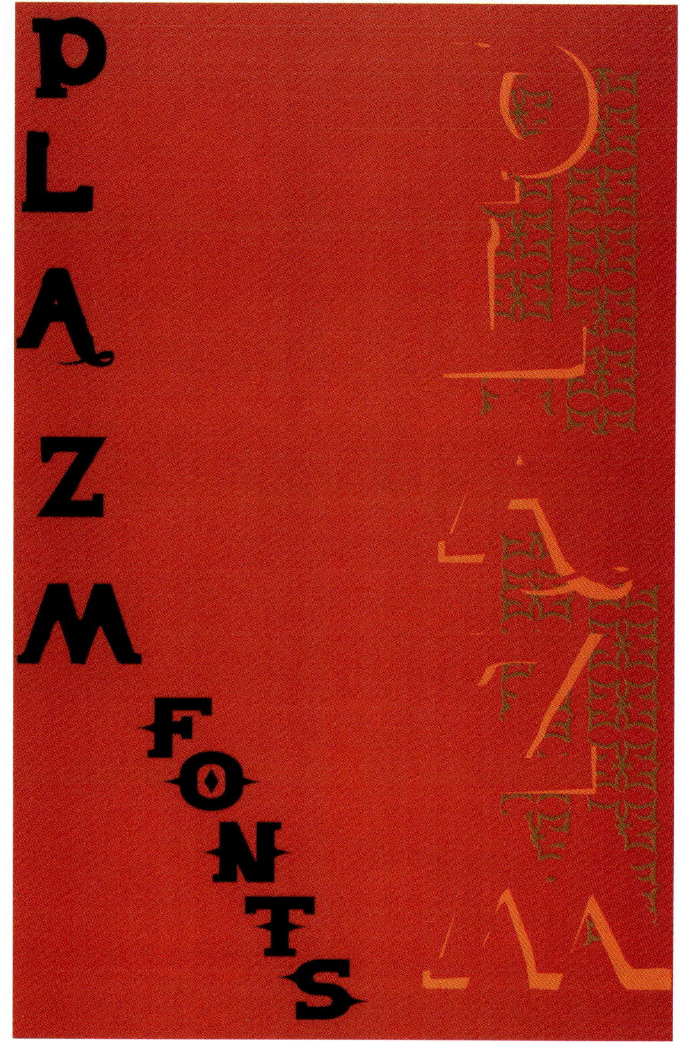

5

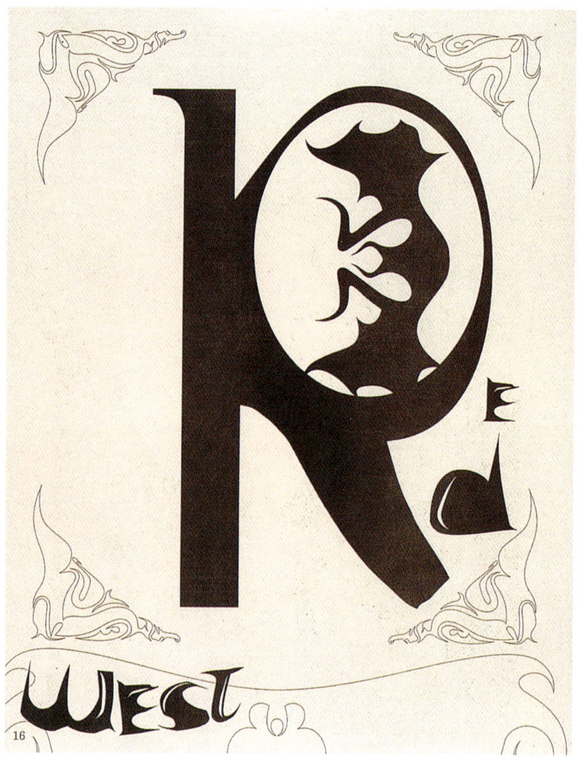

ABCDEFGHIJKLMNOPQRSTUVWXYZ
0123456789(AT¢$NO.%AND)

ABCDEFGHIJKLMNOPQRSTUVWXYZ
abcdefghijklmnopqrstuvwxyz
0123456789 (AT¢$No.%&)

ABCDEFGHIJKLMNOPQRSTUVWXYZ
abcdefghijklmnopqrstuvwxyz
0123456789 (AT¢$No.%AND)

4

4 ✖ Lilyin Saguaro / Lilyin Tupelo / Lilyin Wanted
■ Marcus Burlile
▲ Raw Types

5 ✖ Autumnull
■ Marcus Burlile
▲ Raw Types

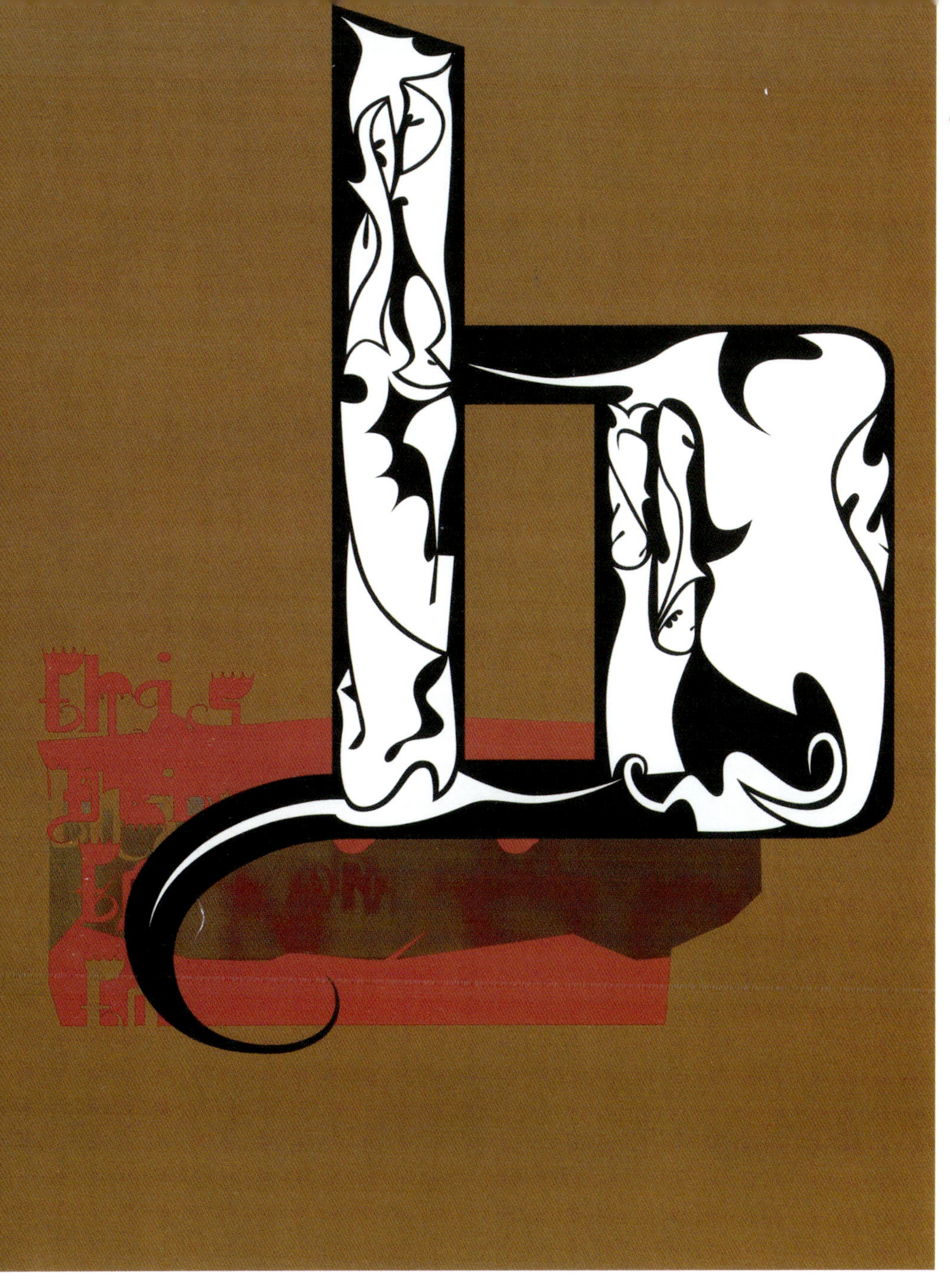

6

aBCdEF
GHiJKLm
NOPQRS
TUVWXYZ
abcdef
ghijklm
nopqrs
tuvwxyz
0123456789
(@¢$%&)

5

4
- ● Plazm Fonts postcard
- ■ Marcus Burlile
- ✖ Lilyin Saguaro / Lilyin Tupelo / Lilyin Wanted
- ★ Plazm Fonts

5
- ● Red West
- ■ Marcus Burlile
- ✖ Autumnull / Custom Lettering
- ★ Plazm Fonts

6
- ● This Belonging to B
- ■ Marcus Burlile
- ✖ Flytrap / Flytrap Brier / Custom Lettering
- ★ Plazm Magazine / Champion Paper

1

ABCDEFG
HIJKLMNO
PQRSTU
VWXYZ

abcde
fghijklmn
opqrstu
vwxyz

0123456789
«!@®©$£¢?%&*»

2

ABCDEFG
HIJKLMNO
PQRSTU
VWXYZ

abcde
fghijklmn
opqrstu
vwxyz

0123456789
«!@®©$£¢?%&*»

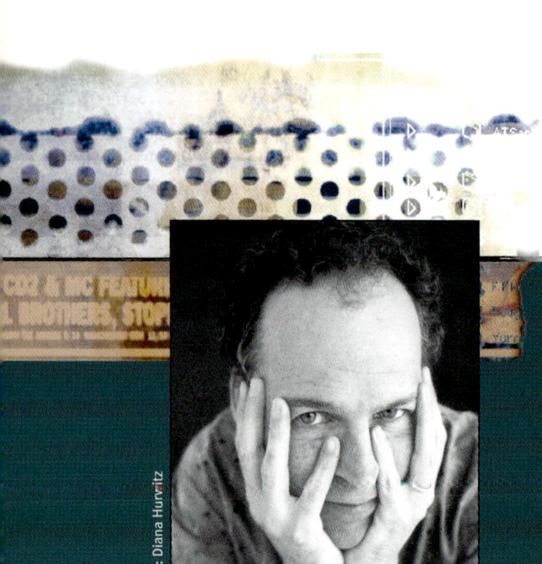

photo: Diana Hurvitz

greg thompson

Taking something apart is the original way to find out what's inside, how it works. Stuff also falls apart if left alone long enough, and sometimes the natural process is accelerated by someone intentionally creating a bit of mayhem.
Deterioration is unavoidable and even exciting, but it presupposes putting things together and polishing them up a bit. What's the fun deconstructing a bunch of debris? I like putting things together.

A graduate of Art Center College of Design, Thompson designed products and music environments for legendary LA music industry recording studios, producers and artists, including Cherokee Studios, producer Bill Schnee, Dan Fogelberg and Supertramp.
In the late 1980s Thompson was caught up in the sweeping changes that PostScript and the Macintosh brought to the Chicago publishing industry. While working with early adapter corporate clients such as Playboy, and Ameritech, design shops such as Bagby Design and Boller/Coates, and typesetters such as Typesmiths and Davidsons Graphics, Thompson discovered an old love – drawing letters.
Thompson contributed many original typeface designs to the fledgling Font Bureau, including the hugely popular Bodega Sans and Bodega Serif families. He continues to independently work with clients on all three coasts and develop original typefaces.

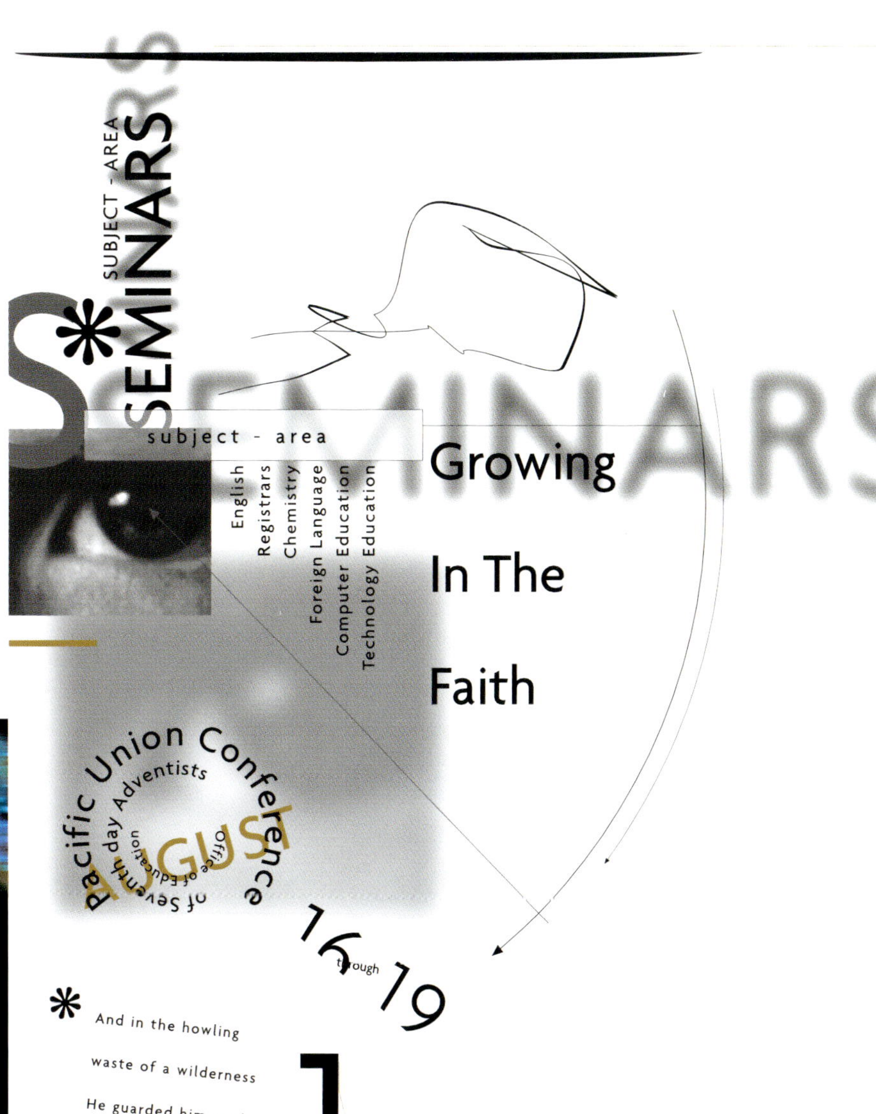

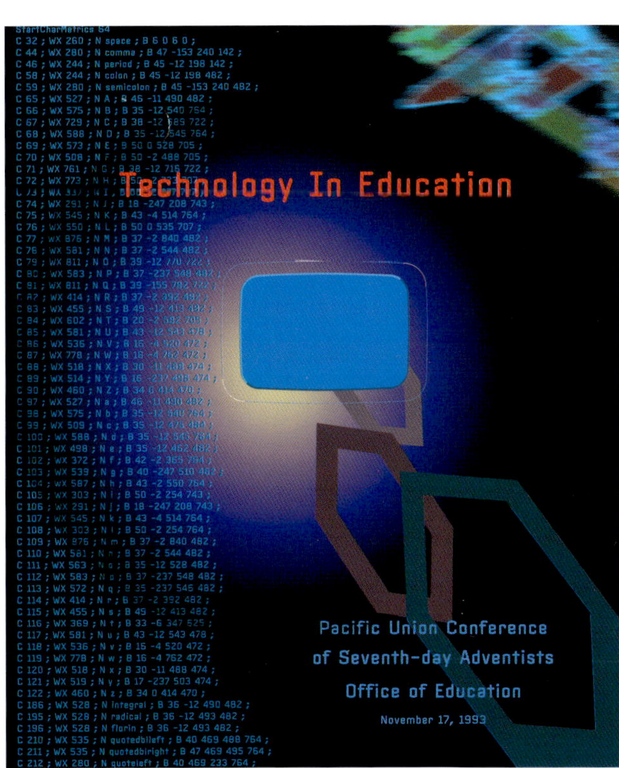

1 ✖ Agenda Medium (a 16 weight family)
■ Greg Thompson
▲ Font Bureau, Inc.

1 ● SAS 1992 Cover
■ Greg Thompson
✖ Agenda Medium and Light
★ Pacific Union Conference of SDA
◆ Greg Thompson

2 ✖ Clicker
■ Greg Thompson
▲ Font Bureau, Inc.

2 ● Technology In Education Cover
■ Greg Thompson
✖ Clicker
★ Pacific Union Conference of SDA
◆ Greg Thompson

1

ABCDEFGHIJ
KLMNOPQRSTUVWXYZ
abcdefghij
klmnopqrstuvwxyz
0123456789
(¢*$%&?!)

2

ABCDEFGHIJKLMNOP
QRSTUVWXYZ
ABCDEFGHIJKLMNOP
QRSTUVWXYZ
0123456789
(¢*$%&?!)

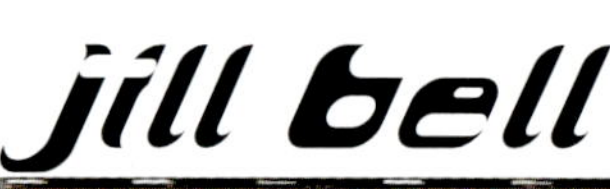

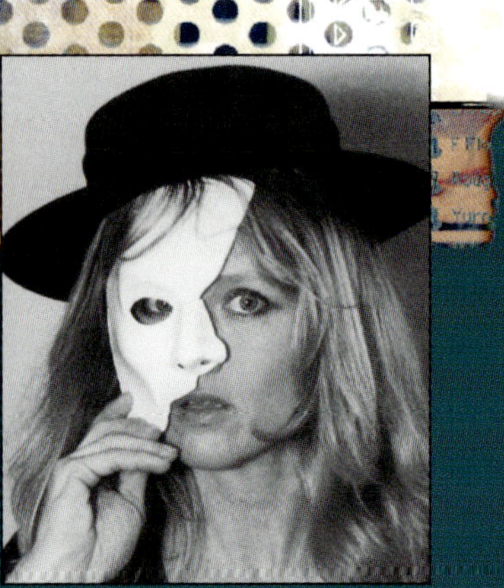

I have always been a proponent of what seems to be basically an eastern philosophy of lettering: that the irregularities and human qualities are to be valued and cherished, rather than smoothed away by engraving, white-out or bezier curves. I'm definitely a "display" type of gal. I am always glad when my clientele wants work that looks handlettered and irregular, handwritten and funky, that shows non-computer origins. Mine is the middle path: a melding of my formal lettering training and pure spontaneity. I endeavour to bring a flow, casualness, and life to my lettering and fonts, while still maintaining an elegance of structure and form within the characters and their family. Like a zen master, you train in your art with patience and regularity, with the best teachers that you can, and then you put it all aside and just be there in the moment with your letterforms during the act of creation.

Jill Bell has specialized in creating letterforms for over 20 years. Her studio creates handlettered logotypes, titles and lettering for advertising, entertainment, and businesses. She has created typefaces for ITC, licensed fonts to Adobe and Creative Alliance/Agfa, as well as developed exclusive fonts for businesses such as Disney, and Johnson and Johnson. She does design work for print and for the Web. Her love of signpainting, western and zen calligraphy and graffiti has influenced her style and work as much as the Trajan column, or Gutenberg. She graduated from UCLA with a degree in English, and Otis/Parsons in Advertising and Graphic Design, and worked for Saul Bass doing production after graduation. She has her own business, Jill Bell Design, located in Los Angeles. She writes, speaks and teaches as an adjunct to her lettering and design business.

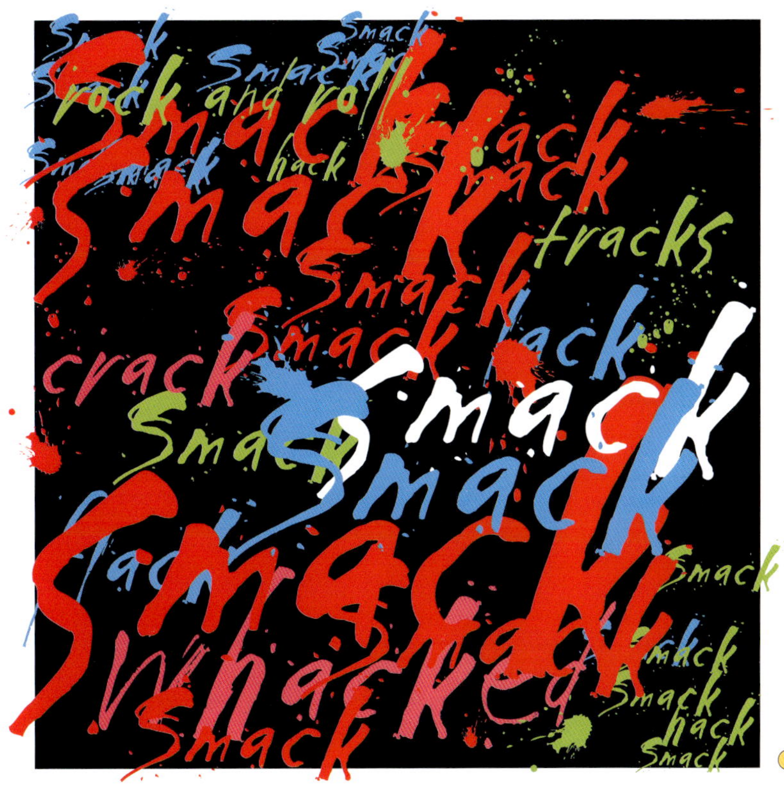

1

ABCDEFG
HIJKLMNOPQ
RSTUVWXYZ
abcdefghijklm
nopqrstuvwxyz
0123456789
(¢*$%&?!)

3

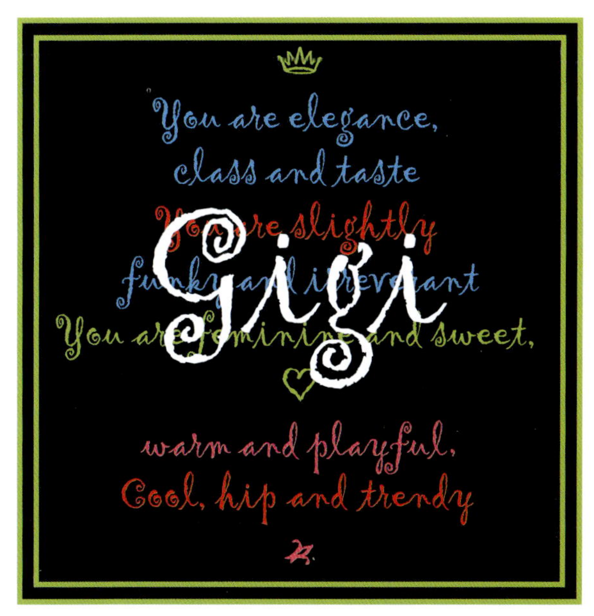

2

1 ✖ ITC Smack
■ Jill Bell
▲ ITC

2 ✖ ITC Carumba Hot Caps
■ Jill Bell
▲ ITC

3 ✖ ITC Gigi
■ Jill Bell
▲ ITC

1 ● ITC Smack sampler
■ Jill Bell
✖ ITC Smack
★ Publish Magazine

2 ● TCI Gigi Sampler
■ Jill Bell
✖ ITC Gigi
★ Publish Magazine

1

A B C D E F G H I J K L M N O P Q R S T U V W X Y Z
a b c d e f g h i j k l m n o p q r s t u v w x y z 0 1 2 3 4 5 6 7 8 9

A B C D E F G H I J K L M N O P Q R S T U V W X Y Z
a b c d e f g h i j k l m n o p q r s t u v w x y z 0 1 2 3 4 5 6 7 8 9

A B C D E F G H I J K L M N O P Q R S T U V W X Y Z
a b c d e f g h i j k l m n o p q r s t u v w x y z 0 1 2 3 4 5 6 7 8 9

A B C D E F G H I J K L M N O P Q R S T U V W X Y Z
a b c d e f g h i j k l m n o p q r s t u v w x y z 0 1 2 3 4 5 6 7 8 9

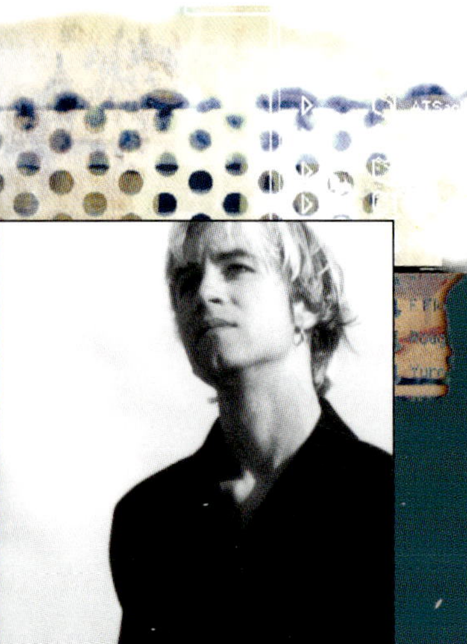

don zinzell

Zinzell Design

Type design is communication, it's science, it's sculpture, it's art, it's culture. Within graphic design, type is more than just one element that interconnects with other elements to make up a whole. The proliferation of type styles is a very important movement; it has triggered issues within communication; it has increased the recognition of type in relation to photography and illustration. Type is an open system that begs for speculation, experimentation and interpretation. The inspiration to create type is endless: quantum physics, metaphysics, chaos theory, found objects, etc...

Don Zinzell, New York City based independent designer, is a true graphic alchemist. Extensive use of his own typeface design and photography, as well as the surreal utilitarian feel of his work, make him a multifaceted graphic originator. His deft use of metaphors and the layers of complexity behind simple surfaces give his work a cerebral modern edge.
Zinzell's graphic design and art direction projects have encompassed a diverse spectrum of industry giants such as Bloomingdale's, Sony, Tommy Hilfiger and Tourneau, as well as numerous smaller companies.

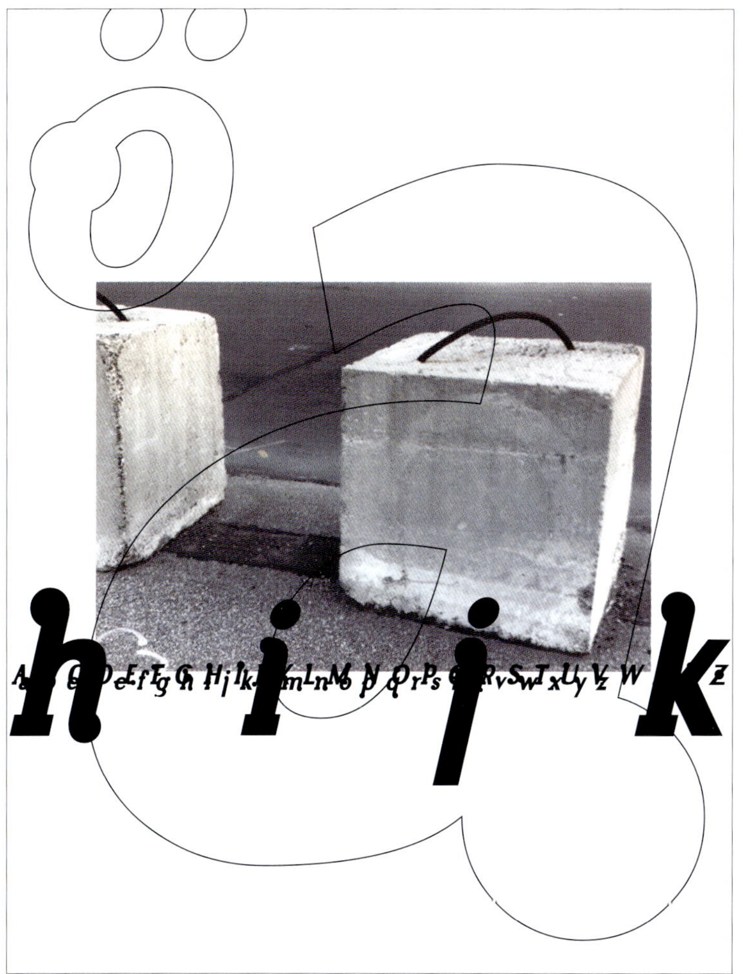

1

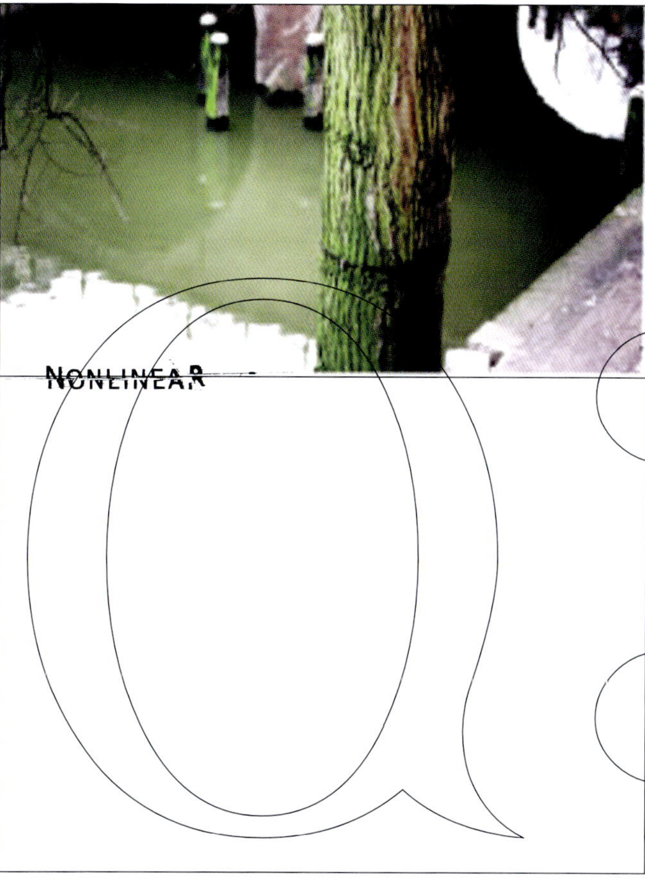

2

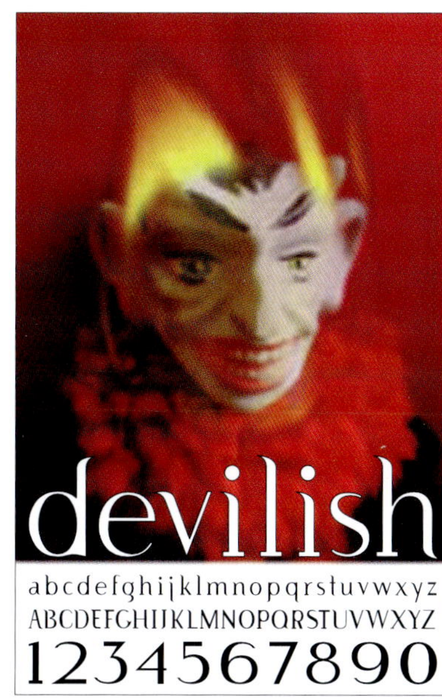

3

1 ✖ Devilish / Devilish bubble
■ Don Zinzell
▲ Zinzell Design

1 ● The cement bubble (Devilish bubble promo)
■ Don Zinzell
✖ Devilish bubble bold
★ Zinzell Design
◆ Don Zinzell

2 ● Devilish canal (Devilish promo)
■ Don Zinzell
✖ Devilish and photocopied type
★ Zinzell Design
◆ Don Zinzell

3 ● Devilish poster (Devilish promo)
■ Don Zinzell
✖ Devilish
★ Zinzell Design
◆ Don Zinzell

2

ABCDEFGHIJKLMNOPQRSTUVWXYZ
abcdefghijklmnopqrstuvwxyz0123456789
ABCDEFGHIJKLMNOPQRSTUVWXYZ
abcdefghijklmnopqrstuvwxyz

ABCDEFGHIJKLMNOPQRSTUVWXYZ0123456789

3

2 ✖ Zero
■ Don Zinzell
▲ Zinzell Design

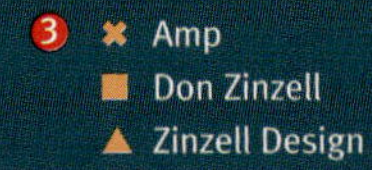

3 ✖ Amp
■ Don Zinzell
▲ Zinzell Design

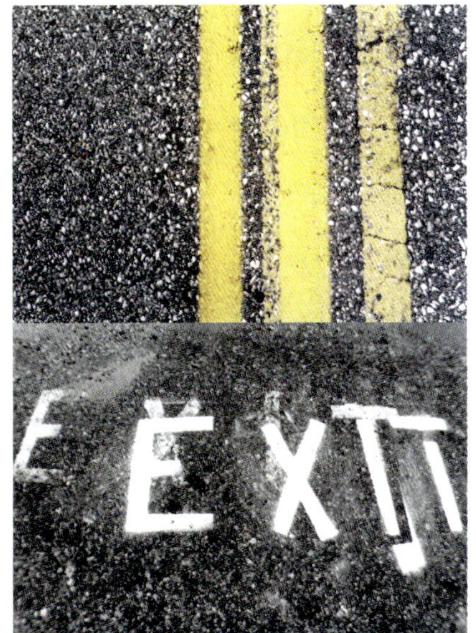

4

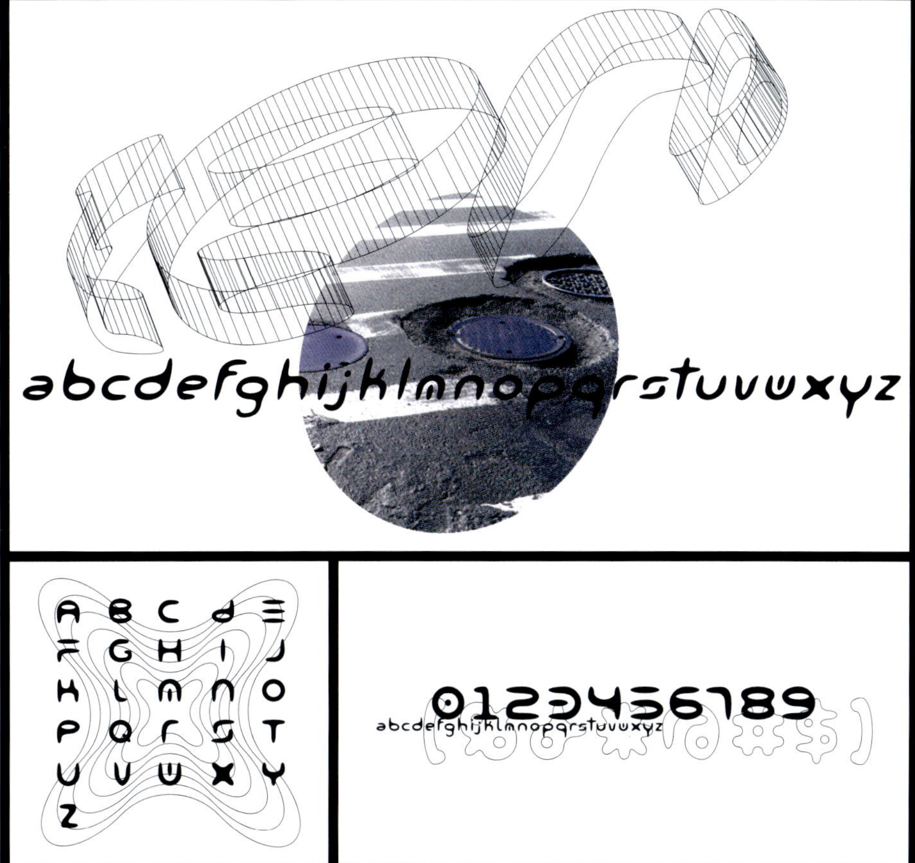

5

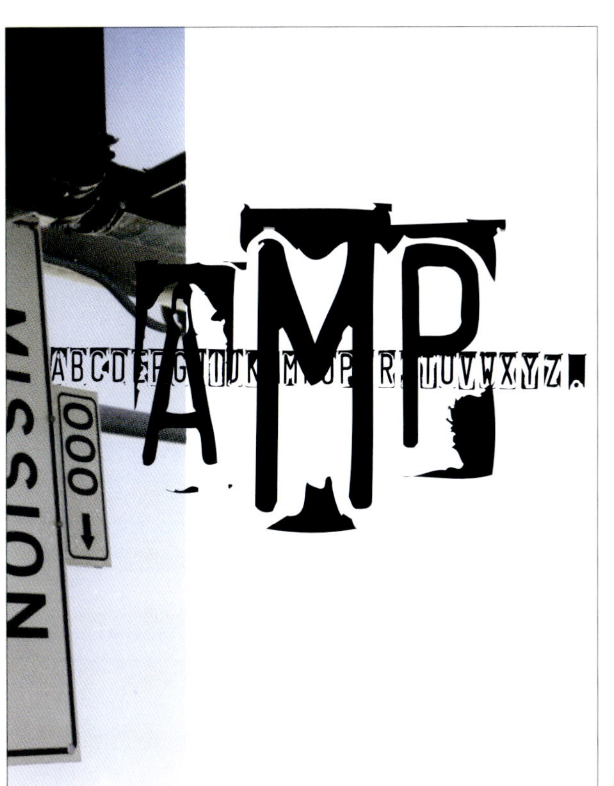

6

4
- Pavement misprints
- Don Zinzell
- found type - pavement
- Zinzell Design
- Don Zinzell

5
- zero ad (promo)
- Don Zinzell
- zero / zero italic
- Zinzell Design
- Don Zinzell

6
- Amp ooo
- Don Zinzell
- Amp
- Zinzell Design
- Don Zinzell

A B C D E F G H I J K L M N O P Q R S T U V W X Y Z
a b c d e f g h i j k l m n o p q r s t u v w x y z 0 1 2 3 4 5 6 7 8 9

4

a b c d e f g h i j k l m n o p q r s t u v w x y z
a b c d e f g h i j k l m n o p q r s t u v w x y z
a b c d e f g h i j k l m n o p q r s t u v w x y z

5

A B C D E F G H I J K L M N O P Q R S T U V W X Y Z
a b c d e f g h i j k l m n o p q r s t u v w x y z 1 2 3 4 5 6 7 8 9 0

6

4 ✖ Gamma Ray
■ Don Zinzell
▲ Zinzell Design

5 ✖ Five Regular
■ Don Zinzell
▲ Zinzell Design

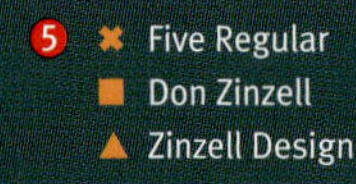

6 ✖ Typo
■ Don Zinzell
▲ Zinzell Design

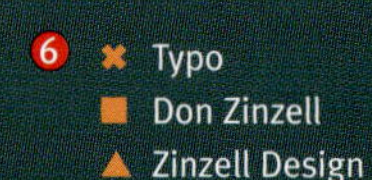

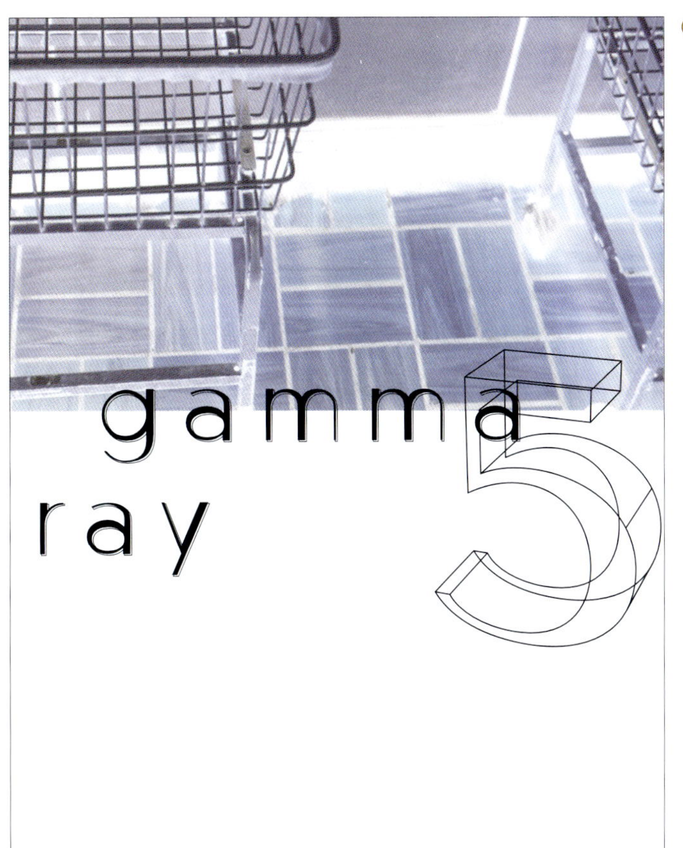

7

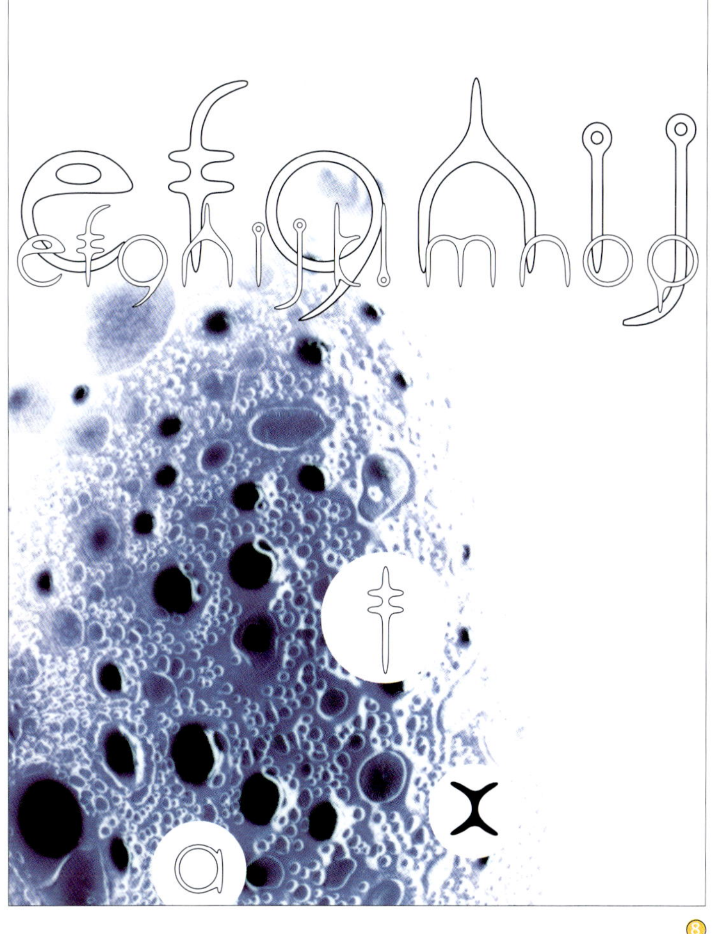

8

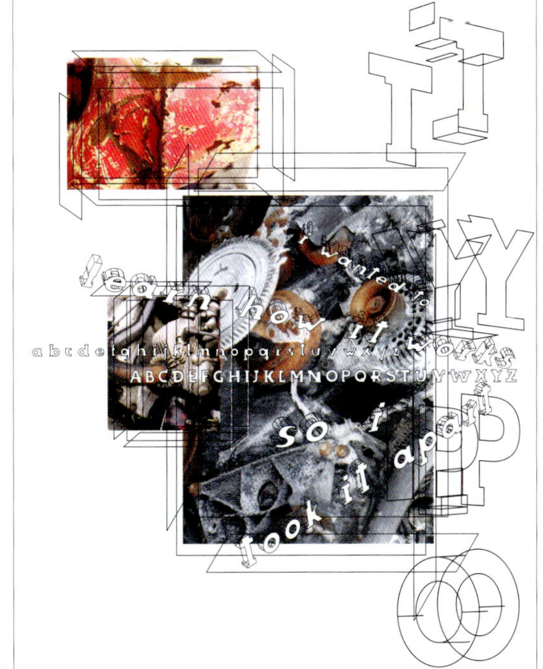

9

7
- ● Gamma Ray 5 (Gamma Ray promo)
- ■ Don Zinzell
- ✖ Gamma Ray
- ★ Zinzell Design
- ◆ Don Zinzell

8
- ● Five organic (Five organic promo)
- ■ Don Zinzell
- ✖ Five
- ★ Zinzell Design
- ◆ Gavin Wilson

9
- ● Learn how it works (Typo promo)
- ■ Don Zinzell
- ✖ Typo
- ★ Zinzell Design
- ◆ Don Zinzell

ABCDEFGHIJKLMNOP
QRSTUVWXYZ
abcdefghijklmnopq
rstuvwxyz
0123456789 (@¢$#%&)

1

ABCDEFGHIJKLMNOP
QRSTUVWXYZ
abcdefghijklmnopq
rstuvwxyz
0123456789 (@¢$#%&)

2

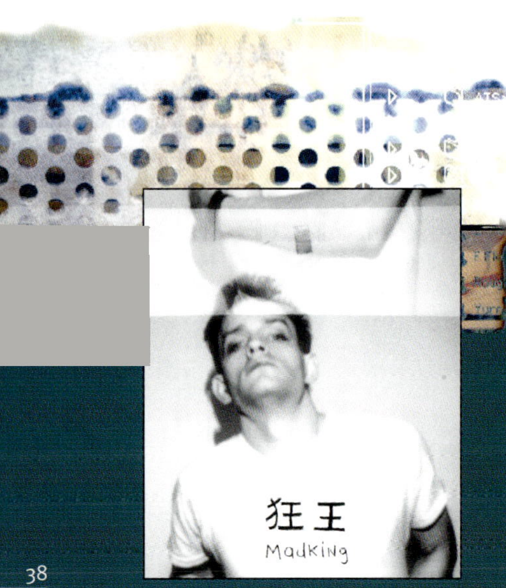

elliott earls

The Apollo Program

Look at the work. Look at "the thing": "Excerpts from EYE SLING SHOT LIONS" is an interactive digital composition conceived and constructed around the Quicktime Media Layer, Max2 and Supercard technologies. During live performance, a melange of typography, sound, video fragments, interactive digital video, simulated live performance, short films and pop music are controlled via midi and interwoven with live poetry, sub-urban hip-hop and spoken word texts. Custom built interface elements link Elliott to computer controlled video and typography, through the extensive use of piezio electric elements. Utilizing CD-ROM and LCD projection, "Excerpts from EYE SLING SHOT LIONS" is programmed to be modal. Not only is it a performance, it's a product... a shiny disc full of ones and zeros ready to be taken home the night of the performance, and put into your Walkman2 or your Mac.

Earls has recently performed at Opera Totale In Venice, Culture Mart in Soho, "Living Surfaces" in Park City, Utah, and at The Walker Art Center. Earls received his M.F.A. from Cranbrook Academy of Art. He is the founder of The Apollo Program. As a typographer, Earls' type design is distributed by Emigre Inc. His posters entitled "The Conversion of Saint Paul," "Throwing Apples at the Sun," and "She a Capulet" are in the permanent collection of the Cooper-Hewitt National Design Museum. His CD-ROM entitled "EYE SLING SHOT LIONS," was shown at; The 97 New York Video Festival at Lincoln Center, Plazzo Della Triennale di Milano, at Nightwave in Italy, during the Remaking History symposium at the American Center for Design, at Fabrica in Treviso, and most recently at Sig-graph in Los Angeles. Earls' commercial clients include; Nonesuch Records, Little Brown & Co., The Criterion Collection, etc.

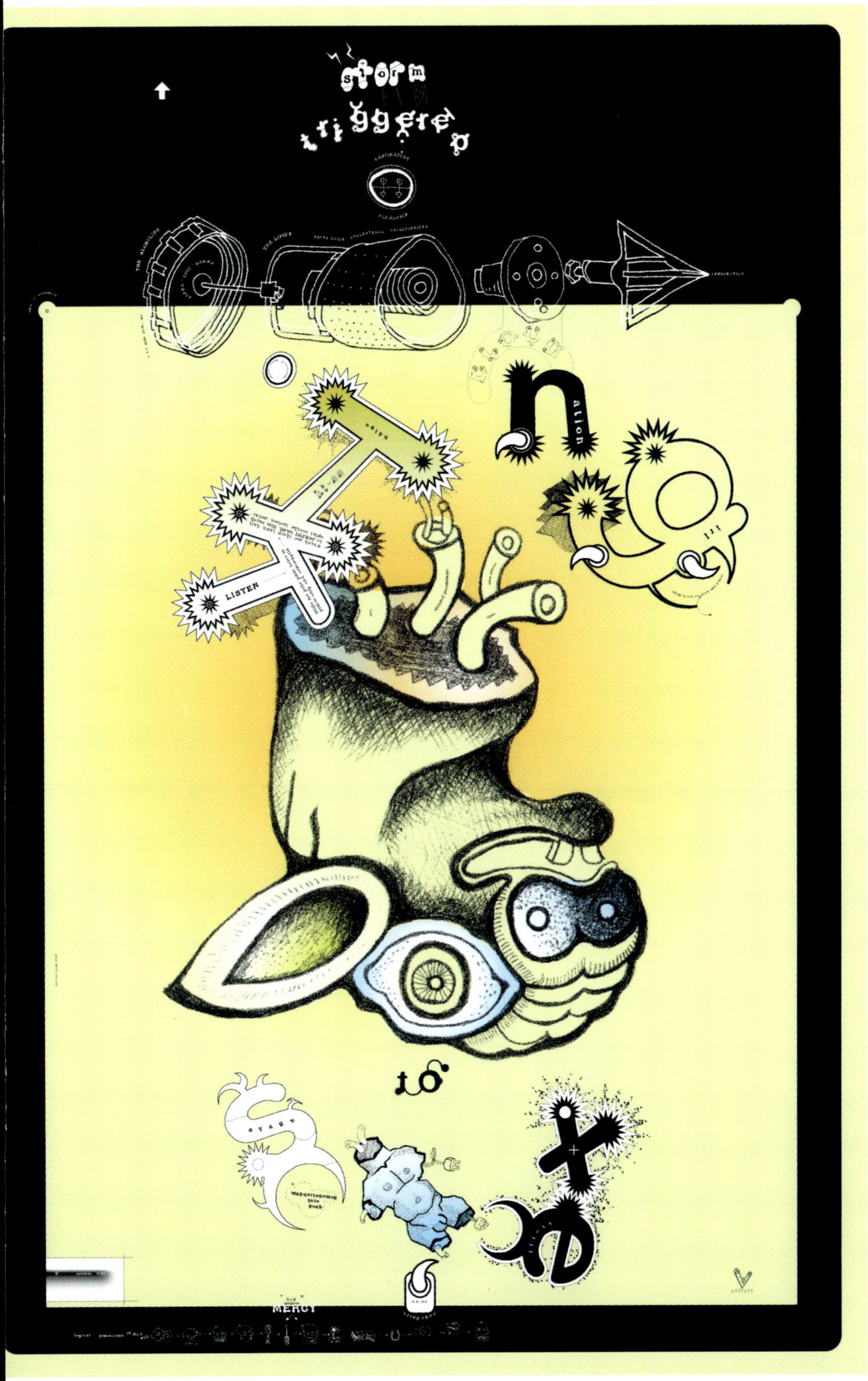

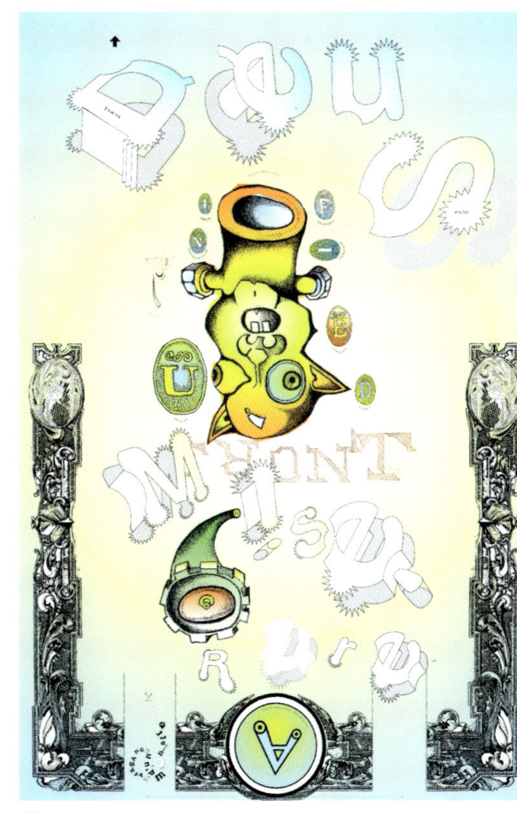

2

1

1 ✖ Jigsaw Dropshadow
■ Elliott Peter Earls at The Apollo Program
▲ Emigre Inc.

2 ✖ Subluxation Perma
■ Elliott Peter Earls at The Apollo Program
▲ Emigre Inc.

1 ● Storm Triggered Cloud King to Sex
■ Elliott Peter Earls
✖ Jigsaw Three D Dropshadow / Venus Dioxide
★ The Apollo Program
◆ Elliott Peter Earls

2 ● Domine Deus Noster, Miserere Nobis (Lord Our God Have Mercy)
■ Elliott Peter Earls
✖ Jigsaw Three D Dropshadow / Venus Dioxide / Typhoid Mary Three D Dark
★ The Apollo Program
◆ Elliott Peter Earls

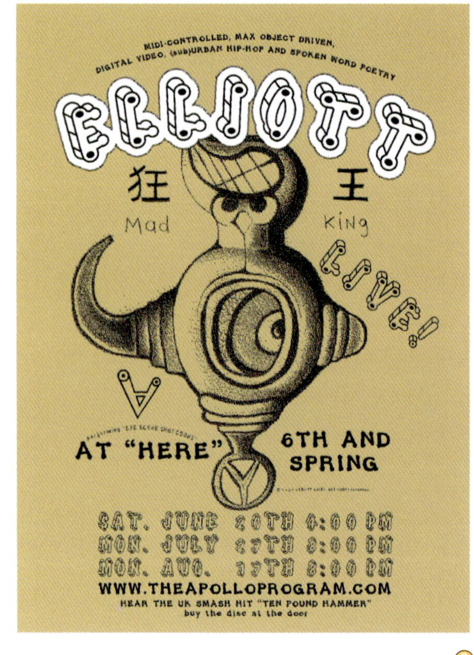

3

4

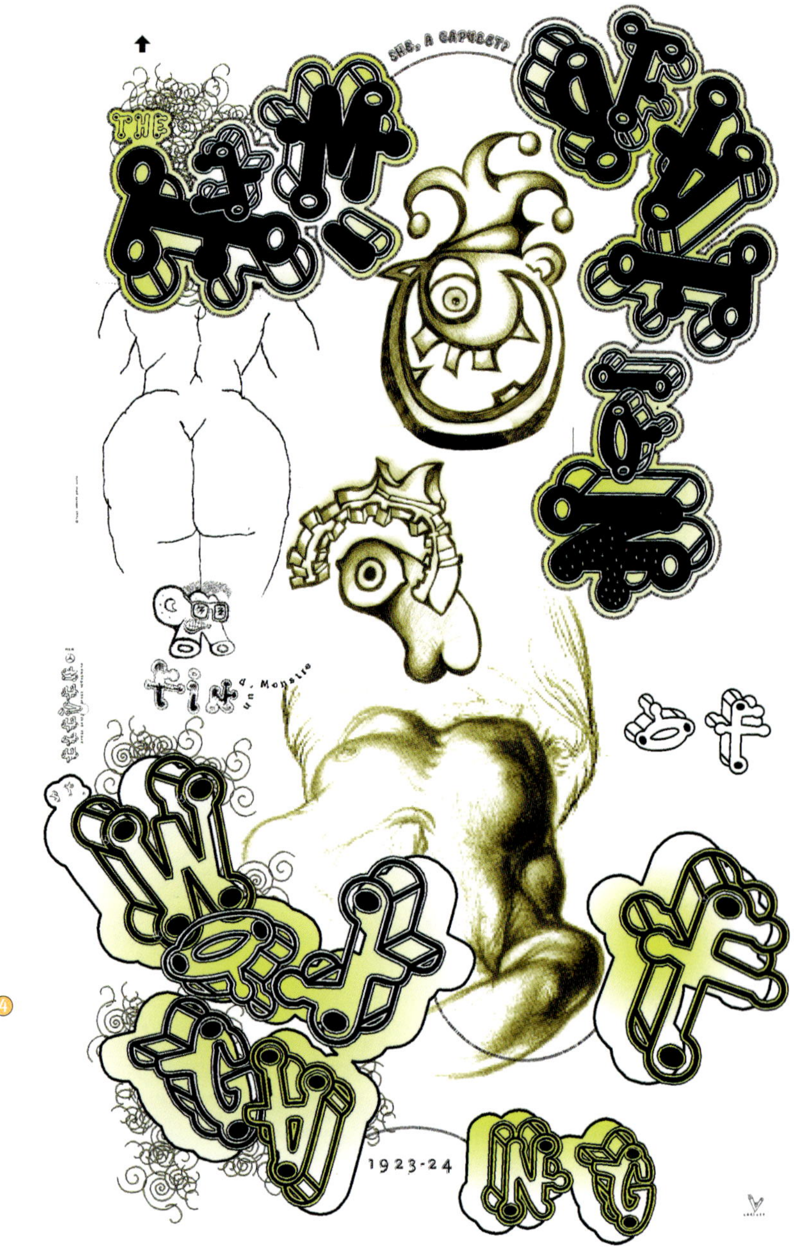

ABCDEFGHIJKLMNOPQRSTUVWXYZ
abcdefghijklmnopqrstuvwxyz
0123456789 (@¢$#%&)

3

ABCDEFGHIJKLMNOPQRSTUVWXYZ
abcdefghijklmnopqrstuvwxyz
0123456789 (@¢$#%&)

3 ✖ Typhoid Mary Three D Dark / Typhoid Mary Three D Light
■ Elliott Peter Earls at The Apollo Program
▲ Emigre Inc.

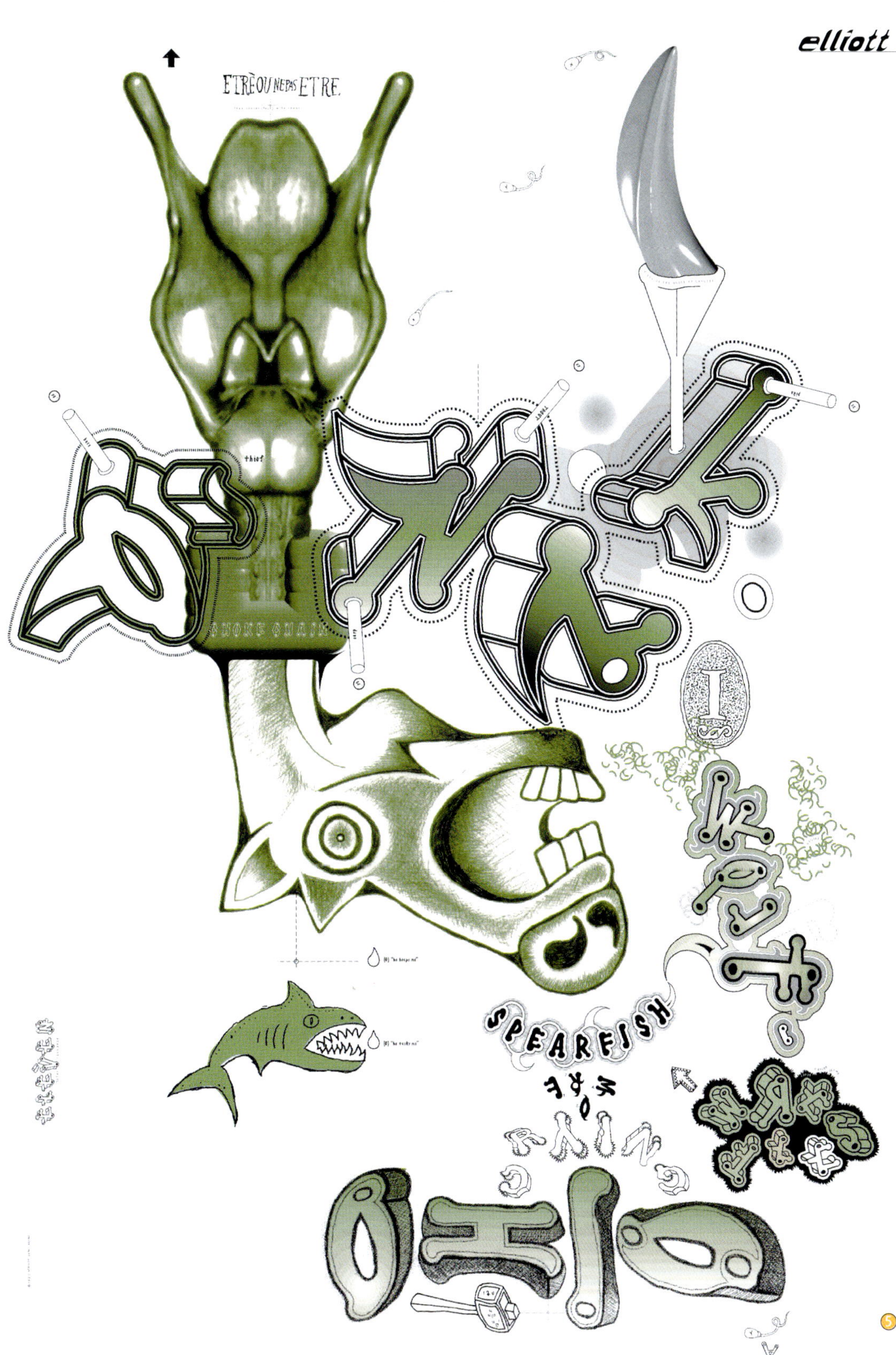

3
- Performance poster
- Elliott Peter Earls
- Typhoid Mary Three D Light
- The Apollo Program
- Elliott Peter Earls

4
- The Temptation of St. Wolfgang (She a Capulet?)
- Elliott Peter Earls
- Typhoid Mary Three D Light
- The Apollo Program
- Elliott Peter Earls

5
- Only I Wolf-wrestle Spearfish from Crying Ohio
- Elliott Peter Earls
- Jigsaw / Jigsaw Three D Dropshadow
- The Apollo Program
- Elliott Peter Earls

ABCDEFGHIJKLMNOP
QRSTUVWXYZ
abcdefghijklmnopq
rstuvwxyz
0123456789 (@¢$#%&)

4

ABCDEFGHIJKLMNOP
QRSTUVWXYZ
abcdefghijklmnopq
rstuvwxyz
0123456789 (@¢$#%&)

ABCDEFGHIJKLMNOP
QRSTUVWXYZ
abcdefghijklmnopq
rstuvwxyz
0123456789 (@¢$#%&)

5

4
- Blue Eye Shadow
- Elliott Peter Earls at The Apollo Program
- Emigre Inc.

5
- Venus Dioxide / Venus Dioxide Outline
- Elliott Peter Earls at The Apollo Program
- Emigre Inc.

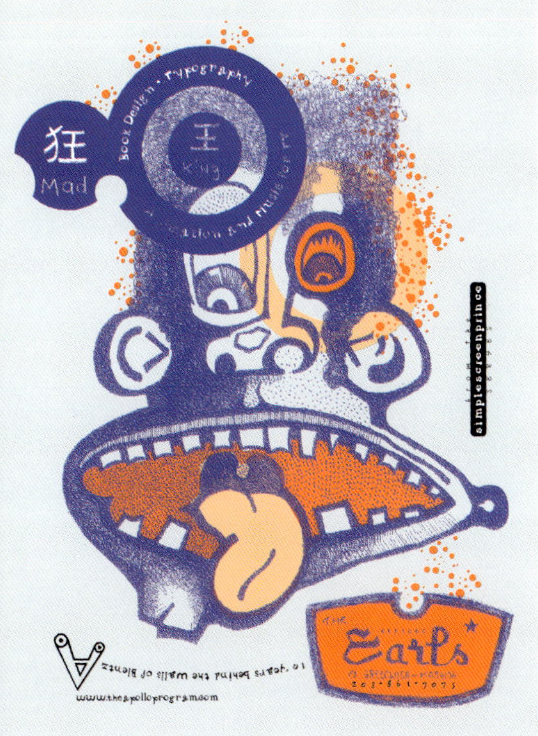

6

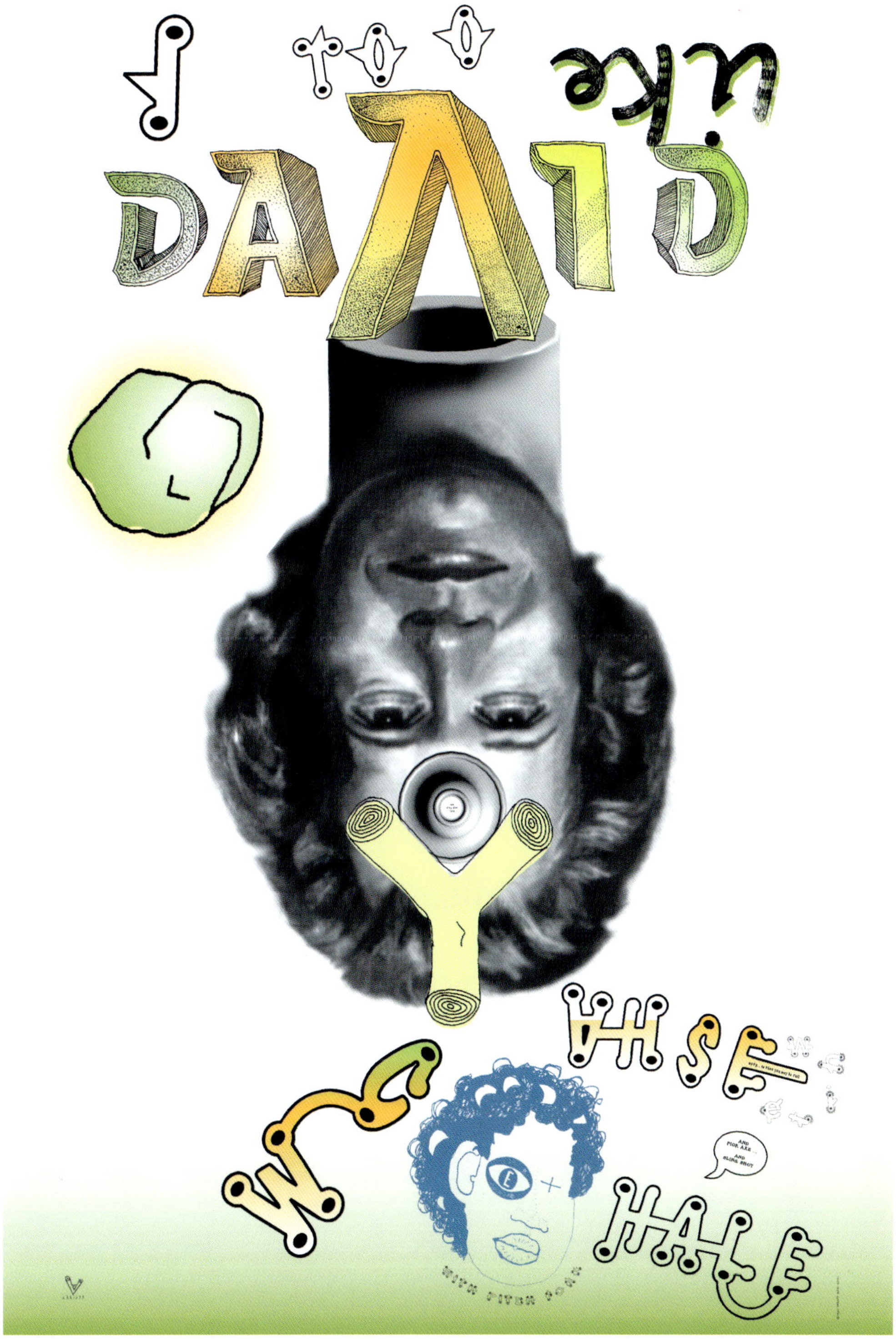

7

6
- ● Poster
- ■ Elliott Peter Earls
- ★ The Apollo Program
- ◆ Elliott Peter Earls

7
- ● I Too, Like David, Chase White Whale with Pitch Fork and Pick Axe and Sling Shot
- ■ Elliott Peter Earls
- ✖ Jigsaw Three D Dropshadow / Venus Dioxide / Typhoide Mary Three D Dark
- ★ The Apollo Program
- ◆ Elliott Peter Earls

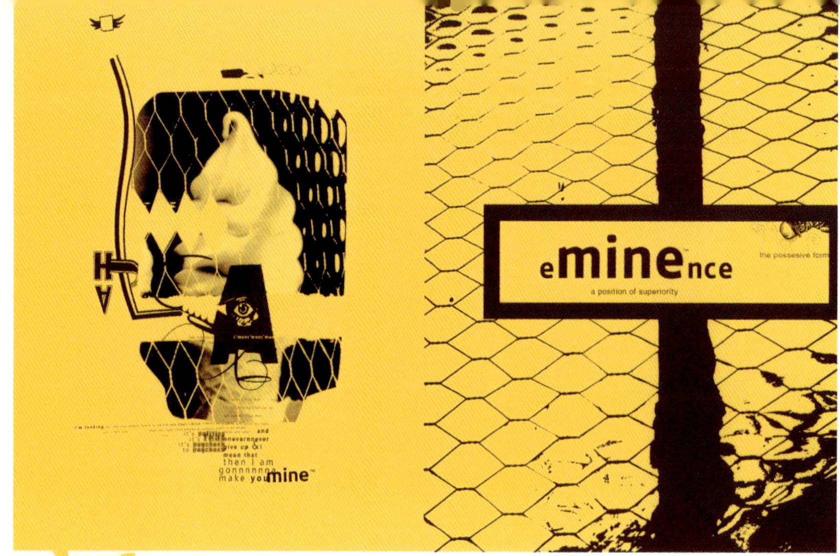

>Participant 4, Martin Venezky >Participant 5, Carlos Segura

Due to prior corporate commitments the work of Round 1, particpant 6 cannot appear.

MINE

CAPITALIS PIRATA Capitalis Pirata, a shareware font designed by Roland Henss. Individual letterforms are "borrowed" from international corporate logos. The font challenges ownership of form as well as context based meaning.

<Participant 6, Marcus Burlile

ABCDEFGHIJKL
MNOPQRSTUV
WXYZ0123456

plazm

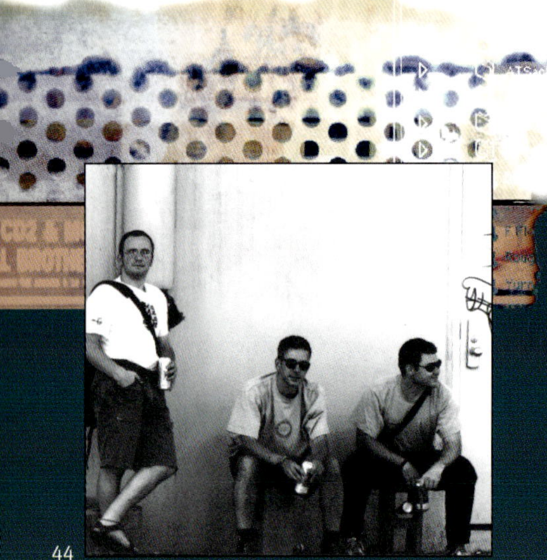

Joshua Berger, Niko Courtelis, Pete McCracken

Socialists in capitalist clothing. Helping others help each other. What's good for the goose is good for the gander. Concentrate on the moment.

Plazm Media Collective is comprised of three interlinked divisions, with a fourth in development. They are: Plazm Magazine, Plazm Fonts, Plazm Design, and Plazm.com. The principals are Joshua Berger, Niko Courtelis, and Pete McCracken, all of whom have conventional design/art school backgrounds. The three met in Portland, Oregon, somewhere between microbrewed beer, subversive activities and freelancing at Wieden & Kennedy. Plazm Magazine was founded in 1991 "to provide a forum for free expression, a location for discourse in our artistic community, and a printed laboratory for critical theory and grassroots artistic endeavor." Since its inception, Plazm has seen design as a tool to heighten the impact of submitted works. As the magazine has evolved, and the designer's role has become more pronounced, Plazm continues to encourage coequal collaboration between designers and artists. We view our design method as one artist interpreting another's work. Plazm Magazine's experiments in design led to typographic innovations as well, and in 1993 Plazm launched a digital type foundry. Plazm now has a core group of talented font designers, developing new experimental typefaces. New designers regularly submit samples which are reviewed monthly. Hand processes figure prominently in the creation of unique, individual type solutions. Silkscreen and letterpress tools are often utilized at McCracken's studio, Crack Press. Plazm Design applies a collaborative creative process and Plazm style to commercial projects.

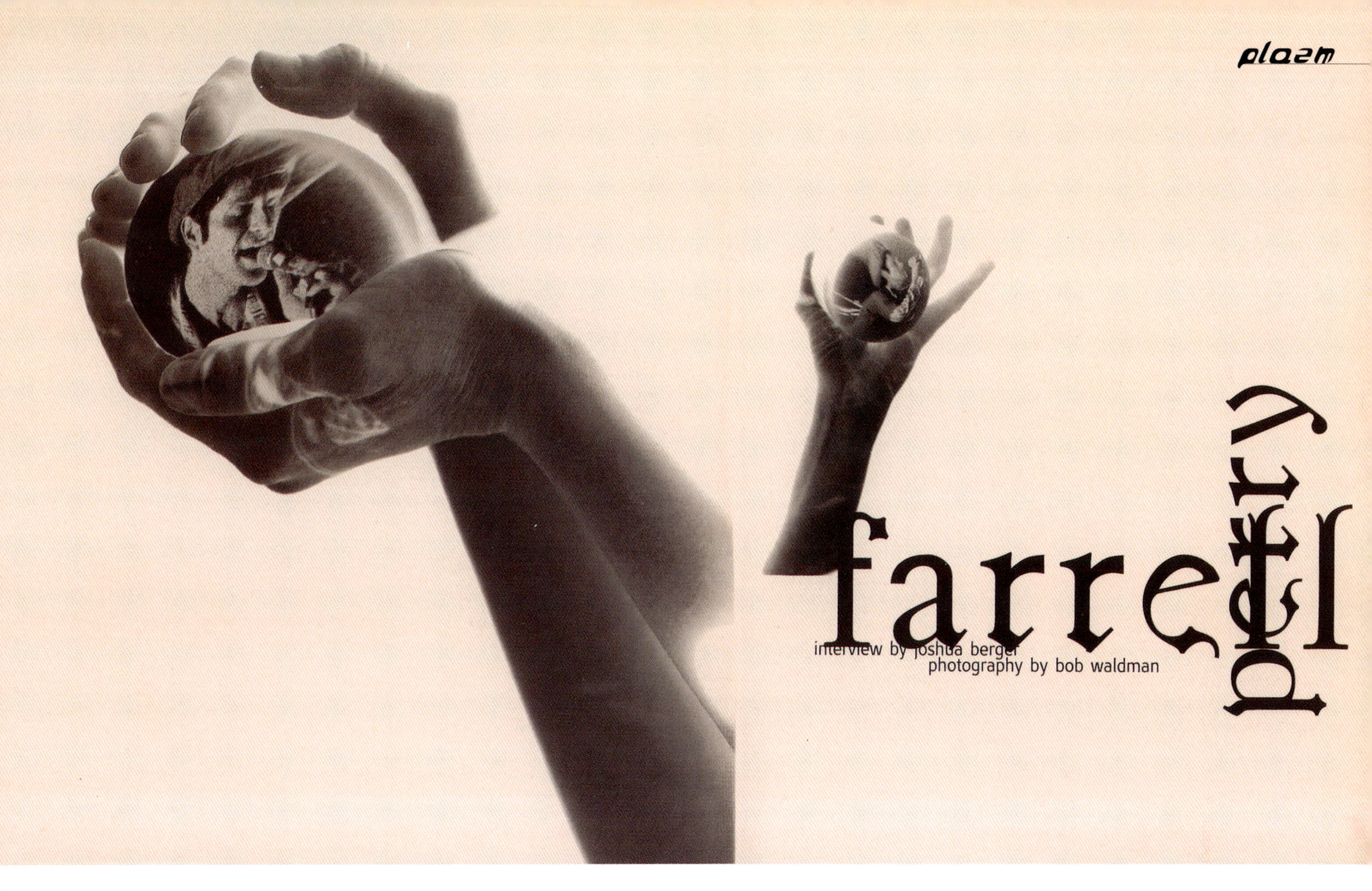

2

ABCDEFGHIJKLMNOPQRSTUVWXYZ
abcdefghijklmnopqrstuvwxyz
0123456789 (@¢$#%&)

3

ABCDEFGHIJKLMNOPQRSTUVWXYZ
abcdefghijklmnopqrstuvwxyz
0123456789 (@¢$#%&)

1
- ✖ Capitalis Pirata
- ■ Roland Hess
- ▲ Plazm Fonts

2
- ✖ Hybrid
- ■ Christian Küsters
- ▲ Plazm Fonts

3
- ✖ Interface One (a2 weight family)
- ■ Christian Küsters
- ▲ Plazm Fonts

1
- ● Mine™ (Promotional book, spread)
- ■ Joshua Berger / Niko Courtelis / Pete McCracken / Carlos Segura / Martin Venezky
- ✖ Capitalis Pirata
- ★ Champion International Paper

2
- ● Perry Farell Spread, Plazm 13
- ■ Joshua Berger / Niko Courtelis / Pete McCracken
- ✖ Hybrid / Roscent
- ★ Plazm Magazine

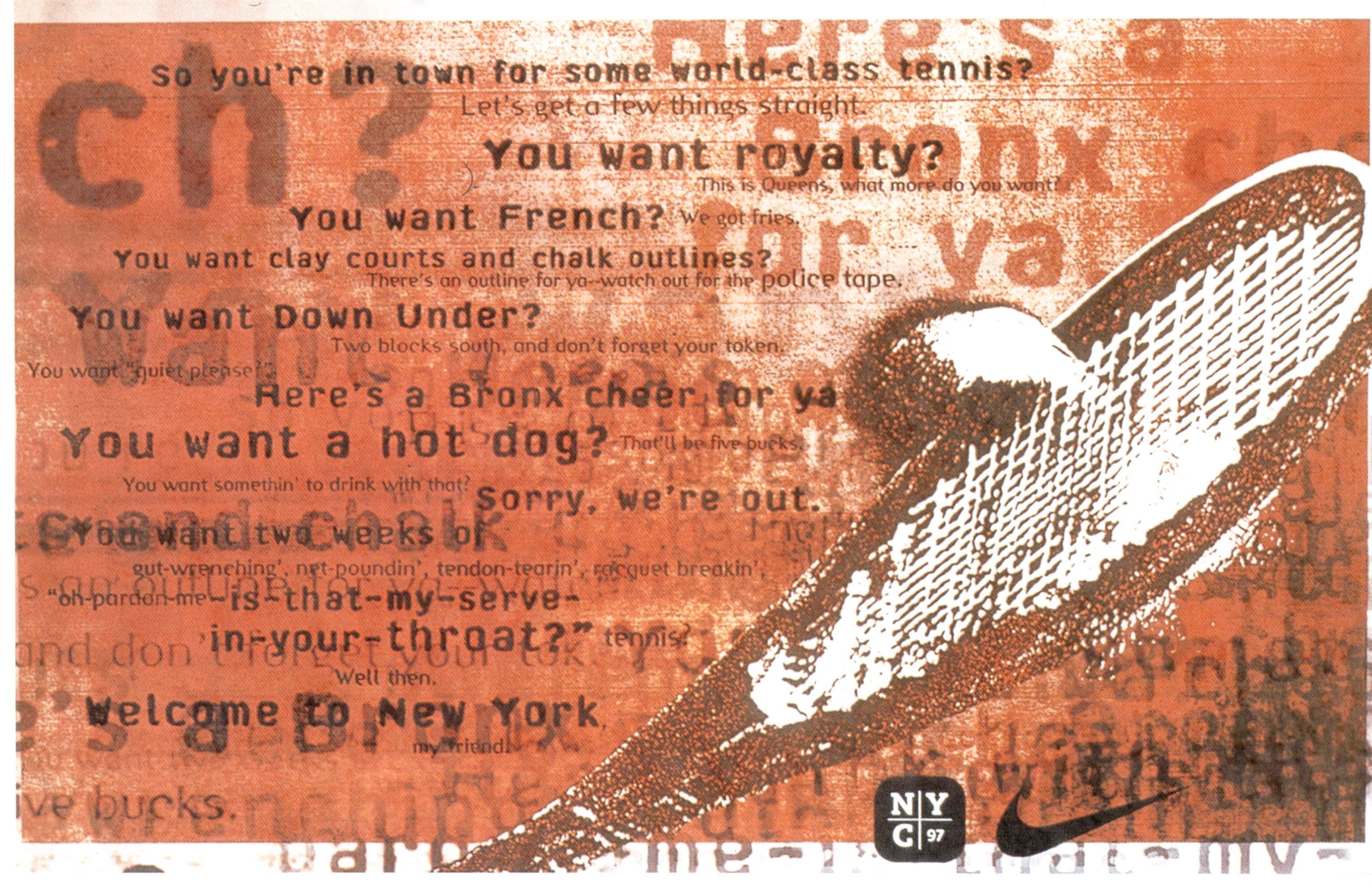

4

ABCDEFGHIJKLMNOPQRSTUVWXYZ
ABCDEFGHIJKLMNOPQRSTUVWXYZ
abcdefghijklmnopqrstvwxyz
0123456789 (@¢$#%&)

5

ABCDEFGHIJKLMNOPQRSTUVWXYZ
abcdefghijklmnopqrstvwxyz
0123456789 (@¢$#%&)

4
- ✖ Credit (a 3 weight family)
- ■ Angus R. Shamal
- ▲ Plazm Fonts

5
- ✖ MTVPE
- ■ Joshua Berger / Niko Courtelis / Pete McCracken / Riq Mosqueda
- ▲ Plazm Fonts

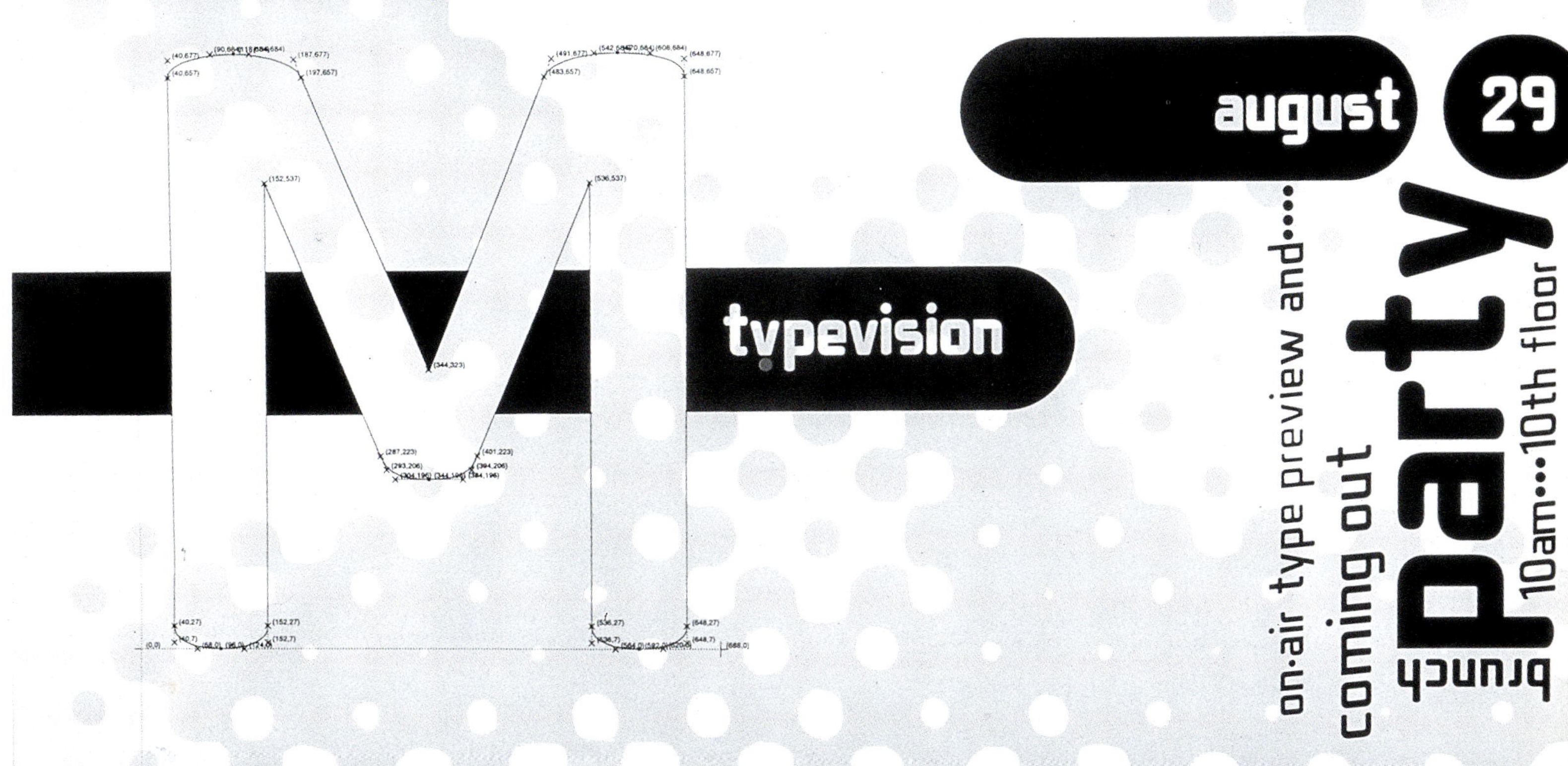

4

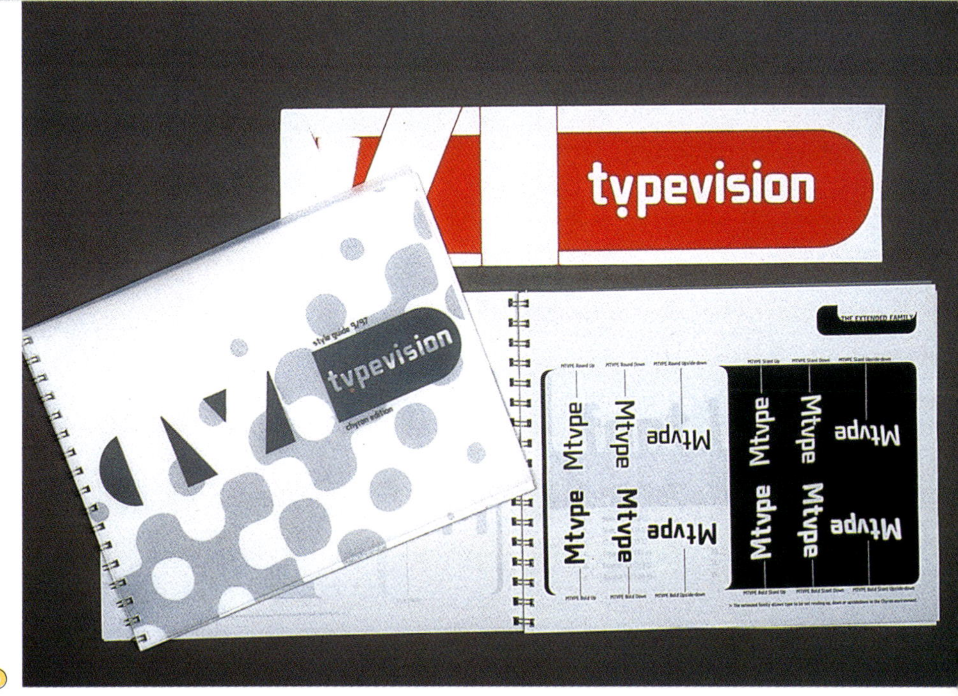

5

3 ● Nike US Open poster
■ Joshua Berger / Niko Courtelis / Pete McCracken
✖ Credit (light / regular / bold), Censor Sans
★ Nike

4 ● MTVPE, Announcement poster
■ Joshua Berger / Niko Courtelis / Pete McCracken
✖ MTVPE Slant / Bold / Bold Slant
★ MTV Networks

5 ● MTVPE, Style guide
■ Joshua Berger / Niko Courtelis / Pete McCracken
✖ MTVPE Slant / Bold / Bold Slant
★ MTV Networks

1

ABCDEFGHIJKLMNOPQRSTUVWXYZ
abcdefghijklmnopqrstuvwxyz
0123456789
«!@®©$£¢?%&*»

2

ABCDEFGHIJ
KLMNOPQRST
UVWXYZ
abcdefghij
klmnopqrst
uvwxyz
0123456789
«!@®©$£¢?%^&*»

ABCDEFGHIJ
KLMNOPQRST
UVWXYZ
abcdefghij
klmnopqrst
uvwxyz
0123456789
«!@®©$£¢?%^&*»

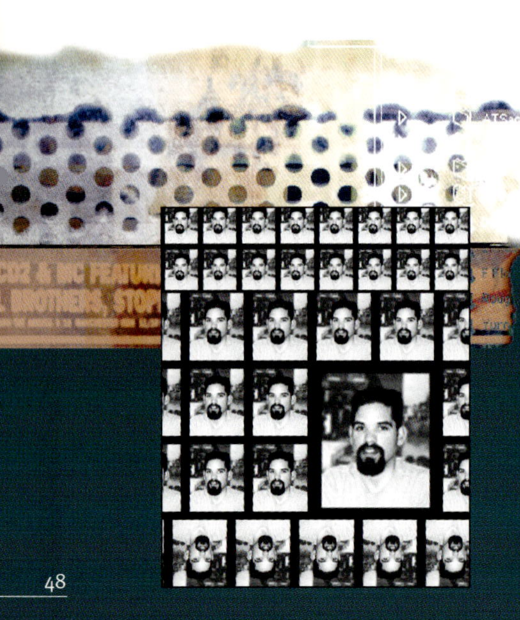

psy/ops

Yes, the "Psychological Operations" theme allows for some entertaining marketing possibilities, but at the root of it there is the statement, the reminder, that typography affects people's choices and behavior in serieous ways. Psy/Ops draw on San Francisco, its home base, for inspiration. It is a city, after all, whose unique history and goegraphy have made for a landscape of wonderfully strange juxtapositions and concentrated diversity. An interest in rare revivals fuels Psy/Ops, also edits fonts for other designers and originates proprietary alphabets for corporations. Such projects include the creation of the official Dr. Seuss* font set for Dr. Seuss* Enterprises and Esprit de Corp; redesign of the recreational and cartographic pictograms used by the USDA Forest Service; and custom lettering and symbols for Ammirati Puris Lintas UK, B Magazine, & Suzan Briganti Inc.

Psy/Ops was formalized in 1995 by Rodrigo Xavier Cavazos, whose typographic dabbling dates back to the mid-eighties with the discovery of a program for the Apple II series called MultiScribe: a combination bitmap font editor and word processor. Cavazos attributes his general fascination with reproducible type to the toy rotary press he had as a kid; however, it was his working apprenticeship under Oakland-based illustrator, hand letterer, and printmaker Ernest G. Kwiat that he considers pivotal. Along with type design, Cavazos also explores the world of letterpress printing and teaches digital type workshops. During the summer you can find him at nearby Yerba Buena Gardens. Yup, he's the guy over by the fountain tweaking serifs on a Powerbook.

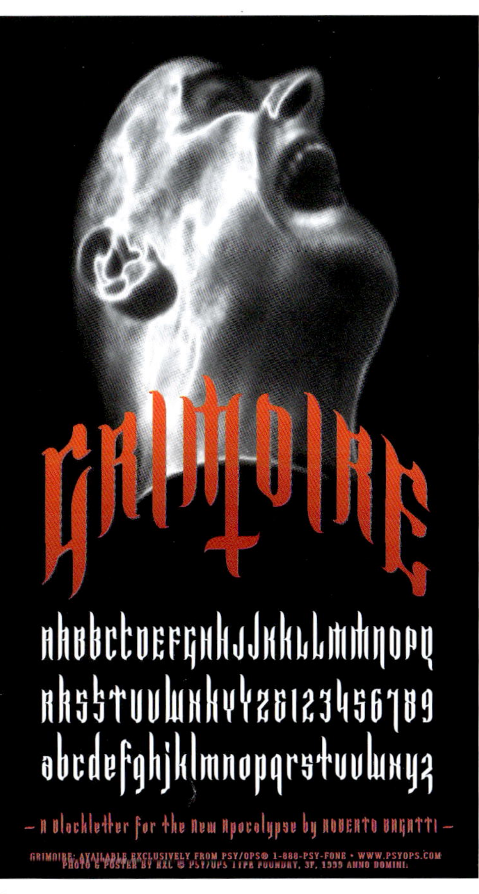

①

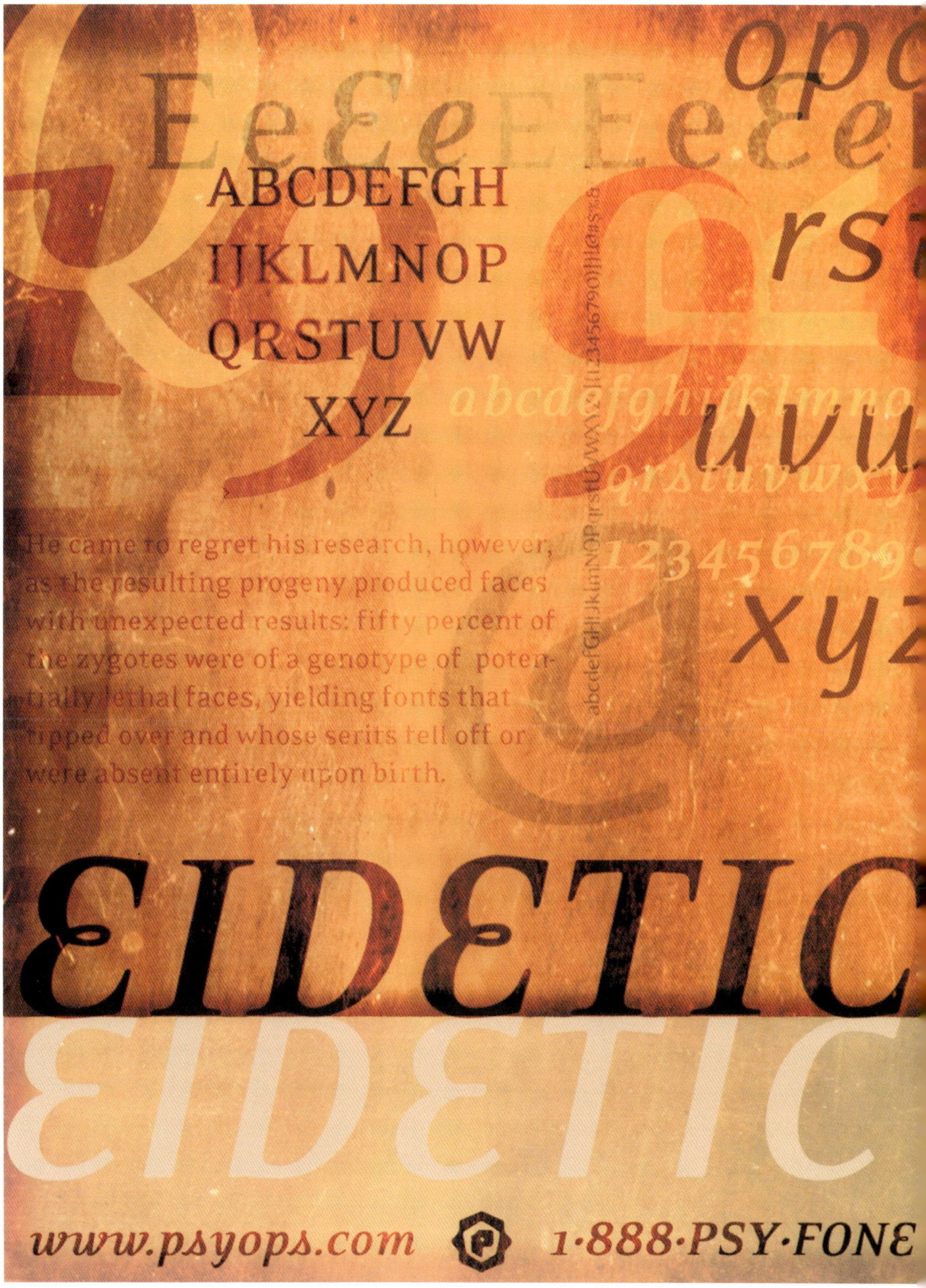

ABCDEFGH
IJKLMNOP
QRSTUVW
XYZ

He came to regret his research, however, as the resulting progeny produced faces with unexpected results: fifty percent of the zygotes were of a genotype of potentially lethal faces, yielding fonts that tipped over and whose serifs fell off or were absent entirely upon birth.

EIDETIC

www.psyops.com 1·888·PSY·FONE

②

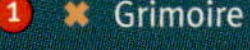

❶ ✖ Grimoire
■ Roberto Bagatty
▲ Psy/Ops type foundry

❷ ✖ Eidetic Modern Regular / Eidetic Serif Regular (a 10 weight family)
■ Rodrigo Cavazos
▲ Psy/Ops type foundry

① ● Grimoire Broadside
■ Rodrigo Cavazos
✖ Grimoire, Kricivi Bold
★ Psy/Ops type foundry
◆ Rodrigo Cavazos

② ● Eidetic poster
■ Ruth Askevold
✖ Eidetic Serif / Eidetic Modern
★ Psy/Ops
◆ Ruth Askevold

3

ABCDEFGHIJKLMNOPQRSTUVWXYZ
abcdefghijklmnopqrstuvwxyz
0123456789
«!@®©$£¢?%&*»

ABCDEFGHIJ	ABCDEFGHIJ
KLMNOPQRS	KLMNOPQRS
TUVWXYZ	TUVWXYZ
abcdefghij	abcdefghij
klmnopqrst	klmnopqrst
uvwxyz	uvwxyz
0123456789	0123456789
«!@®©$£¢?%^&*»	«!@®©$£¢?%^&*»

4

3
- Table Manners Regular (a 2 weight family)
- Robert Beck
- Psy/Ops type foundry

4
- Alembic Regular One / Alembic Regular Two (a 8 weight family)
- Rodrigo Cavazos
- Psy/Ops type foundry

4

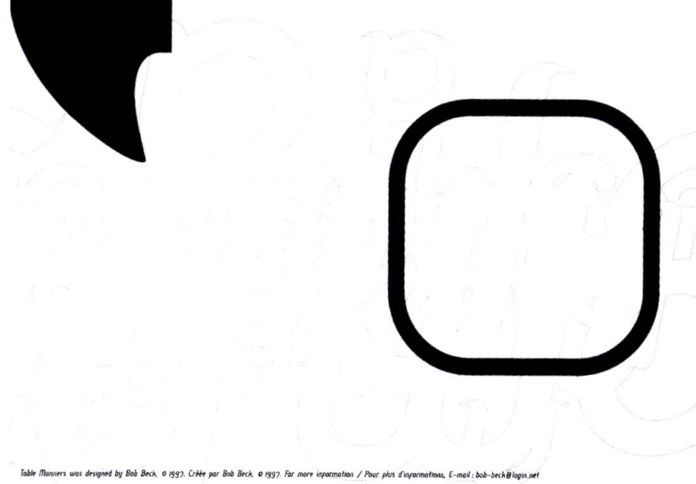

Table Manners was designed by Bob Beck, © 1997. Créée par Bob Beck, © 1997. For more information / Pour plus d'informations, E-mail : bob-beck@login.net

3

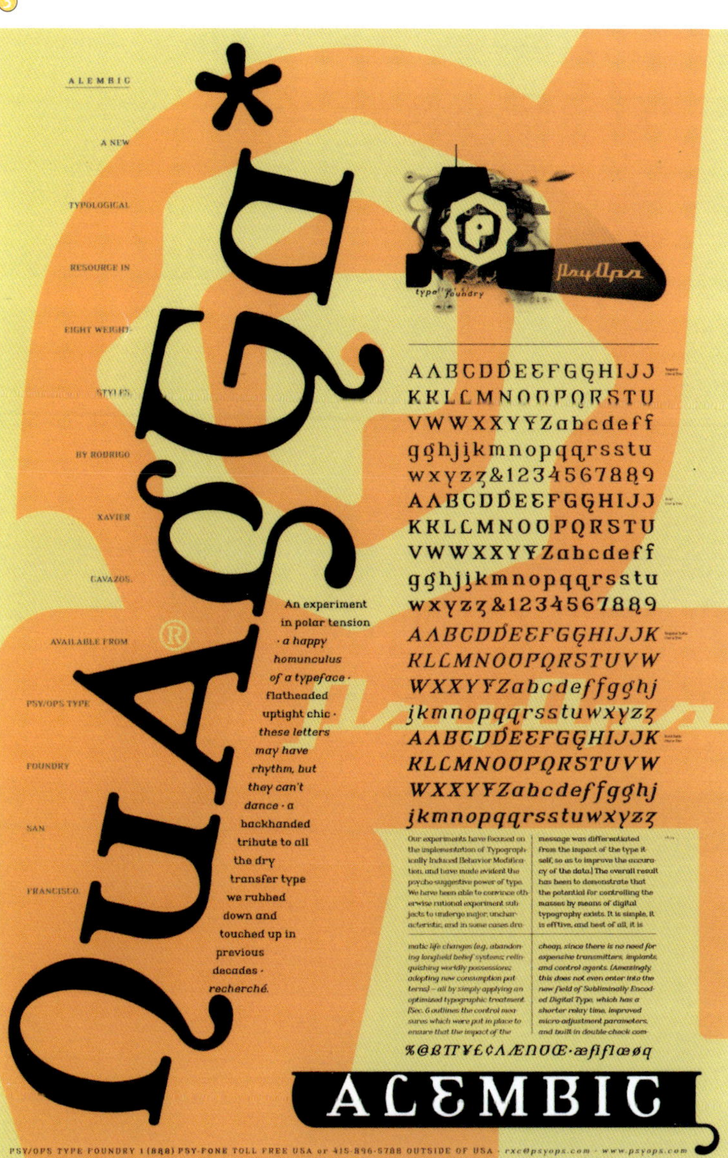

3
- ● QuAgGa posteer
- ■ Rodrigo Cavazos
- ✖ Alembic One & Two
- ★ Psy/Ops
- ◆ Rodrigo Cavazos

4
- ● Table Manners postcard
- ■ Robert Beck
- ✖ Table Manners Regular / Italic
- ★ Psy/Ops
- ◆ Robert Beck

5

ABCDEFGHIJ
KLMNOPQRS
TUVWXYZ
abcdefghij
klmnopqrst
uvwxyz
0123456789
«!@®©$£¢?%&*»

ABCDEFGHIJ
KLMNOPQRS
TUVWXYZ
abcdefghij
klmnopqrst
uvwxyz
0123456789
«!@®©$£¢?%&*»

ABCDEFGHIJKLMNOPQRSTUVWXYZ
abcdefghijklmnopqrstuvwxyz
0123456789
«!@®©$£¢?%&*»

6

5 ✖ VM74 Regular / Irregular
■ Rodrigo Cavazos
▲ Psy/Ops type foundry

6 ✖ Oculus A Gauge (a 12 weight family)
■ Rodrigo Cavazos
▲ Psy/Ops type foundry

7

ABCDEFGHIJKLMNOPQRSTUVWXYZ
abcdefghijklmnopqrstuvwxyz
0123456789
«!@®©$£¢?%&*»

ABCDEFGHIJ
KLMNOPQRS
TUVWXYZ
ABCDEFGHIJ
KLMNOPQRST
UVWXYZ
0123456789
«!@®©$£¢?%&*»

ABCDEFGHIJ
KLMNOPQRS
TUVWXYZ
ABCDEFGHIJ
KLMNOPQRST
UVWXYZ
0123456789
«!@®©$£¢?%&*»

8

7 ✖ Perceval Regular (a 4 weight family)
■ Michel Valois
▲ Psy/Ops type foundry

8 ✖ Trillium Regular / Gilded (a 4 weight family)
■ Rodrigo Cavazos
▲ Psy/Ops

abCdEFGHiJkLMNoPQRStUVWXYZ

0123456789@®©¢$&?

abCdEFGHiJkLMNoPQRStUVWXYZ

0123456789@®©¢$&?

1

2

ABCDEFGHIJKLMNOPQRSTUVWXYZ
abcdefghijklmnopqrstuvwxyz
0123456789@®©¢$&?

ABCDEFGHIJKLMNOPQRSTUVWXYZ
abcdefghijklmnopqrstuvwxyz
0123456789@®©¢$&?

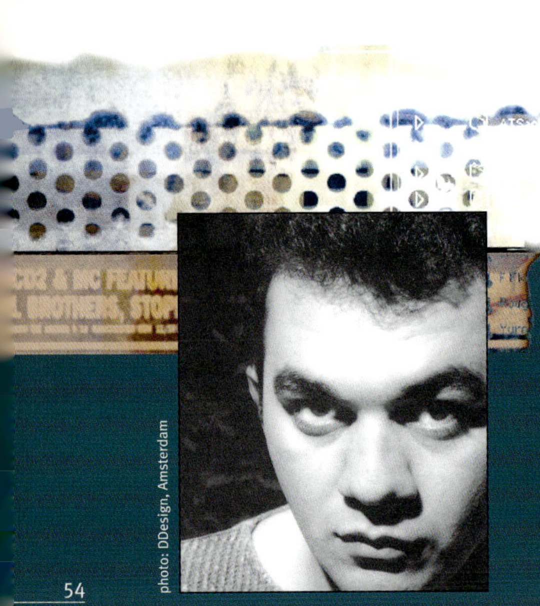

photo: DDesign, Amsterdam

angus r. shamal

ARS Design

Looking back at the last 10 years of type design, one cannot ignore the tendency toward individual expression and creation of work that is more personal and self-conscience.
Being a designer, I do realize that a big and important part of this profession is staying tuned with the developments and needs of the industry as well as those of society. But, I do sometimes wish I could see more work that derived from a serious and more individual typographical background, rather than following certain trends. I find it very exciting to see new and original typefaces that make good use of the old fundamentals of the type-design tradition and very efficiently meet with the challenges of this century and the one to follow. I'm pleased to see that besides the big font foundries, there are enough small foundries and individual designers that follow this approach.

Angus R. Shamal (1972) is a graphic designer and a type designer running ARS Design, a one-man design studio based in Amsterdam. Among other projects, the studio produces CD- & Record-covers to different Dutch Labels like: Staalplaat, Lab Records & Getto Trax; numerous Books & Book-covers to major Book-publishers in Amsterdam, and art-direction and design for Radio 100 – a local Amsterdam radio-station. The work of ARS Design combines a great attention to typography with strong graphical presence and imagery.
Angus R. Shamal also designs his own high quality typefaces, which are released under his foundry name – ARS Type™. The ARS Type™ collection includes about 20 font families that range from very extensive text fonts to experimental display fonts.

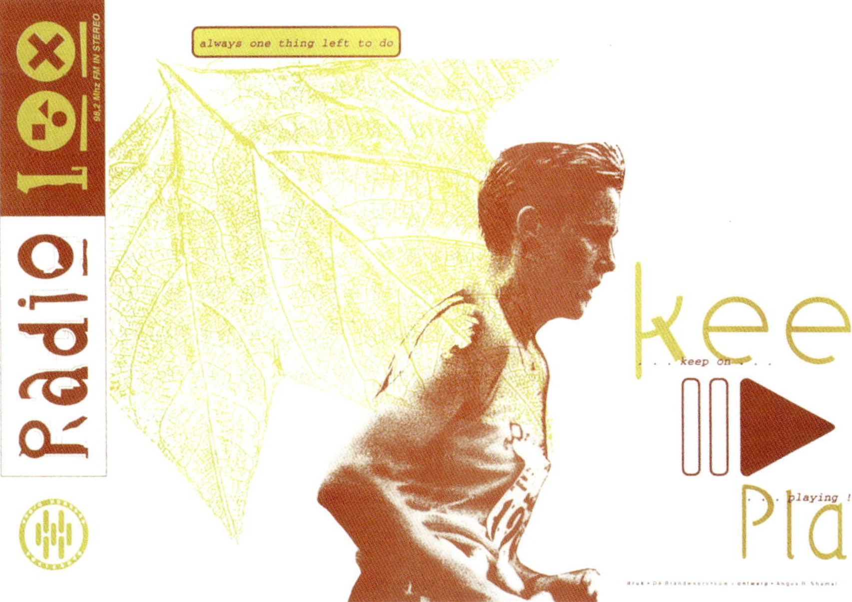

1

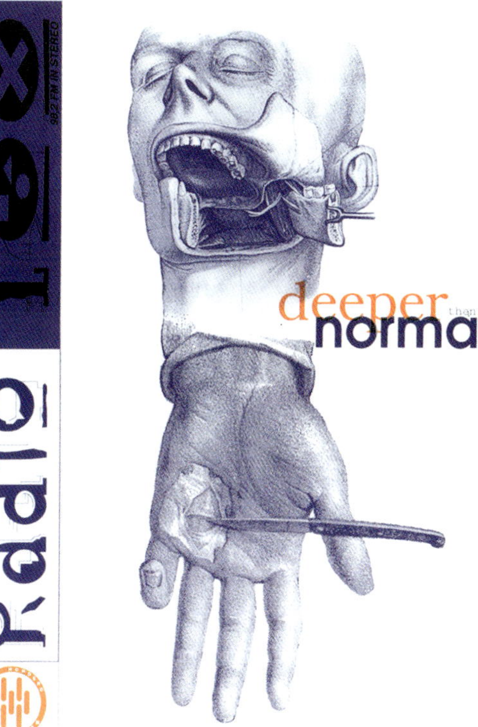

2

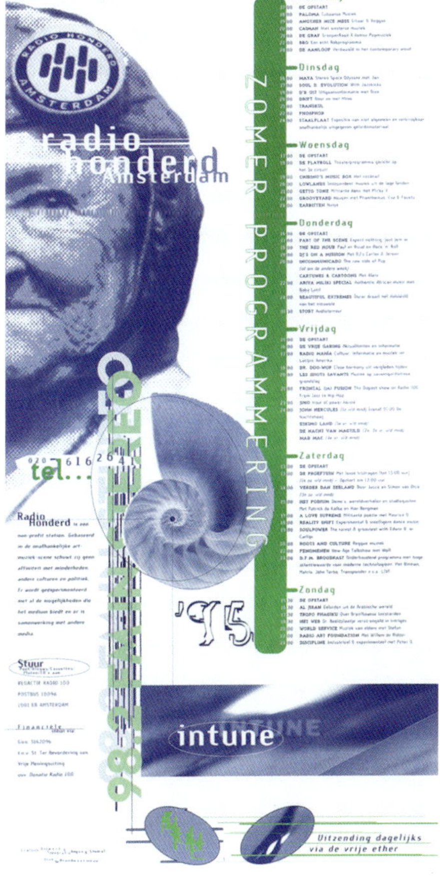

3

1 ✖ Humain Synthetica / Graphica (a 2 weight family)
■ Angus R. Shamal
▲ ARS Type™

2 ✖ Temper Plain / Temper Script Plain (a 4 weight family)
■ Angus R. Shamal
▲ ARS Type™

1 ● Radio 100 poster - keep playing
■ Angus R. Shamal
✖ ARS Humain-Graphica and hand drawn letters
★ Radio 100, Amsterdam
◆ Angus R. Shamal and found artwork

2 ● Radio 100 poster - deeper than normal
■ Angus R. Shamal
✖ ARS Humain-Graphica / ITC Bookman Light / Avant Garde
★ Radio 100, Amsterdam
◆ Angus R. Shamal and found artwork

3 ● Radio 100 programming - summer 95
■ Angus R. Shamal
✖ ARS Temper-Regular/Bold, ARS Humain-Synthetica, ARS Stormy Blue
★ Radio 100, Amsterdam
◆ Angus R. Shamal and found artwork

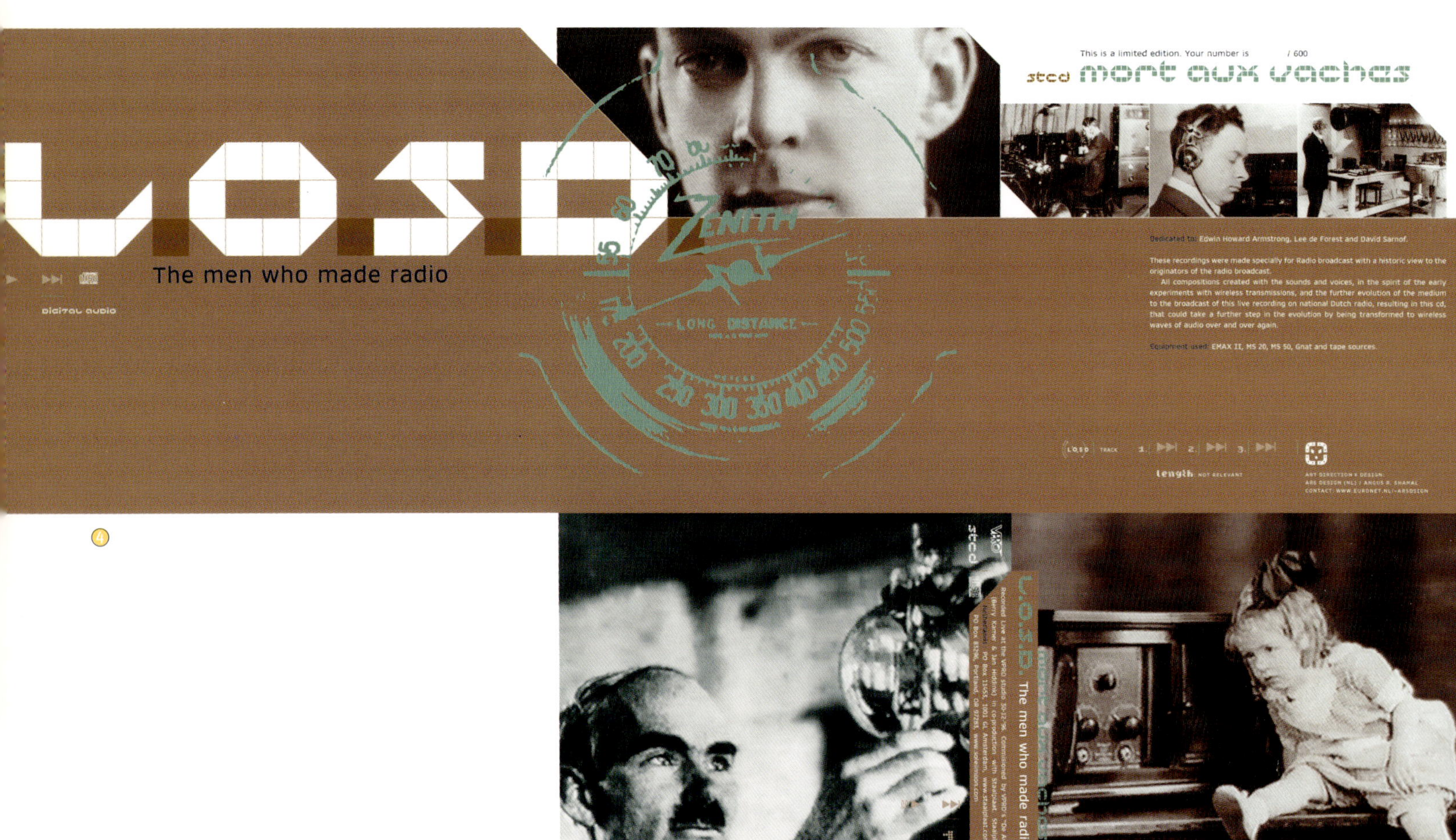

4

5

3

→ abcdefghijklmnopqrstuvwxyzabcde
0123456789 @®©¢$&?¤

→ abcdefghijklmnopqrstuvwxyz
0123456789 @®©¢$&?¤

→ ABCDEFGHIJKLMNOPQRSTUVWXYZABCD
0123456789 @®©¢$&?¤

→ ABCDEFGHIJKLMNOPQRSTUVWXYZ
0123456789 @®©¢$&?¤

3 ✖ ARS Polythene (a family of 8 variants)
■ Angus R. Shamal
▲ ARS Type™

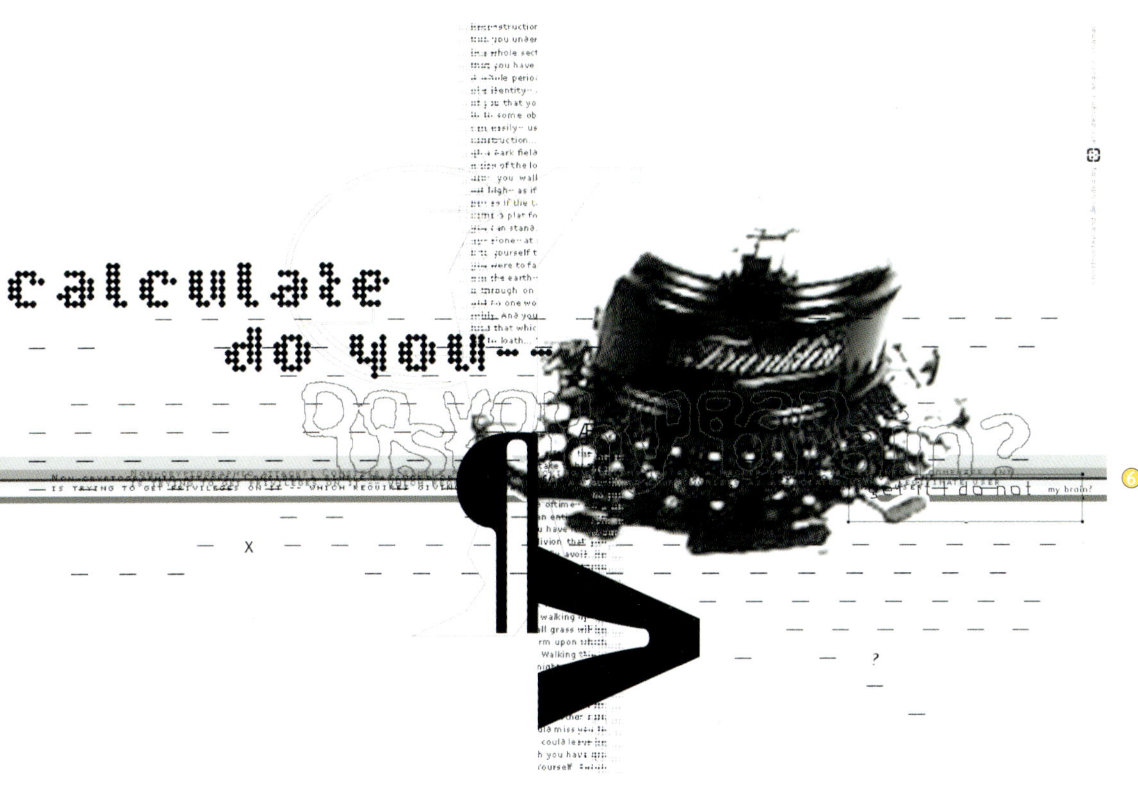

→ a b c d e f g h i j k l m n o p q r s t u v w x y z a b c d
0 1 2 3 4 5 6 7 8 9 @ ® © ¢ $ & ? ¤

→ a b c d e f g h i j k l m n o p q r s t u v w x y z
0 1 2 3 4 5 6 7 8 9 @ ® © ¢ $ & ? ¤

→ A B C D E F G H I J K L M N O P Q R S T U V W X Y Z A B C
0 1 2 3 4 5 6 7 8 9 @ ® © ¢ $ & ? ¤

→ A B C D E F G H I J K L M N O P Q R S T U V W X Y Z
0 1 2 3 4 5 6 7 8 9 @ ® © ¢ $ & ? ¤

4
- ● L.O.S.D. - The men who made radio (spread)
- ■ Angus R. Shamal
- ✖ ARS Polythene-Round Bold / ARS Folder / ARS Tunera Regular
- ★ Staalplaat
- ◆ Angus R. Shamal and found artwork

5
- ● L.O.S.D. - The men who made radio (CD cover)
- ■ Angus R. Shamal
- ✖ ARS Polythene-Round Bold / ARS Folder / ARS Tunera Regular
- ★ Staalplaat
- ◆ Angus R. Shamal

6
- ● Catalog spread - Plazm Fonts
- ■ Angus S. Shamal
- ✖ ARS Polythene-Round Bold / ARS Credit / ARS Platrica / ARS Censor-Sans
- ★ Plazm Media
- ◆ Angus R. Shamal

4

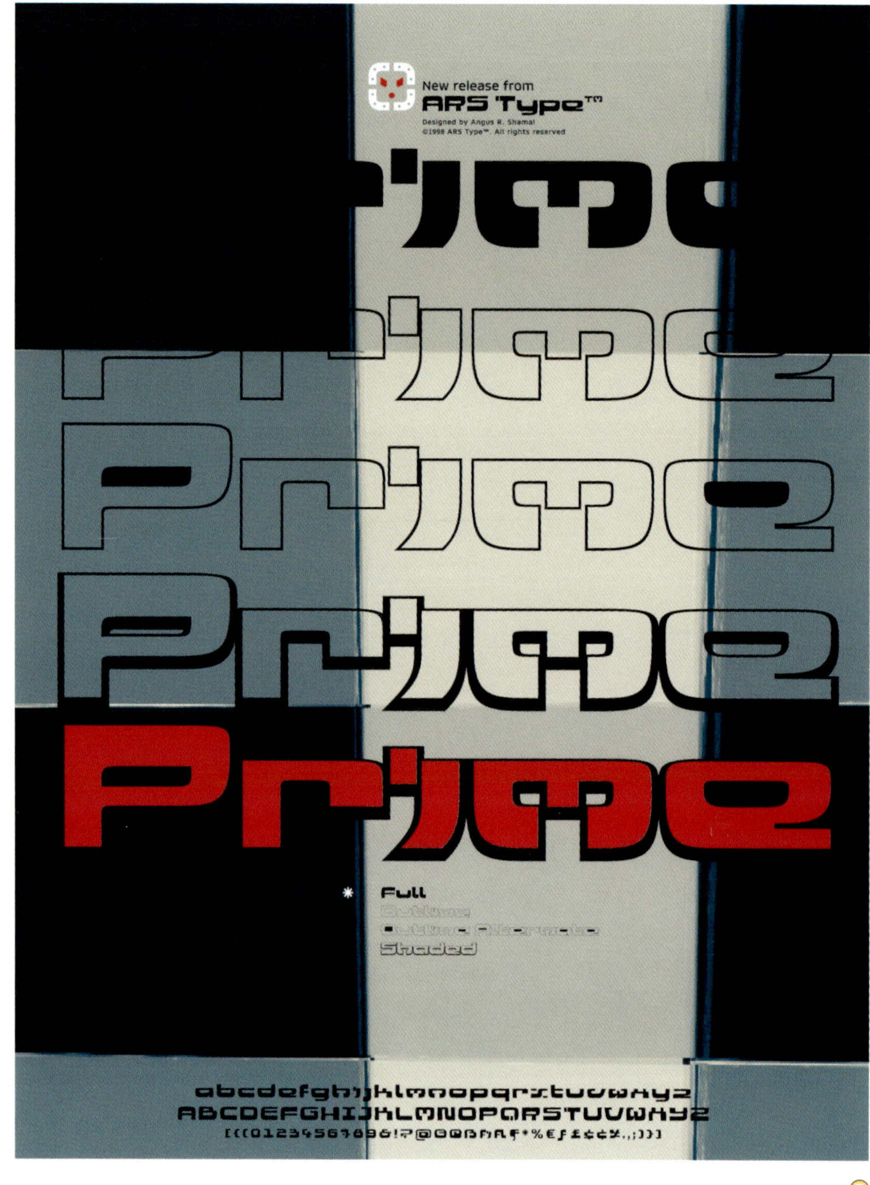

7

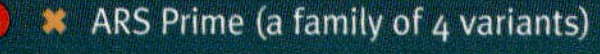

4 ✖ ARS Prime (a family of 4 variants)
■ Angus R. Shamal
▲ ARS Type™

5 ✖ ARS Kamp Sans & Serif (a family of 10 variants)
■ Angus R. Shamal
▲ ARS Type™

8

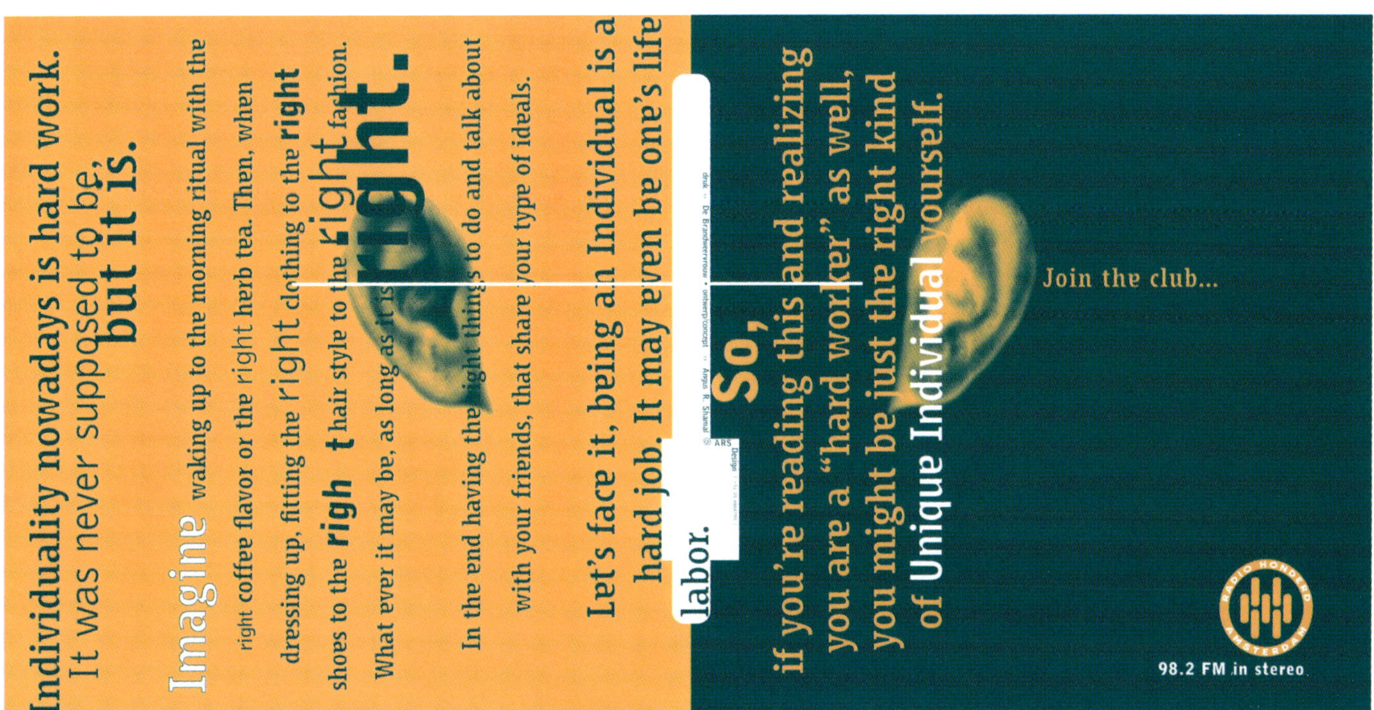

9

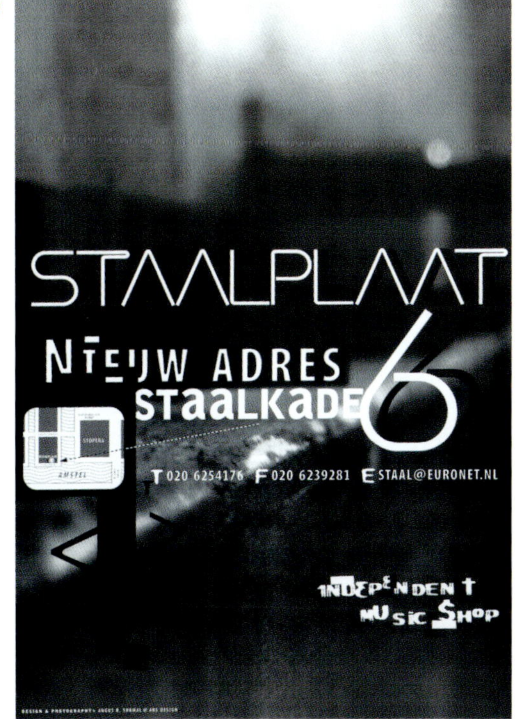

ABCDEFGHIJKLMNOPQRS
TUVWXYZ
abcdefghijklmnopqrstuvwxyz
0123456789@®©¢$&?
ABCDEFGHIJKLMNOPQRS
TUVWXYZ
abcdefghijklmnopqrstuvwxyz
0123456789@®©¢$&?

5

7
- ● Promotion poster, font release: ARS Prime
- ■ Angus R. Shamal
- ✖ ARS Prime (Full, Outline, Shaded, Alternate)
- ★ ARS Type ™
- ◆ Angus R. Shamal

8
- ● Radio 100 - programming Spring 96
- ■ Angus R. Shamal
- ✖ ARS Kamp Regular / Serif, Bell Gothic Black
- ★ Radio 100, Amsterdam
- ◆ Angus R. Shamal

9
- ● Staalplaat - Announcement poster
- ■ Angus R. Shamal
- ✖ Custom font (Staalplaat) / ARS Credit Bold / ARS Kamp Regular / Bell Gothic Black
- ★ Staalplaat, Amsterdam
- ◆ Angus R. Shamal

1

ABCDEFGHI
JKLMNOPQR
STUVWXYZ
abcdefghij
klmnopqrst
uvwxyz
0123456789
«!@®$¢?%&»

2

ABCDEFGHI
JKLMNOPQR
STUVWXYZ
abcdefghij
klmnopqrst
uvwxyz
0123456789
«!@@®$¢?&»

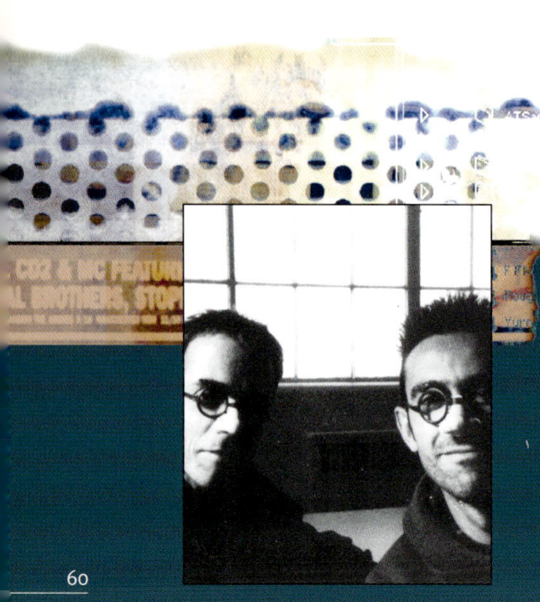

2rebels

Denis Dulude & Fabrizio Gilardino

Dirty, blurry, scratched up and cut through, 2Rebels' designs are edgy. Caught between the classical and the chaotic, and just on the cusp of legibility, their irreverant fonts fly in the face of tradition, suggesting past visions and sights unseen instead. A challenge to the accepted and understandable. A rebellion for the noisier aesthetics of the unknown led by 2Rebels' initial iconoclasts, Denis Dulude and Fabrizio Gilardino.

Back in 1995, Dulude and Gilardino buckled down in a Montréal basement to create an outlet for experimental design. 2Rebels emerged, an experiment in turning print into pictures suddenly underway. Since, their fonts have made headway across several continents–continents from where more rebels have come to meet them at the frontier of the font revolution. From there, the experiment continues...

Denis Dulude is a Canadian graphic designer based in Montréal, Canada. He graduated from his self-taught classes in 1993. To avoid job rejections, in 1993 he founded his own graphic studio, K.O. création. His clients range from software to dance companies. Denis Dulude founded the digital typefoundry 2Rebels in January 1995.

Fabrizio Gilardino is an Italian graphic designer currently based in Montréal, Canada. After graduating from the Istituto Europeo di Design in Milan in 1986 he worked for a variety of studios as well as a free lance in Milan and Bologna before moving to Montréal in 1990. His clients include record labels, new music / avant garde composers and musicians, art galleries, theatre and dance companies, and various cultural associations. He has been associated with the digital type foundry 2Rebels since its beginnings.

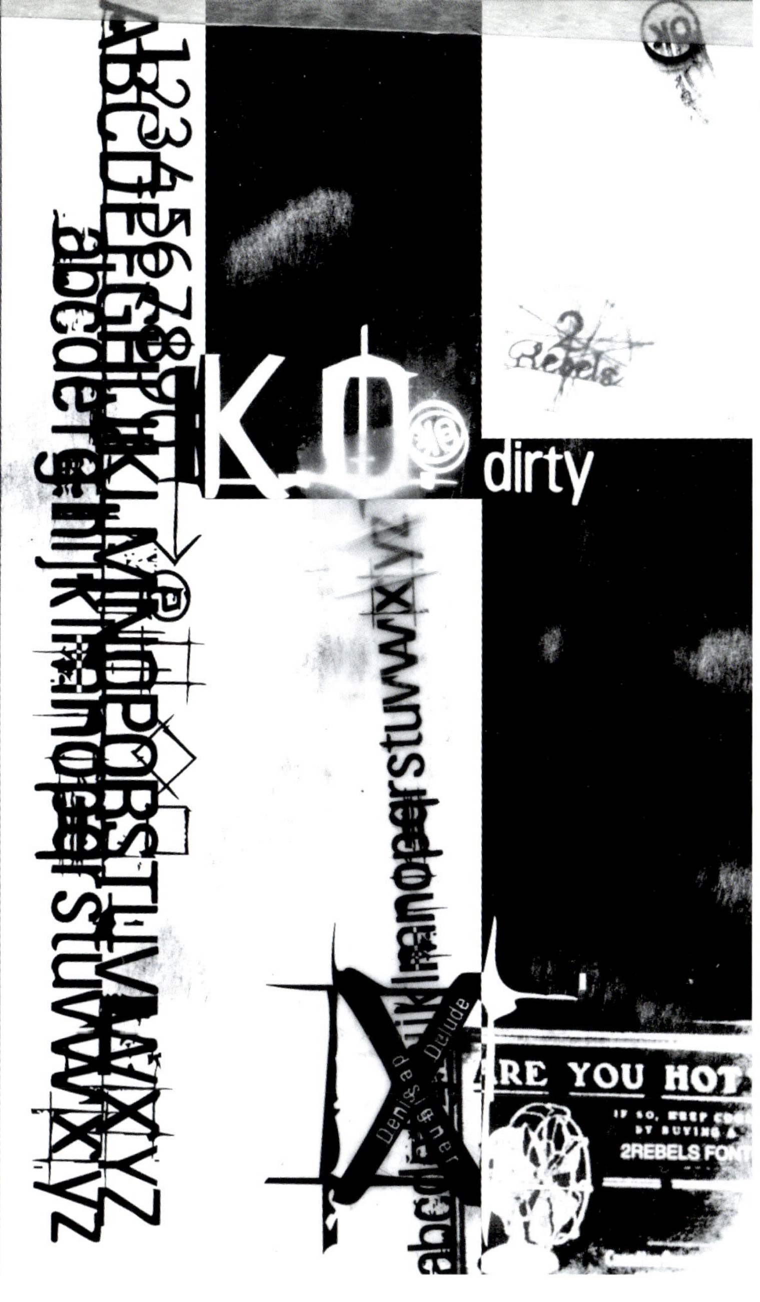

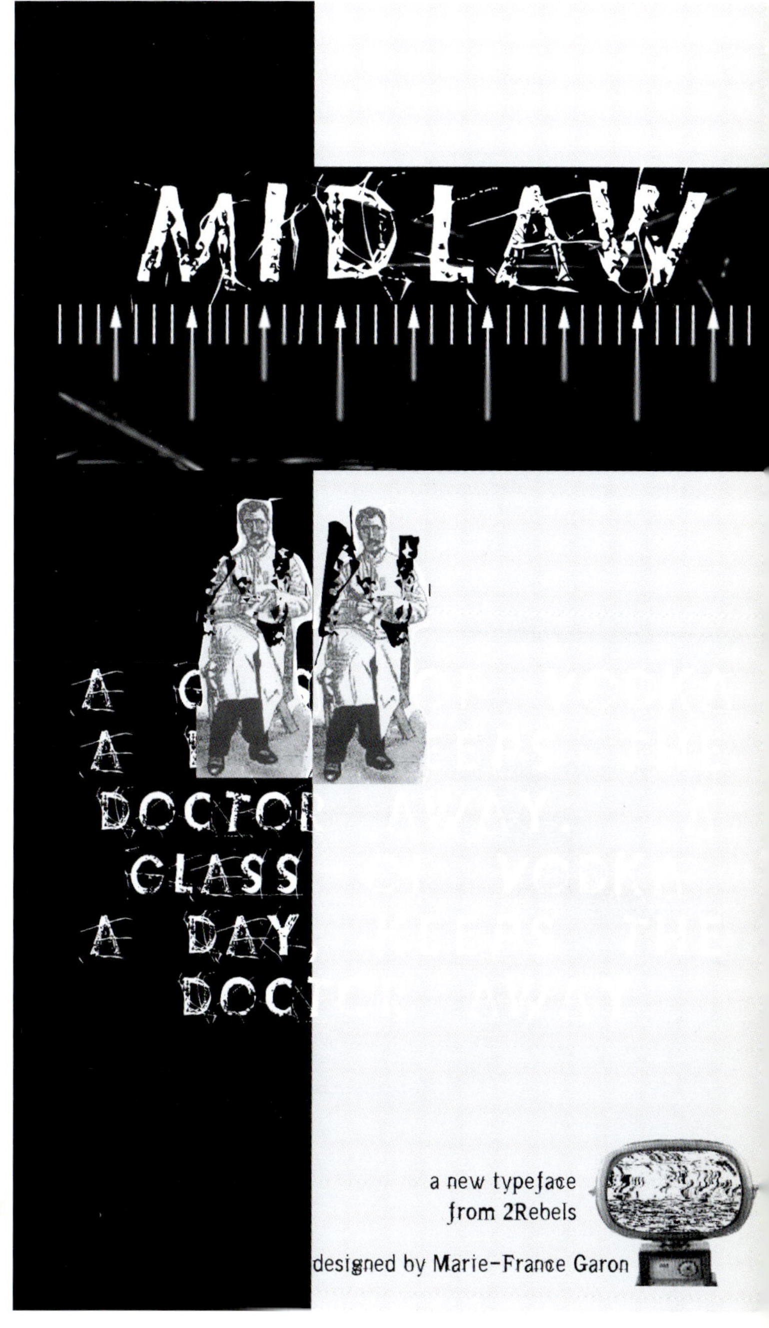

1 Midlaw
Marie France Garon
2Rebels

2 K.O. dirty
Denis Dulude
2Rebels

1 K.O. dirty poster
Denis Dulude
K.O. dirty
2Rebels

2 Midlaw poster
Marie France Garon
Midlaw, Tape
2Rebels

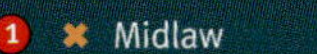

ABCDEFGHIJKLMNOPQRSTUVWXYZ
abcdefghijklmnopqrstuvwxyz
0123456789
«!@®$¢?&» 3

ABCDEFGHIJKLMNOPQRSTUVWXYZ 4
abcdefghijklmnopqrstuvwxyz
0123456789
«!@®$¢?%&kpacf»

ABCDEFGHIJKLMNOPQRSTUVWXYZ 5
0123456789
«!@®$¢?%& POLICE BRUTALITY FUCK THE COPS»

3 Hanbuhrs
Fabrizio Gilardino
2Rebels

4 Scritto Politto Freako
Fabrizio Gilardino
2Rebels

5 Angry
Fabrizio Gilardino
2Rebels

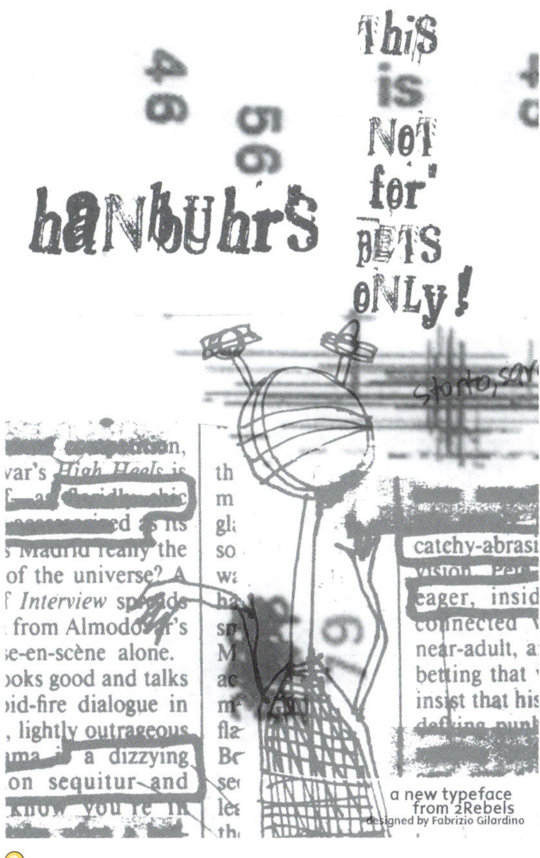

3

4

ABCDEFGHIJKLMNOPQRSTUVWXYZabcdefghijklmnopqrstuvwxyz0123456789

¿ ! & % $ @

SCRITTO POLITTO FREAKO

design Fabrizio Gilardino

VULGAR MODERNISM:

on Movies and Other

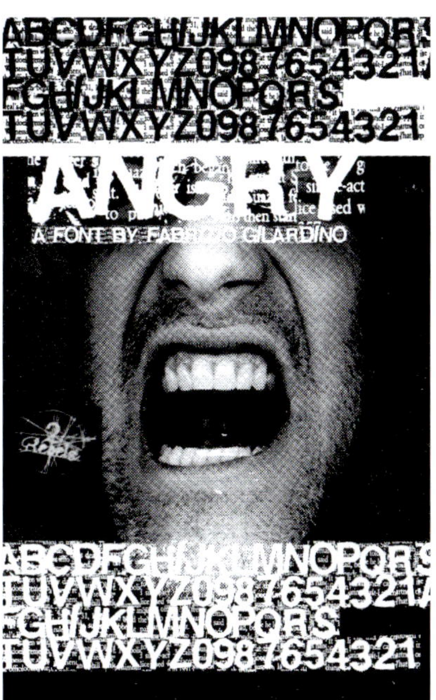

5

3
- Hanbuhrs poster
- Fabrizio Gilardino
- Hanbuhrs, Malcom Bold
- 2Rebels

4
- Scritto poster
- Fabrizio Gilardino
- Scritto Politto Freako
- 2Rebels

5
- Angry poster
- Denis Dulude, Pol Baril
- Angry
- 2Rebels

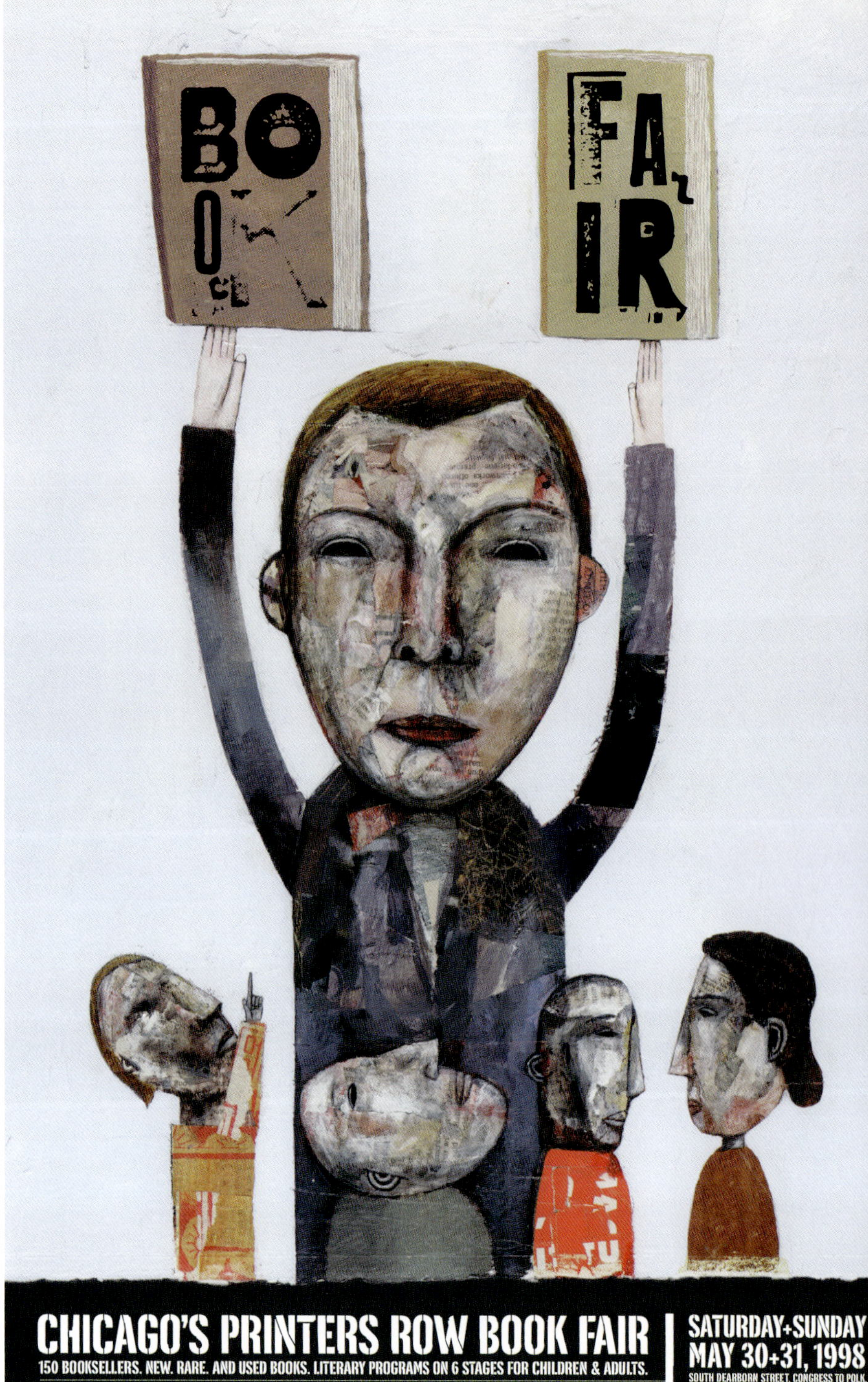

1

ABCDEFGHIJKLMNOPQRSTUVWXYZ
ABCDFGHIJKLMNOP
QRSTUVWXYZ
0123456789

abcdefghijklmnopqrstuvwxyz
ABCDEFGHIJKLMNOPQRSTU-
VWXYZ0123456789

abcdefghijklmnopqrstuvwxyz
ABCDEFGHIJKLMNOPQRSTU-
VWXYZ0123456789

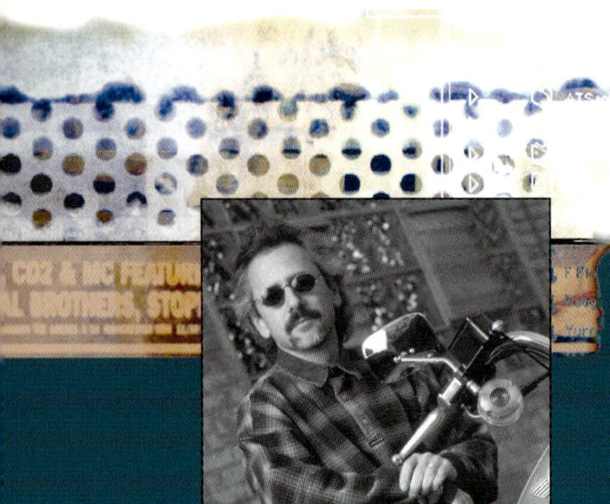

[T-26]

Carlos Segura

In 1994, [T-26] (a new digital type foundry) was born to explore the typographical side of the business. [T-26] is now distributed throughout the world by Fonthaus - USA, 2Rebels - Canada, Agosto - Japan, alt.Type - Singapore, Atomic Type - UK, Cyber Graphics-South Africa, Elsner+Flake - Germany, Faces - UK, Fontshop - San Francisco, Fontworks - UK, Phil's Fonts - USA, Precision Type -USA, Storm Creative - Malta, Signum Art - France, Sunflower Softwares - Fontshop Brazil, The ITF CD, as well as the AGFA/Monotype Creative Alliance CD.

I was born in Cuba, and came to the United States in 1965 when I was nine. I grew up in Miami, and at a very early age (12) got into a band as their drummer. I remained there until I was nineteen. One of my responsibilities was promotions, and when I left, I threw all that stuff into a book and got my first job as a production artist at an envelope company (my job was to design the return-addresses for bank deposit envelopes). My first real break was at an agency in New Orleans, and after a few more job changes, I moved to Chicago (always wanting to move here because I liked the way the name sounded) in 1980. I'm glad I did because that's where I met my wonderful wife. I worked for advertising agencies, such as Marsteller, Foote Cone & Belding, Young & Rubicam, Ketchum, DDB Needham and others, both here and in Pittsburgh, for eleven years until coming to the realization that I was not happy creatively, so I quit and started Segura Inc in 1991 to pursue design, with the goal of trying to blend as much "fine art" into "commercial art" as I could.

3

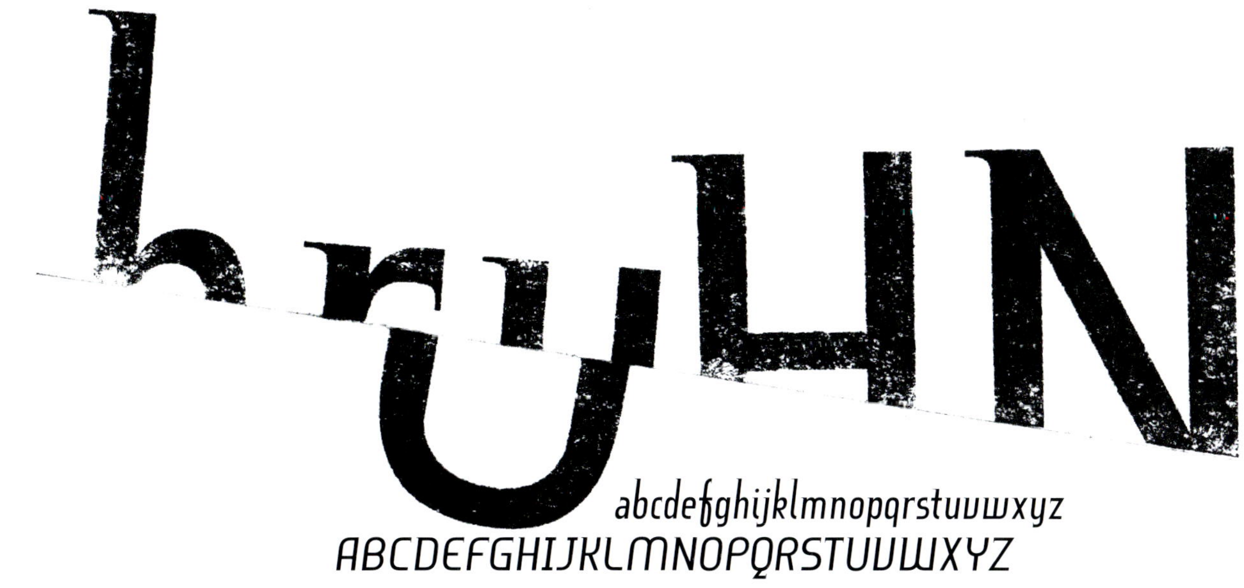

abcdefghijklmnopqrstuvwxyzABCDEFGHIJKLMNOPQRSTUVWXYZ1234567890abcdefghijklmnopqrstuvwxyzABCDEFGHIJKLMNOPQRSTUVWXYZ1234567890

2

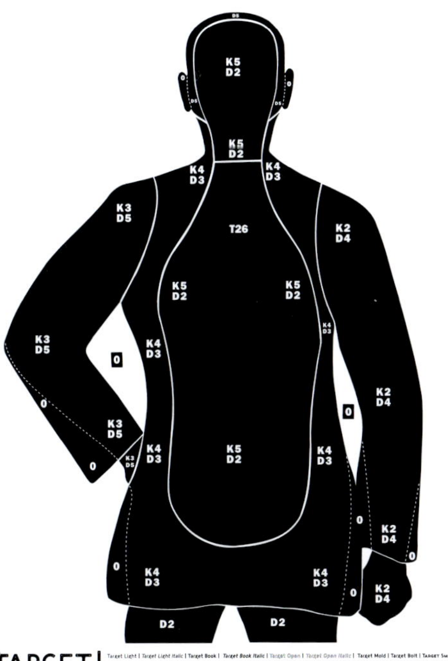

2

3

ABCDEFGHIJKLMNOPQRSTUVWXYZ
abcdefghijklmnopqrstuvwxyz
ABCDEFGHIJKLMNOPQRSTUVWXYZ
abcdefghijklmnopqrstuvwxyz
0123456789 (@¢$№%&)

1
- ✖ Gazz (a 3 weight family)
- ■ Mario Feliciano
- ▲ [T-26] digital type foundry

2
- ✖ Bruhn Script
- ■ Peter Bruhn
- ▲ [T-26] digital type foundry

3
- ✖ Target (a font family of 9)
- ■ Tomi Haaparanta
- ▲ [T-26] digital type foundry

1
- ● Chicago Book Fair (poster)
- ■ Carlos Segura
- ✖ Gazz
- ★ Chicago Book Fair Association
- ◆ Jordan Isip

2
- ● Target poster
- ■ Carlos Segura
- ✖ Target
- ★ [T-26] digital type foundry
- ◆ Carlos Segura

3
- ● Bruhn poster
- ■ Carlos Segura
- ✖ Bruhn Script
- ★ [T-26] digital type foundry

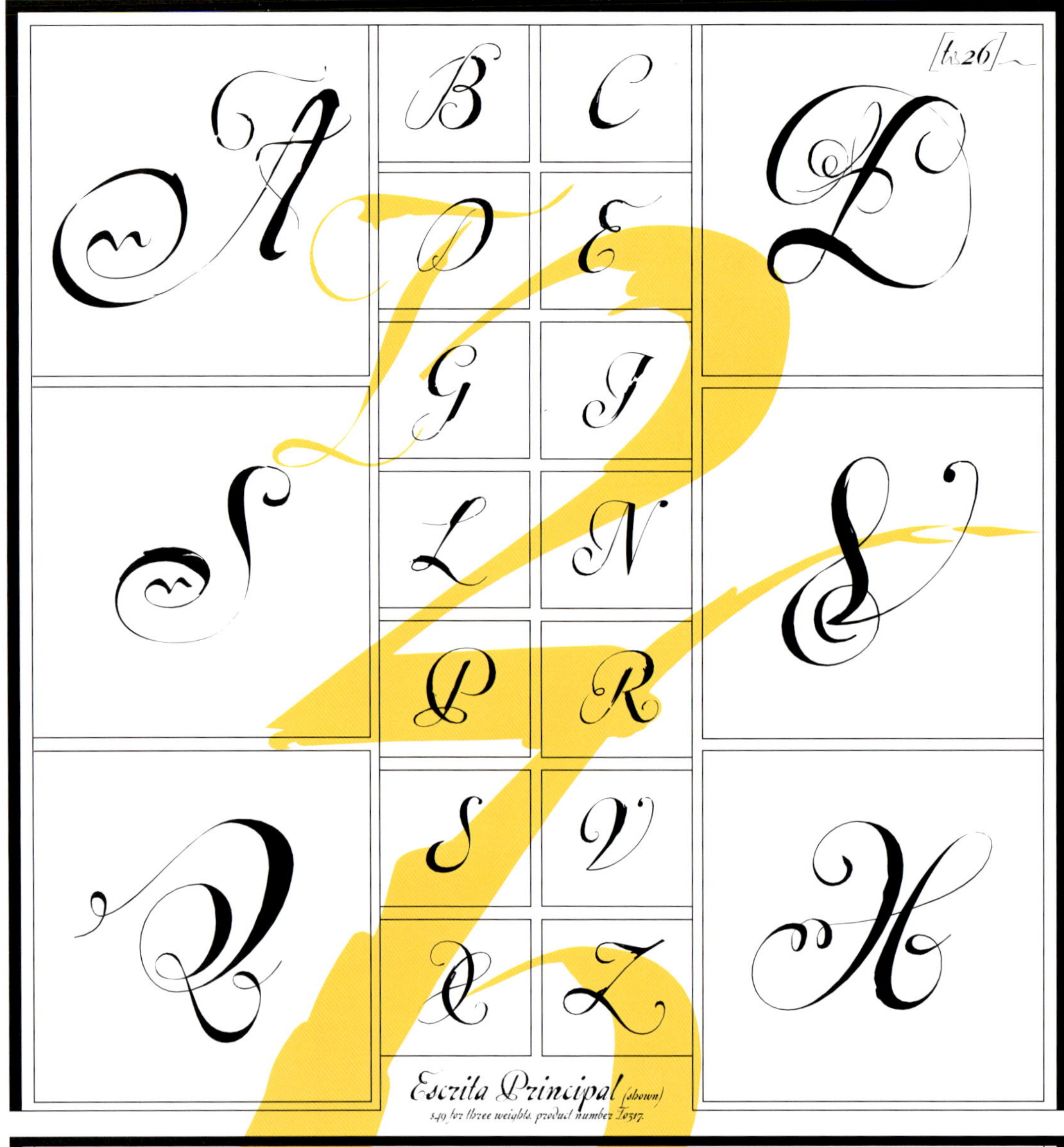

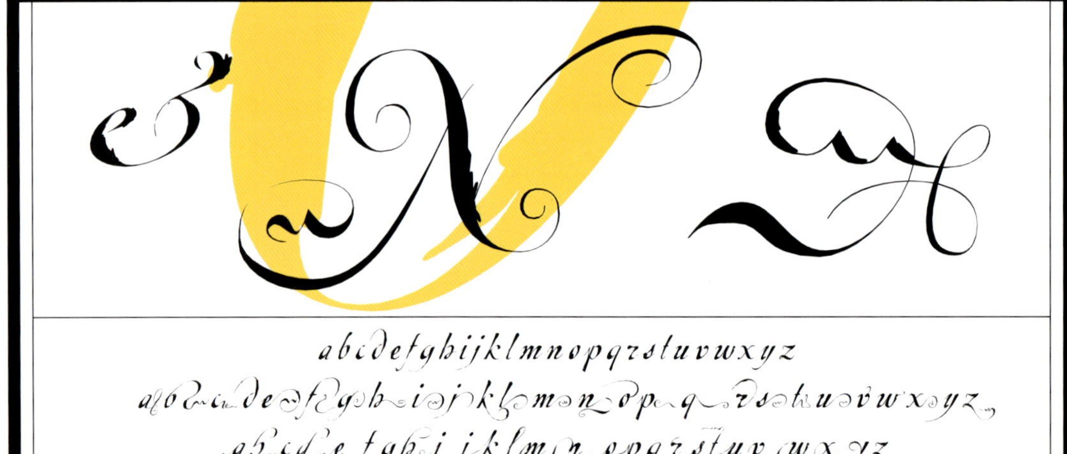

4

Escrita (principais), Escrita (finais) & Escrita (iniciais). Designer: Mario Feliciano. Exclusively from [t-26]

This poster has been letterpressed by Rohner Letterpress. 3759 North Ravenswood, Chicago, Illinois 60613. tel 773.248.0800, fax 773.248.8635, e-mail: bruno@rohner1.com

4 ✖ Escrita (a 3 weight family)
■ Mario Feliciano (font)
Mario Feliciano / Carlos Segura (Escrita poster)
▲ [T-26] digital type foundry

5 ✖ Taser Round (a set of 5 fonts)
■ Jim Marcus
▲ [T-26] digital type foundry

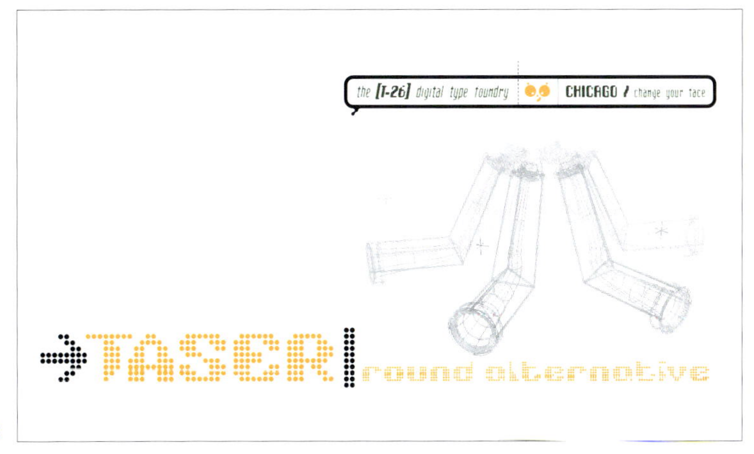

4

5

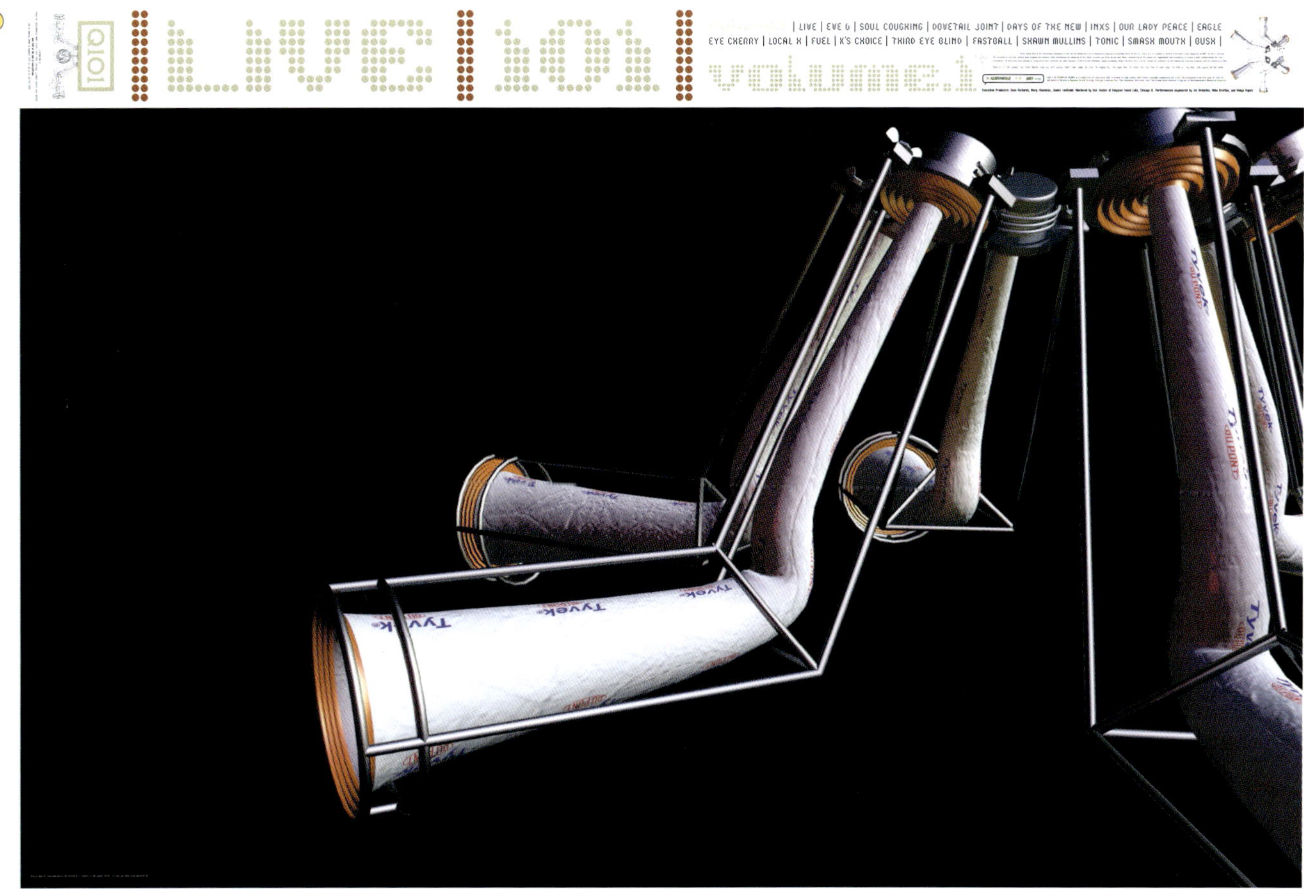

ABCDEFGHIJKLMNOPQRSTUVWXYZ
abcdefghijklmnopqrstuvwxyz
0123456789 [@¢$#%&]

5

4
- ● Taser promotion card
- ■ Carlos Segura
- ✖ Taser
- ★ [T-26] digital type foundry

5
- ● Q101 Live - 101 Poster
- ■ Carlos Segura
- ✖ Taser
- ★ Q101 Radio
- ◆ Eric Ravenstein

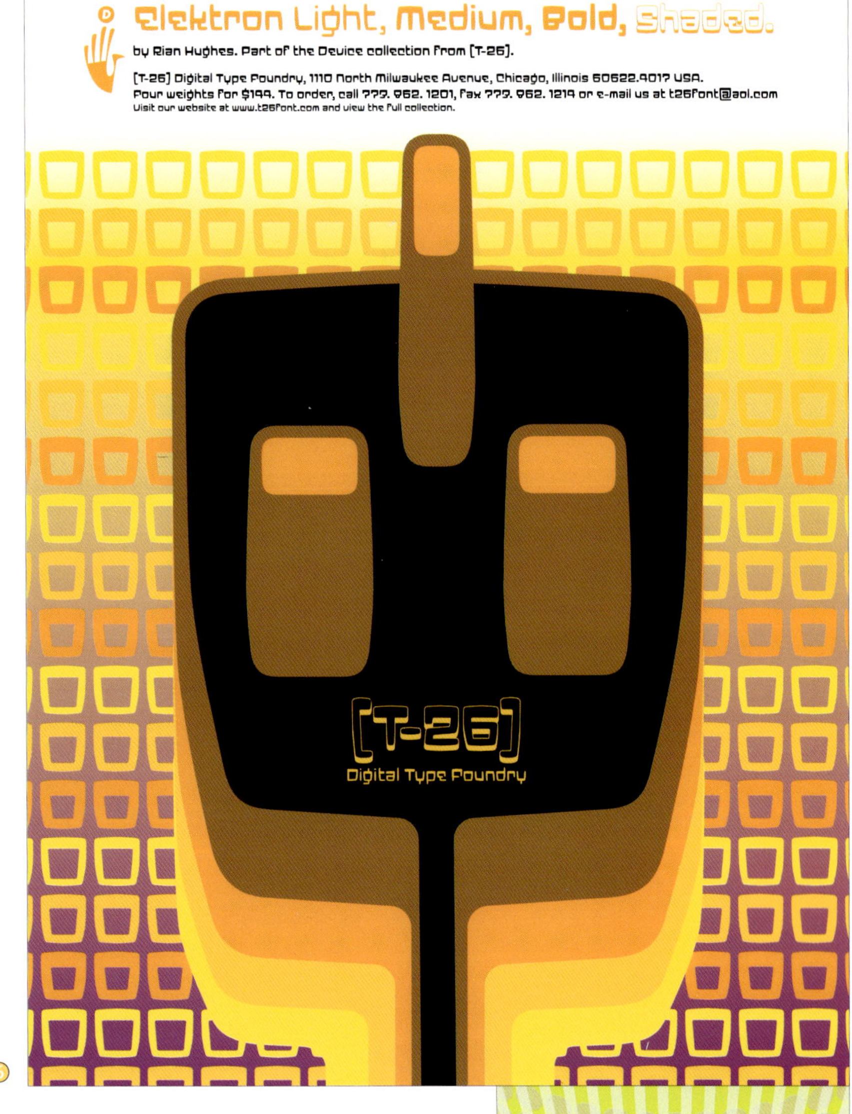

6

ABCDEFGHIJKLMNOPQRSTUVWX
YZabcdefghijklmnopqrstuvwxyz
0123456789 [@¢$#%&]

ABCDEFGHIJKLMNOPQRSTUVWX
YZabcdefghijklmnopqrstuvwxyz
0123456789 [@¢$#%&]

7

6 ✖ Elektron (a 4 weight family)
■ Rian Hughes
▲ [T-26] digital type foundry

7 ✖ Stadia Outline / Regular (a 2 weight family)
■ Rian Hughes
▲ [T-26] digital type foundry

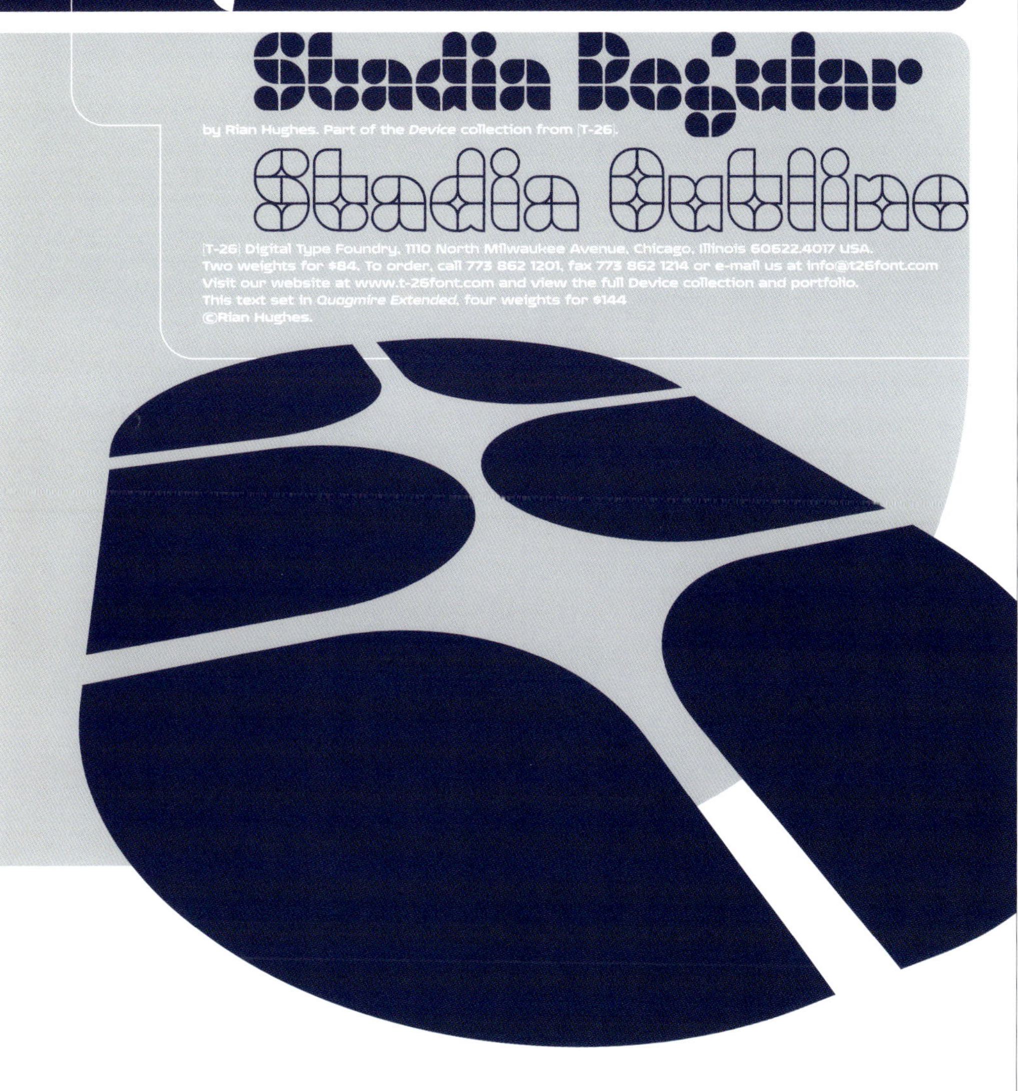

8

ABCDEFGHI
JKLMNOPQ
RSTUVWXYZ
abcdefghi
jklmnopq
rstuvwxyz
0123456789

ABCDEFGHI
JKLMNOPQ
RSTUVWXYZ
abcdefghi
jklmnopq
rstuvwxyz
0123456789

7

6
- ● Elektron postcard
- ■ Rian Huges
- ✖ Elektron
- ★ [T-26] digital type foundry
- ◆ Rian Huges

7
- ● [T-26] digital type foundry promotion card
- ✖ Quad
- ★ [T-26] digital type foundry

8
- ● Stadia poster
- ■ Brent Riley
- ✖ Stadia
- ★ [T-26] digital type foundry
- ◆ Brent Riley

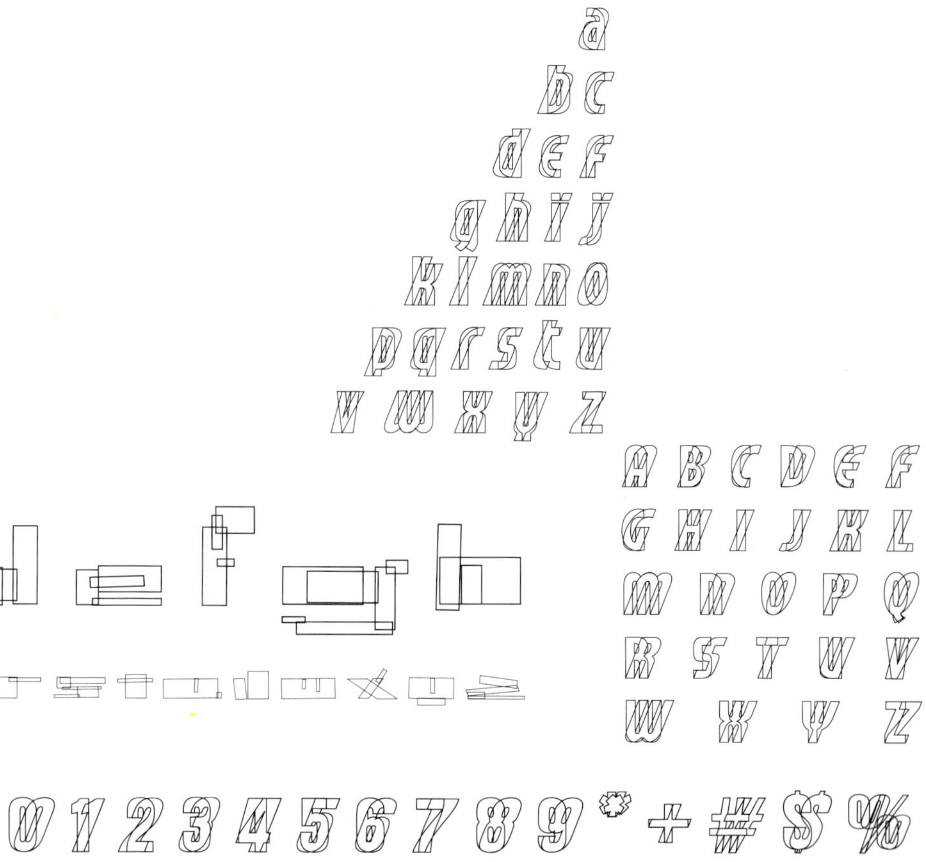

1

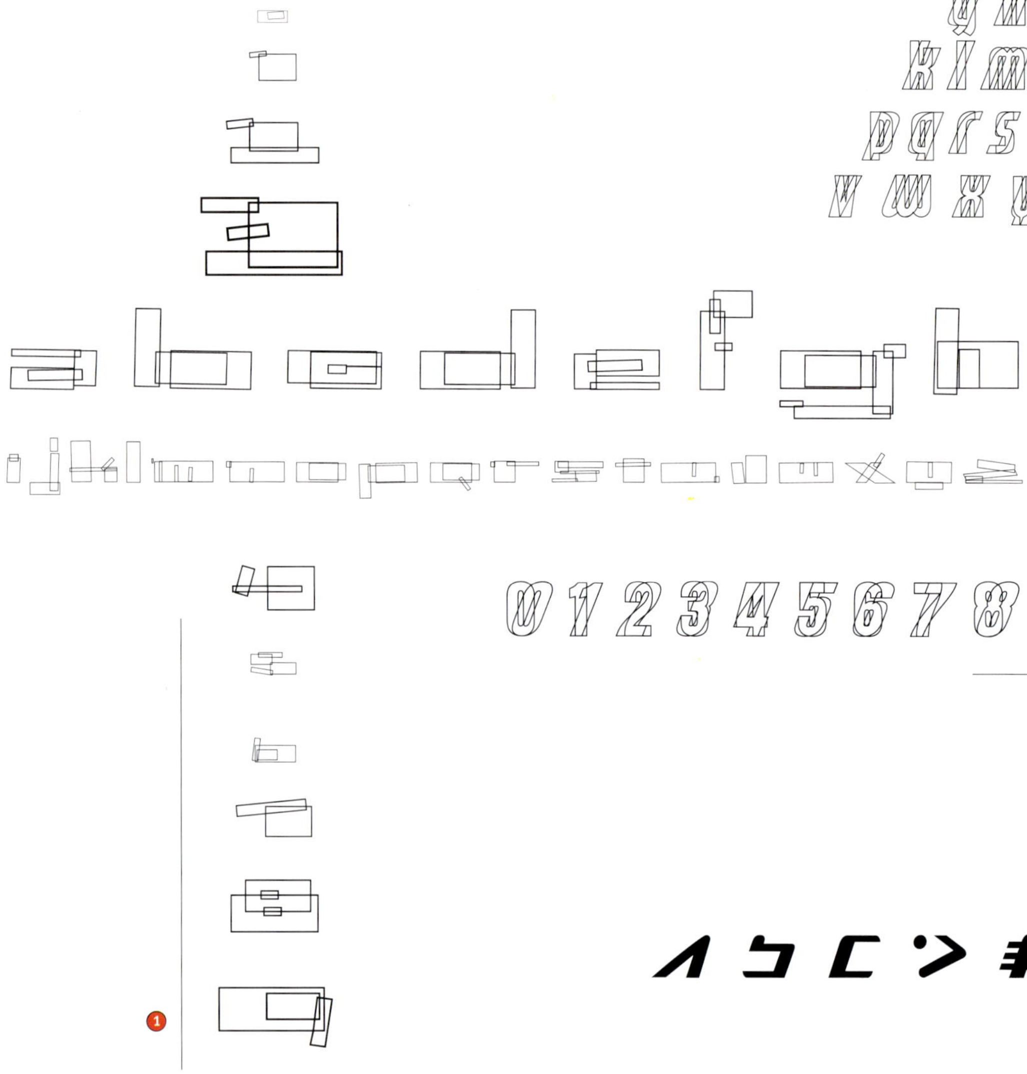

2

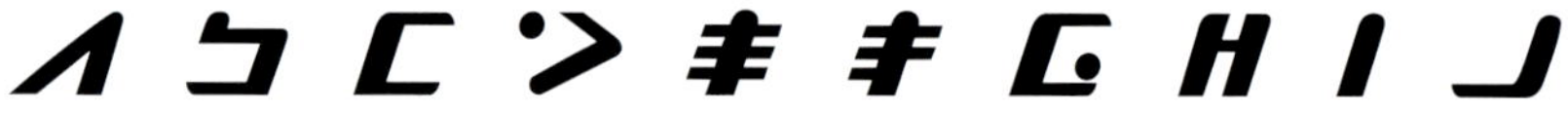

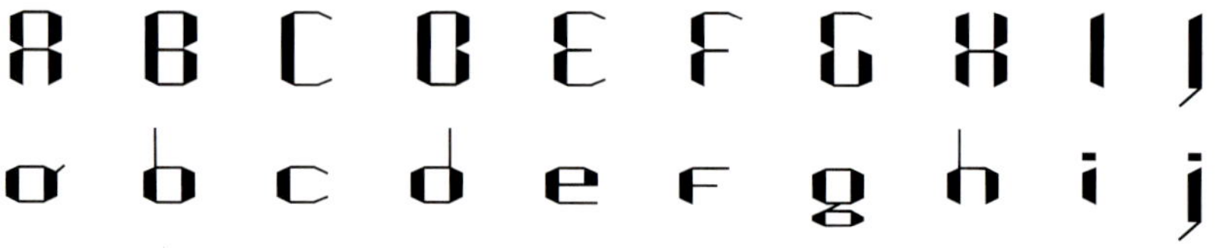

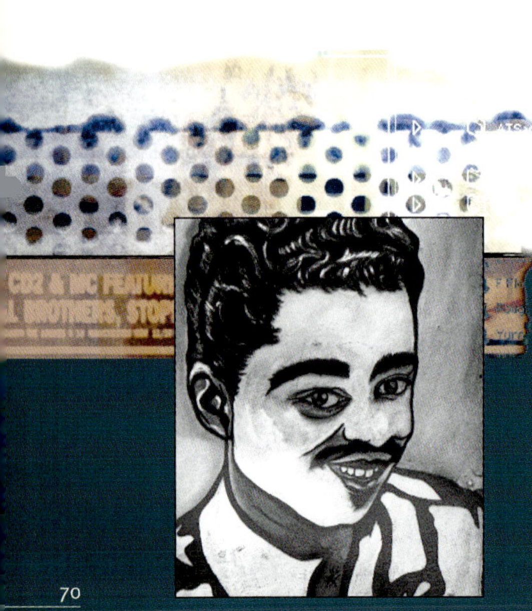

hale+co

James Hale

They say you can tell a type designer's psychological dysfunction by his font. So, little Freud, what do you see in Deth Imperial? At Hale+CO. we love to type. We live type. We collect type. We have 8,500 fonts in our collection. We started designing these 30 or so original masterpieces on the original version of Fontographer. We're talking Altsys, not Macromedia! Then we started marketing our fonts to other designers, but could only capture a small part of the market. If what goes around comes around, we look forward to the day when the true art and craft of fine typography comes back in style. Because by then, we'll be dead.

Formerly Senior Art Director at Beber Silverstein & Partners advertising agency, James Hale has received almost every advertising and design award given, including both Gold and Silver medals from the New York Art Directors Club, Communication Arts, The New York Andys and the Telly Awards. Prior to his five years at Beber Silverstein working on such accounts as Florida Power & Light, Persol Eyewear, NEA, Michele Watches and Helmsley Hotels, Hale worked from 1988-1991 as an art director at world-renowned advertising agency Ogilvy & Mather Worldwide in New York, as well as TMV Networks in New York. Hale was educated at the Academy of Art College in San Francisco, CA, as well as UC Berkeley. He has taught and lectured on advertising, conceptualization and graphic design at the University of Miami, F.I.U., The Portfolio Center of Atlanta, GA and The Miami Ad School. He is also an accomplished oil and acrylic painter and enjoys riding his motorcycle in his free time.

3

A B C D E F G H I J K
L M N O P Q R S
T U V W X Y Z
0 1 2 3 4
5 6 7
8 9

A B C D E F G H I J
K L M N O P Q R
S T U V W X Y Z
a b c d e f g h i j
k l m n o p q r s
t u v w x y z
0 1 2 3 4 5 6 7 8 9

4

k l m n o p q r s t u v w x y z

5

K L M N O P Q R S T U V W X Y Z
k l m n o p q r s t u v w x y z

6

1 Tosca
James Hale
Hale + Co.

2 Ganymede
James Hale
Hale + Co.

3 Deth Imperial
James Hale
Hale + Co.

4 Grand Torino
James Hale
Hale + Co.

5 Beyond Machines
James Hale
Hale + Co.

6 Kineto
James Hale
Hale + Co.

1

A B C D E F G H I J K L M N O P Q R S T U V W X Y Z
a b c d e f g h i j k l m n o p q r s t u v w x y z
1 2 3 4 5 6 7 8 9 0

2

ABCDEFGHIJKLMNOPQRS
TUVWXYZ
abcdefghijklmnopqrstuvwxyz

3

ABCDEFGHIJKLMNOPQRSTUVWXYZ
abcdefghijklmnopqrstuvwxyz
1234567890

javier michalski

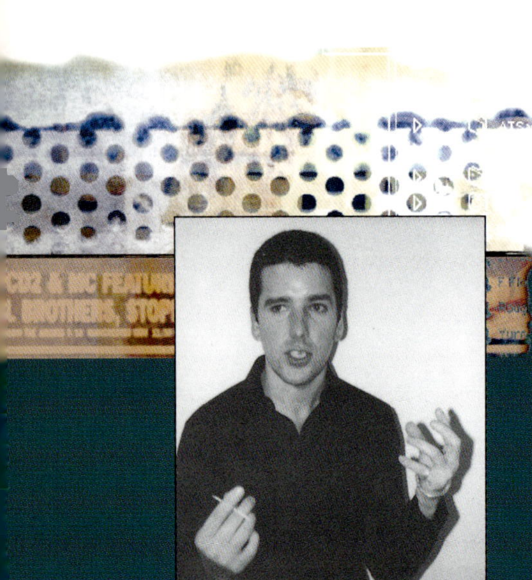

Javier Stanislas Michalski is a painter/typographer who emigrated to NYC from Montreal, Canada. While attending High School in Harlem he was befriended by individuals (Serge, West - FC) who exposed him to Graffiti: a style of writing and drawing that would later be incorporated with his formal studies of painting and typography at The Cooper Union.
Linking both influences, he introduced the attributes of this vernacular into "Graffiti"-oriented campaigns for Nike and Absolut Vodka. He is presently working on a mural for the Parks Dept. of NYC at DeSalvio Playground in the "Little Italy" section of Manhattan.

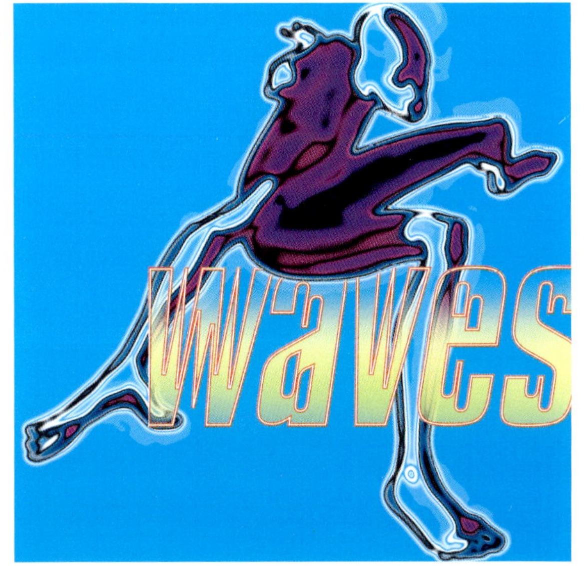

1

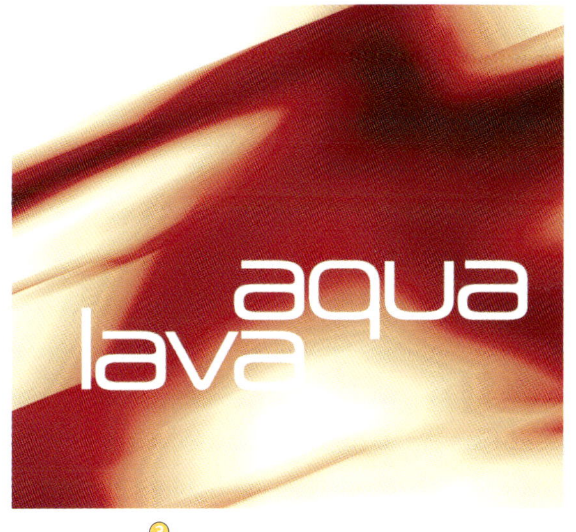

3

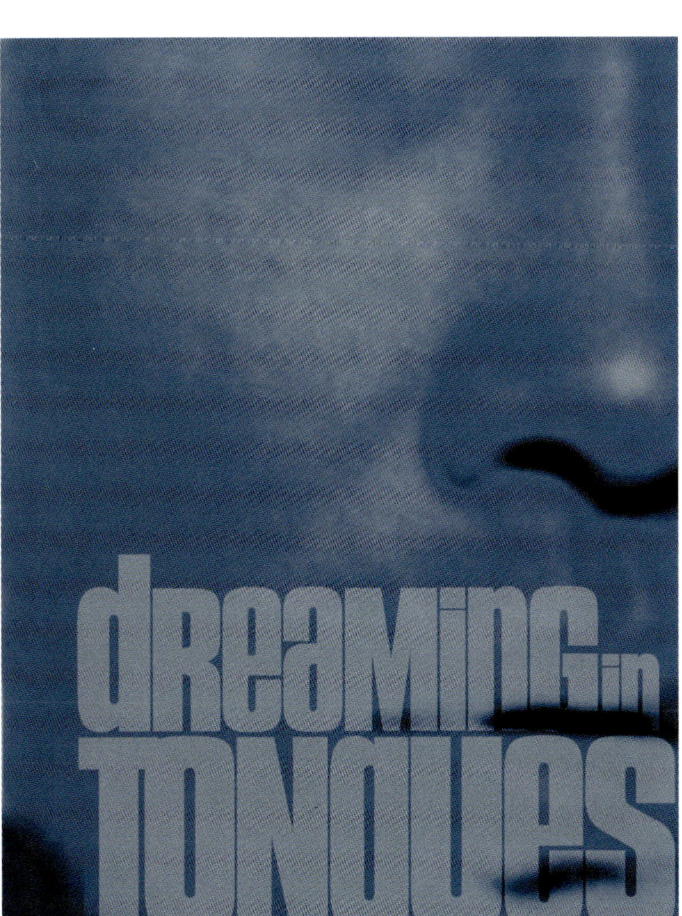

2

4

DJ SPOOKY

SONGS OF A DEAD DREAMER

1
- ✖ Compounda
- ■ Javier Michalski
- ▲ Unreleased

2
- ✖ Michalski Glacial Roman
- ■ Javier Michalski
- ▲ Unreleased

3
- ✖ X-Height
- ■ Javier Michalski
- ▲ Unreleased

1
- ● Waves
- ■ Javier Michalski
- ✖ Compounda
- ★ Liquid Groove
- ◆ Javier Michalski

2
- ● Dreaming in tongues
- ■ Javier Michalski
- ✖ X-Height
- ★ Labirynth Theatre Company NYC
- ◆ Vicki Lavergne

3
- ● Aqualava
- ■ Javier Michalski
- ✖ Michalski Glacial Roman
- ★ Liquid Groove
- ◆ Javier Michalski

4
- ● Dj Spooky, Songs Of A Dead Dreamer.
- ■ Javier Michalski
- ✖ Spooky
- ★ Asphodel Records

A B C D E F G H I J K L M
N O P Q R S T U V W X Y Z
A B C D E F G H I J K L M
N O P Q R S T U V W X Y Z
1 2 3 4 5 6 7 8 9 0 ! " §
$ % & / ( ) = ? # , . ; :
å Å ø ¤ † ¨ ^ ¥ Ø

1

2

A b c d e f g h i j k l m n o p q r
s t u v w x y z a b c d e f g h i j
k l m n o p q r s t u v w x y z
1 2 3 4 5 6 7 8 9 0 ! ( ) = ? , ; :

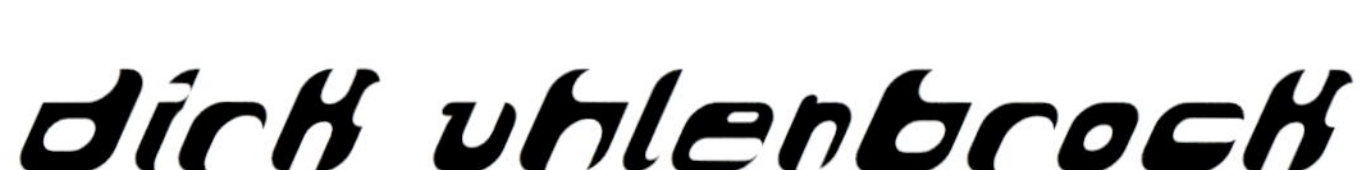

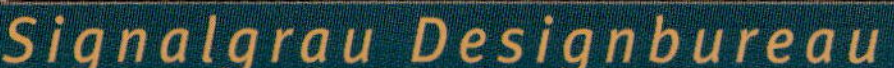

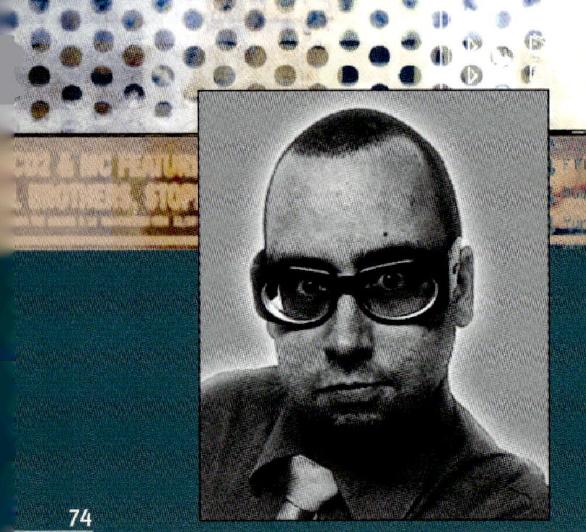

Design for me is like building a castle of sand on the beach. You start with digging holes to get enough material for your building, and then you develop the first rough form. You're going into detail; you try to fix parts of it. Some things break apart and must be rebuilt, the whole thing is altering its shape during its evolution, and then it's finished. The sun is shining; people walk by and take notice of your work. Time after time you add some annexes and one day you'll be the tide, wash it away and build a new one.

Born in 1964 in Essen, Germany, darling of the primary school teacher, several times class president, set free from military service (have you recognized the glasses?), student of communicational design, owner of gut & boese design agency, singer of the band aprioris, father of 4 sons, employee at designverign, married, employee at wysiwyg software design, owner of signalgrau designbureau. That's all.

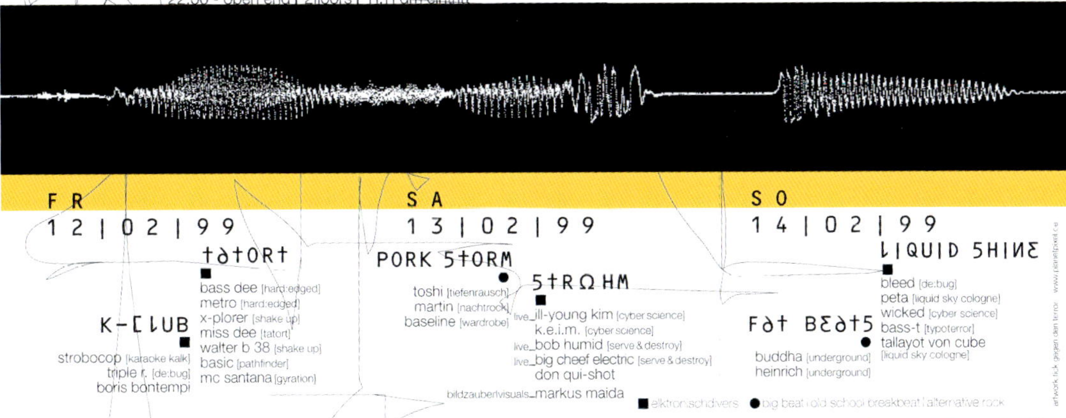

1

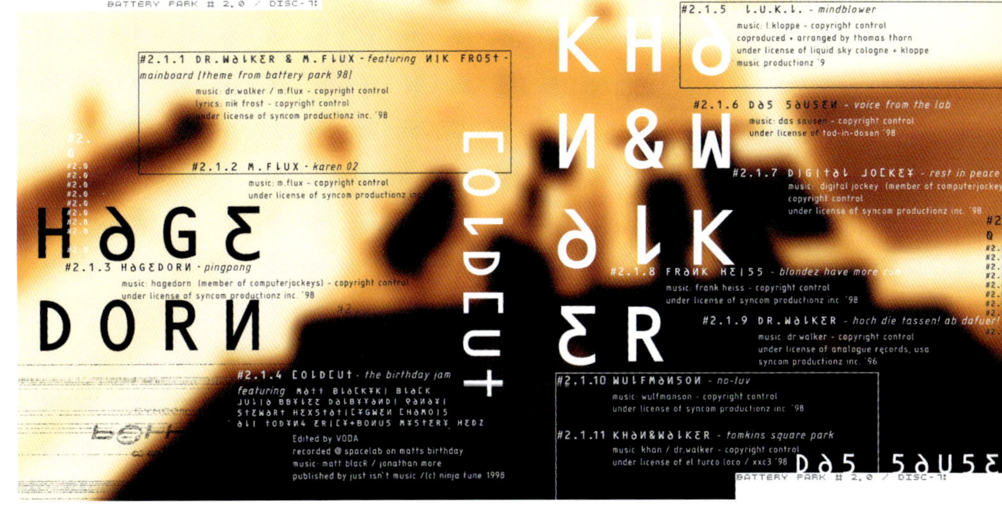

2

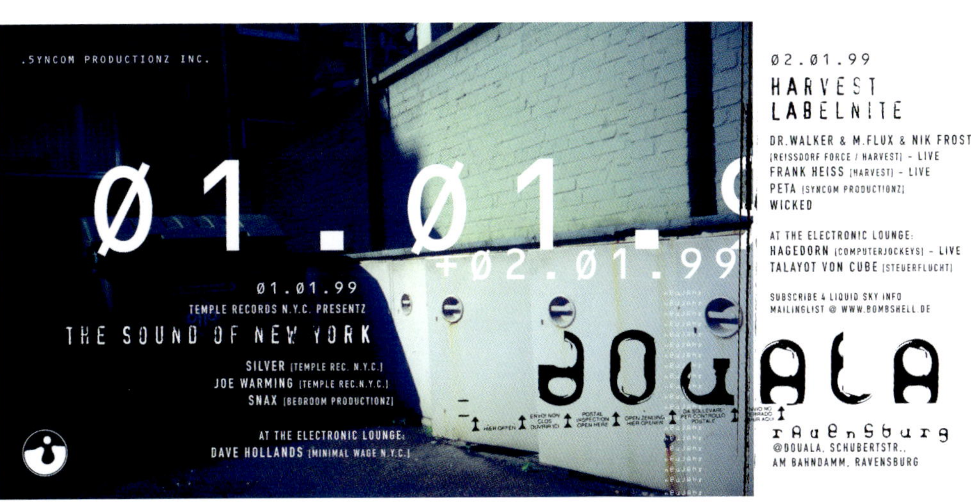

3

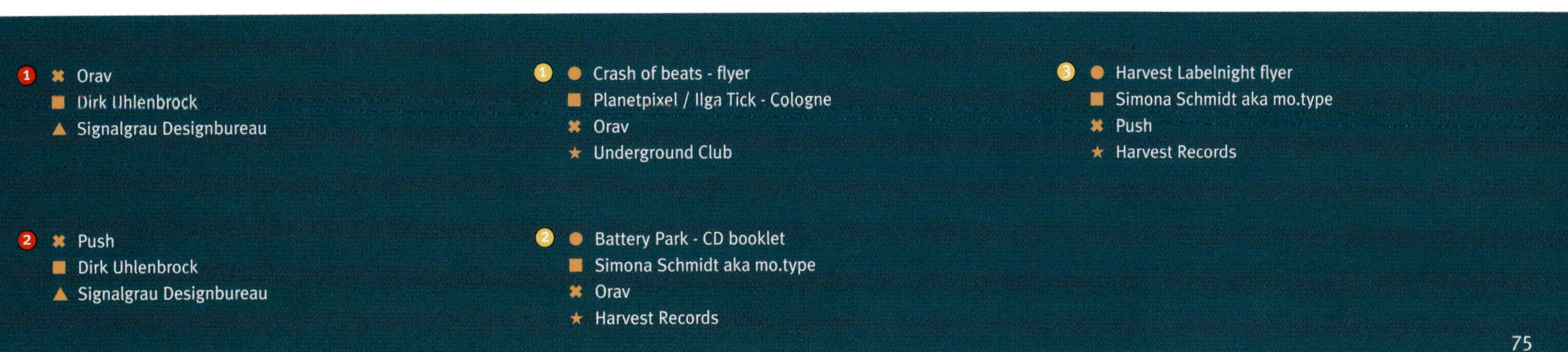

1
- Orav
- Dirk Uhlenbrock
- Signalgrau Designbureau

2
- Push
- Dirk Uhlenbrock
- Signalgrau Designbureau

1
- Crash of beats - flyer
- Planetpixel / Ilga Tick - Cologne
- Orav
- Underground Club

2
- Battery Park - CD booklet
- Simona Schmidt aka mo.type
- Orav
- Harvest Records

3
- Harvest Labelnight flyer
- Simona Schmidt aka mo.type
- Push
- Harvest Records

3

ABCdEFGHIJKLM
NOPQRSTUVWXYZ
abcdefghijklm
nopqrstuvwxyz
1234567890! www.
$%&/()?,.-;:

ABCdEFGHIJKLM
NOPQRSTUVWXYZ
abcdefghijklm
nopqrstuvwxyz
1234567890! www.
$%&/()?,.-;:

ABCdEFGHIJKLM
NOPQRSTUVWXYZ
abcdefghijklm
nopqrstuvwxyz
1234567890! www.
$%&/()?,.-;:

ABCdEFGHIJKLM
NOPQRSTUVWXYZ
abcdefghijklm
nopqrstuvwxyz
1234567890! www.
$%&/()?,.-;:

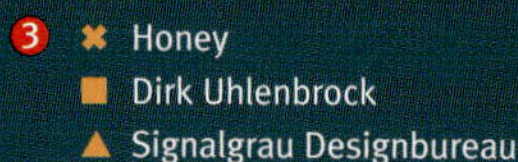

3 Honey
Dirk Uhlenbrock
Signalgrau Designbureau

4

Hallo Freunde!

2

Endlich sind auch die letzten Jahreswechselnachwehen ausgestanden, und so langsam haben auch alle wieder zur täglichen Arbeit gefunden. Unser Mitgefühl gilt allen Gesinnungsgenossen im Mittleren Westen der USA (Chicago & Detroit), die Anfang Januar unter der Saukälte und Schneemassen zu leiden hatten. Da halfen wohl nur warme Gedanken oder die klassische brennende Mülltonne an der Ecke.

Nur wenige Tage später fällt die weiße Pest auch wieder über uns her. Autobahnen sind blockiert, in den Innenstädten herrscht Chaos und in unserer sonst so lebhaften Redaktion wird es plötzlich ganz schön einsam. 13. Januar - der Düsseldorfer Express titelt: Notlandung - 6 Minister an Bord! Beinahe hätten wir vielleicht die Chance bekommen, unsere Wahl vom letzten September noch einmal zu überdenken, nur der Wichtigste hat gefehlt. Chance vertan. Gruß an den Piloten.

Für alle Raver - es soll noch welche geben - haben wir in diesem Monat die absolute After-Hour-Alternative für Euch (After-Hours - das waren Parties, die erst am frühen Morgen begannen, und wo nach kurzer Zwischenstation bei McDoof alle einliefen, die noch nicht müde waren. Meistens waren das die besten und entspanntesten Parties, sowieso!). Wie wäre es mit einer Busfahrt zum Prickingshof nach Haltern? Realsatire par excellence mit einer Ansprache von Bauer Ewald persönlich und die Verpflegung ist gleich mit eingeschlossen, wo gibt es so was noch? (Alle grausamen Einzelheiten auf S. 90!)

Dafür, daß Euch sonst nicht langweilig wird, haben wir natürlich wieder den gewohnten Rundumschlag durch die bunte Welt des Party-Pops. Have fun and rave on!

IMPRESSUM

Herausgeber & Geschäftsleitung: A.E.C. Geronimo Verlag GmbH

Redaktion: A.E.C. Geronimo Verlag GmbH, Raveline Magazin, Arenbergstraße 5, 45701 Herten, Phone: +49-[0]209-96191-0, Phax: +49-[0]209-96191-99, e-Mail: raveline-d@t-online.de

Redaktionsschluss: jeweils am 8. des Vormonats

Anzeigenschluss: jeweils am 12. des Vormonats

Chefredakteur: Dirk Waltmann [V.i.S.d.P.]

Stellv. Chefredakteur: Sven Schäfer

Redaktion: Claus Pieper, Martin Magielka, Christian Beckmann, Sascha von Nahmen, Önder Özkan

Bildredaktion: Stefan Promnik-van den Heuvel

Sekretariat: Gabi Schifkowitz

Redaktionelle Mitarbeit: Andrea Daschner [London], Carsten Pomorin, Carsten Wohlfeld, Daniel Karg, Daniel Najock, Ingo Wiemert, Jerome Kühnert [New York], Jochen Sarembe, Jonas Hager, Jürgen Laarmann, Lang Bros., Mister X (London), Oliver Wallner, René Pera, Silvia Schumacher [San Francisco], Susan Dammhayn, Tati O' Pathi

Fotos: Stefan Promnik-van den Heuvel und die Mitarbeiter der Nightflightseiten

Grafik: Planet Pixel [Köln], Funke Hiller Wülfing GbR, www.planetpixel.de

Tastaturbelegung: Oliver Funke, Ansgar Hiller, Anja Wülfing, Ilga Tick, Tim Saueressig, Markus Schulze

Abuse Pages & more: Andy O/R/E/L [Vienna]

Assistent der Geschäftsleitung: Frank van Lieshaut

Anzeigen: Sebastian Spohr (Leitung), Phone: 0209-96191-32, Fax: 0209-96191-98; Nicole Dominique Bader, Phone: 0209-96191-33

Es gilt die Anzeigenpreisliste vom 01.01.1998

Druck: Druckhaus Meyer & Beckmann GmbH, Gutenbergstraße 2, 33790 Halle / Westf.

Vertrieb: Deutschland / Benelux / Österreich, IPS Pressevertrieb GmbH, Postfach 14 60, 50204 Frechen

Schweiz: All 4 music GmbH, Riedstraße 1, CH-6343 Rotkreuz, Phone: +41-[0]41 - 799 59 50, Phax: +41-[0]41 - 799 59 51

Verantwortliche Leitung Schweiz: Susanne Behrendt

raveline 02/1999

5

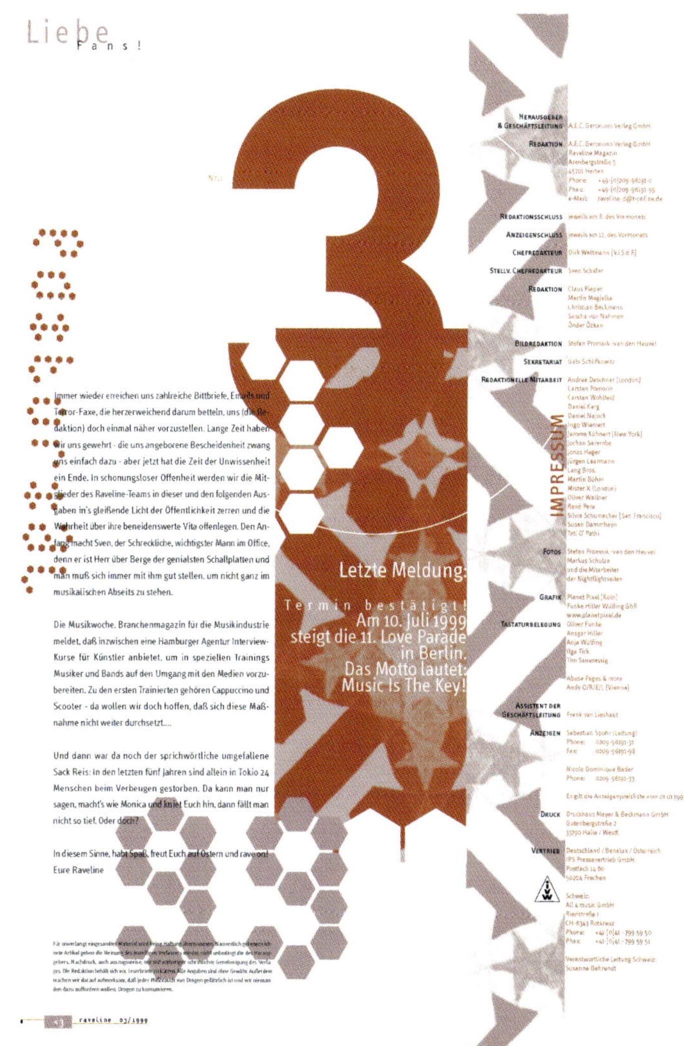
Liebe Fans!

3

Immer wieder erreichen uns zahlreiche Bittbriefe, Emails und Terror-Faxe, die herzerweichend darum betteln, uns (die Redaktion) doch einmal näher vorzustellen. Lange Zeit haben wir uns gewehrt - die uns angeborene Bescheidenheit zwang uns einfach dazu - aber jetzt hat die Zeit der Unwissenheit ein Ende. In schonungsloser Offenheit werden wir die Mitglieder des Raveline-Teams in dieser und den folgenden Ausgaben in's gleißende Licht der Öffentlichkeit zerren und die Wahrheit über ihre beneidenswerte Vita offenlegen. Den Anfang macht Sven, der Schreckliche, wichtigster Mann im Office, denn er ist Herr über Berge der genialsten Schallplatten und man muß sich immer mit ihm gut stellen, um nicht ganz im musikalischen Abseits zu stehen.

Die Musikwoche, Branchenmagazin für die Musikindustrie meldet, daß inzwischen eine Hamburger Agentur Interview-Kurse für Künstler anbietet, um in speziellen Trainings Musiker und Bands auf den Umgang mit den Medien vorzubereiten. Zu den ersten Trainierten gehören Cappuccino und Scooter - da wollen wir doch hoffen, daß sich diese Maßnahme nicht weiter durchsetzt....

Und dann war da noch der sprichwörtliche umgefallene Sack Reis: In den letzten fünf Jahren sind allein in Tokio 24 Menschen beim Verbeugen gestorben. Da kann man nur sagen, macht's wie Monica und kniet Euch hin, dann fällt man nicht so tief. Oder doch?

In diesem Sinne, habt Spaß, freut Euch auf Ostern und rave on!
Eure Raveline

Letzte Meldung:
Termin bestätigt!
Am 10. Juli 1999 steigt die 11. Love Parade in Berlin.
Das Motto lautet: Music Is The Key!

IMPRESSUM

raveline 03/1999

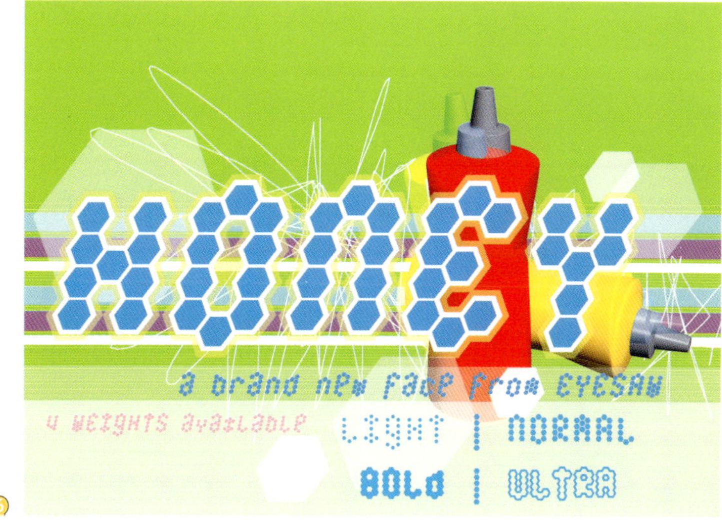

6

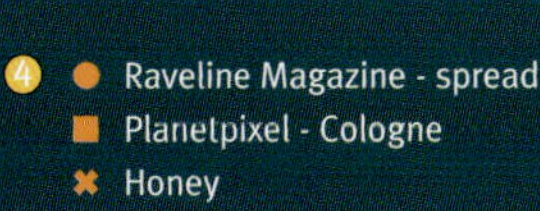

4 ● Raveline Magazine - spread
■ Planetpixel - Cologne
✖ Honey
★ Geronimo Verlag

5 ● Raveline Magazine - spread
■ Planetpixel - Cologne
✖ Honey
★ Geronimo Verlag

6 ● Honey
■ Dirk Uhlenbrock
✖ Honey
★ Signalgrau Designbureau - Selfpromo

4

abcdefghijklm
nopqrstuvwxyz
abcdefghijklm
nopqrstuvwxyz

5

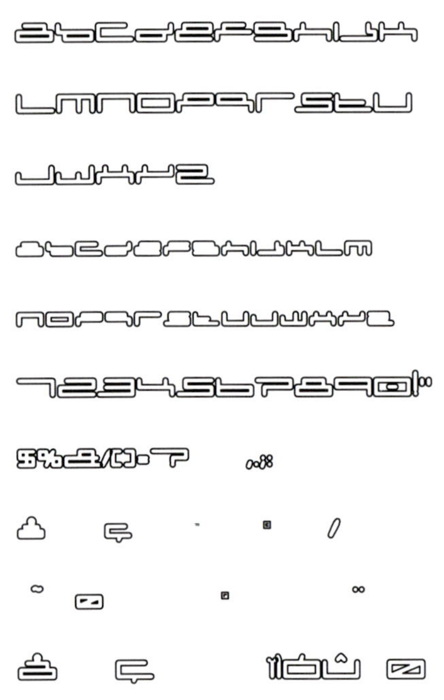

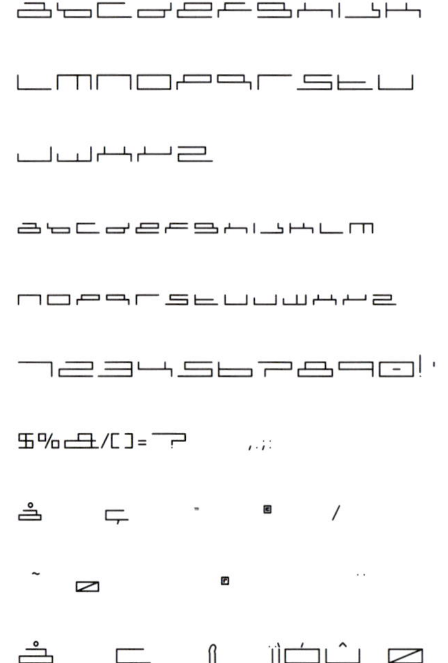

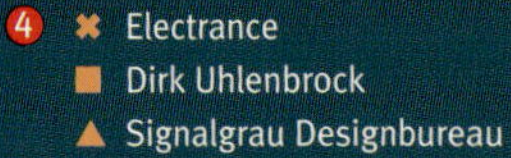

4 Electrance
Dirk Uhlenbrock
Signalgrau Designbureau

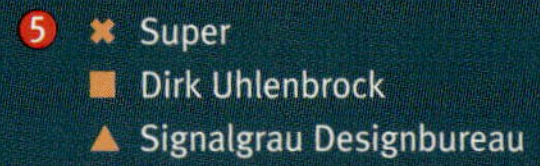

5 Super
Dirk Uhlenbrock
Signalgrau Designbureau

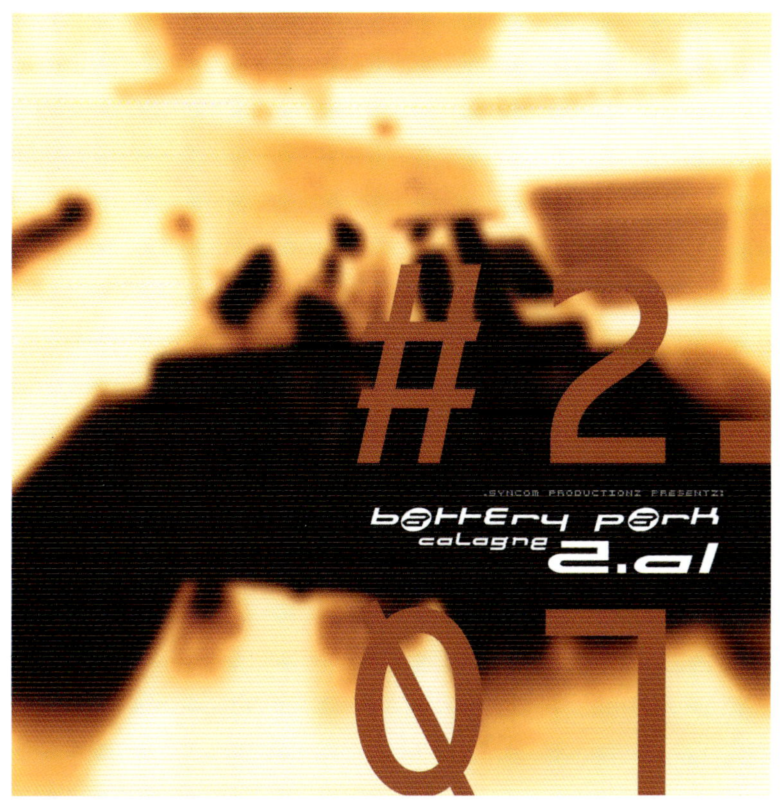

7

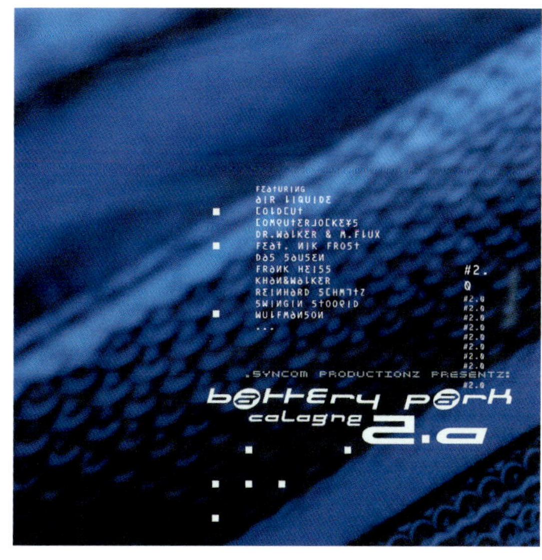

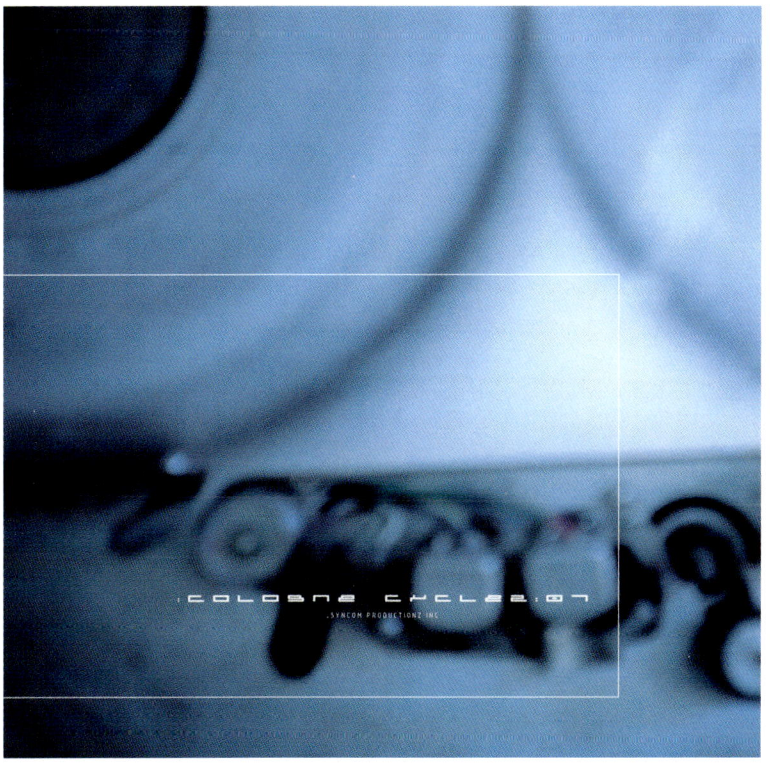

8

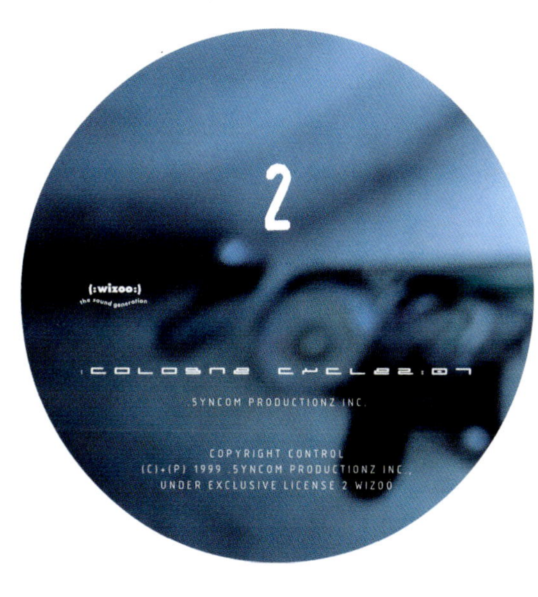

7
- ● Battery Park -Cover and label
- ■ Simona Schmidt aka mo.type
- ✖ Electrance
- ★ Harvest Records

8
- ● Cologne Cycles - Cover and label
- ■ Simona Schmidt aka mo.type
- ✖ Super Normal
- ★ Wizoo Records

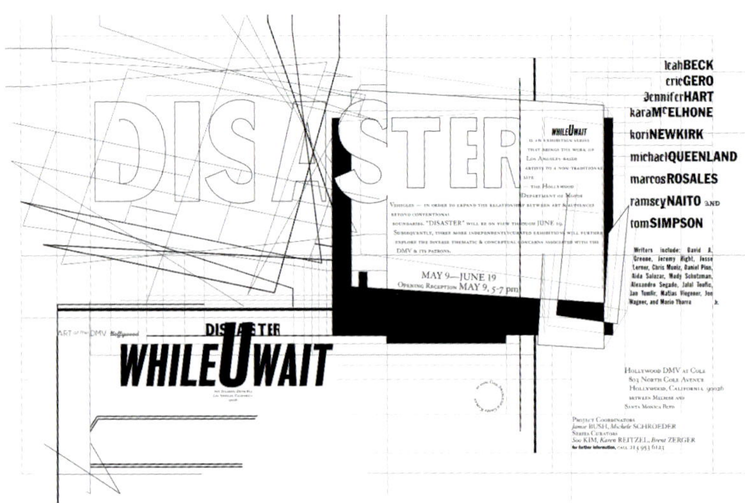

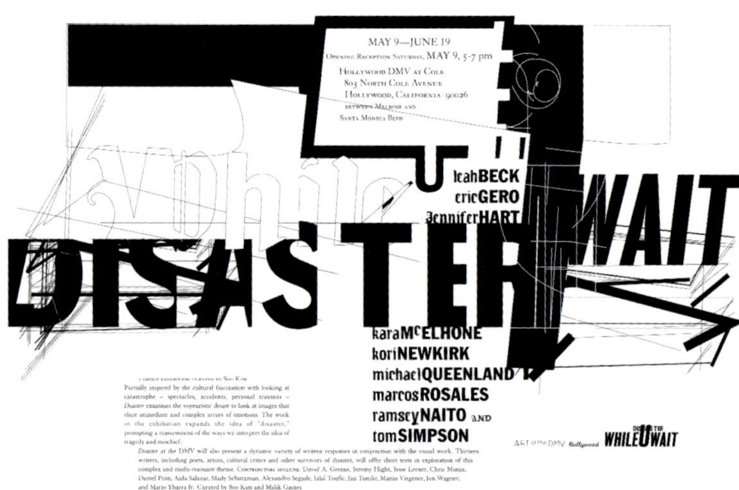

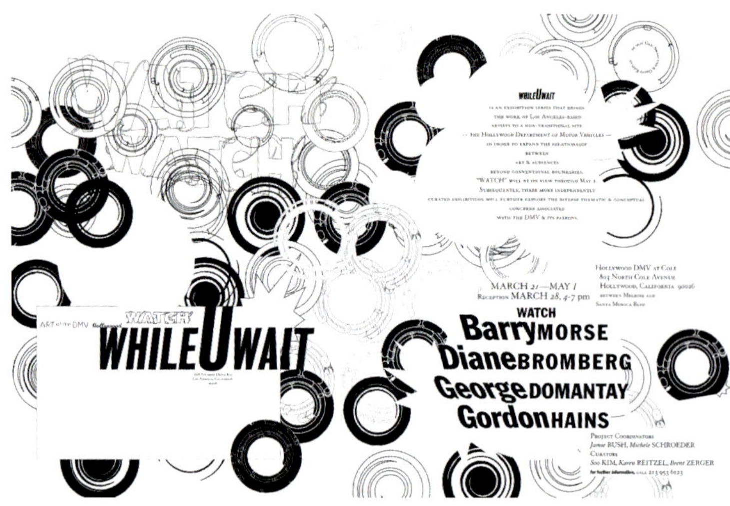

Aa Bb Cc Dd Ee Ff Gg Hh
Ii Jj Kk Ll Mm Nn Oo Pp
Qq Rr Ss Tt Uu Vv Ww
Xx Yy Zz

geoff Kaplan

General Working Group

Metaphorically our design philosophy goes as follows: pick the most congested intersection in your town, wait for a car wreck, pick up the carnage, run.

My general approach in designing the three fonts is one of collision, comparison and contrast. Identifying social, historical and cultural dialectics, and then, let the trains wreck, the forms are then dug out of the carnage.

Geoff Kaplan graduated from Carnegie Mellon and obtained his MFA from Cranbrook. Kaplan started General Working Group in 1998. He has produced projects for Cranbrook Academy of Art, Channel One, The Walker Arts Center, Reebok, Chronicle Books, and in-scene graphics for Any Given Sunday. He teaches at both CalArts and Art Center.

1

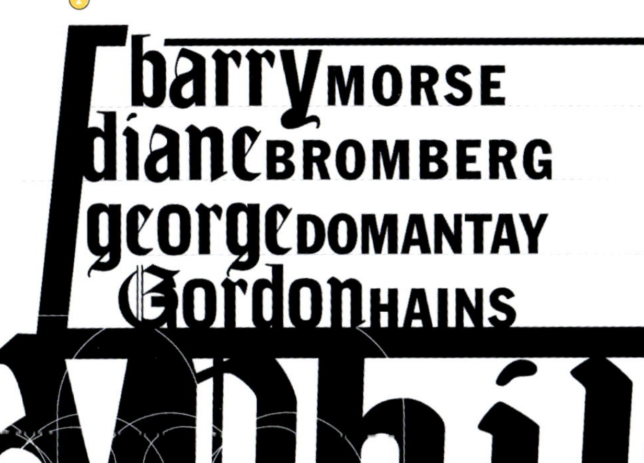

MARCH *21*—MAY *1*
RECEPTION MARCH *28*, *4-7* pm

HOLLYWOOD DMV AT COLE
803 NORTH COLE AVENUE
HOLLYWOOD, CALIFORNIA 90026
BETWEEN MELROSE AND
SANTA MONICA BLVD

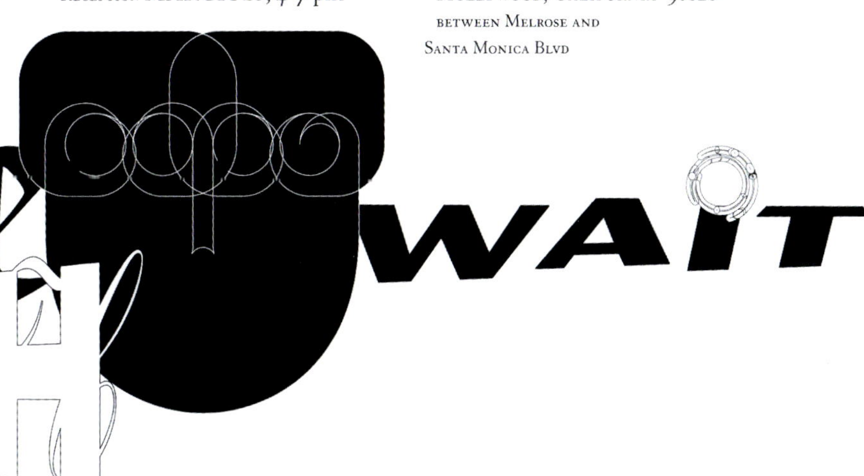

The four artists whose work comprises the group exhibition "Watch" are inspired by the process of their own accumulation or cumulative creation of objects over time. Referencing or documenting the experience of time in specific increments, repetition of sameness versus difference intones a common theme. In addition, each artwork is the result of a careful attention to formal appeal, and the presentation of unusual elements and materials are composed with a clear sense of order defined by either a linear or circular impression of time.

Each work is visually engaging and invites lengthy inspection. In doing so, viewers are given the opportunity to transform the usual DMV experience of breaking up time by glancing at one's watch into a more pleasant encounter where time becomes more fluid.

WATCH
ART at the DMV Hollywood WHILEUWAIT

1 Sucker, but
Geoff Kaplan
General Working Group

1 WhileUWait (poster series)
Gail Swanlund / Geoff Kaplan, General Working Group
Sucker, but / Cyberkitch
WhileUwait, coordinators Jamie Bush / Michele Schroeder

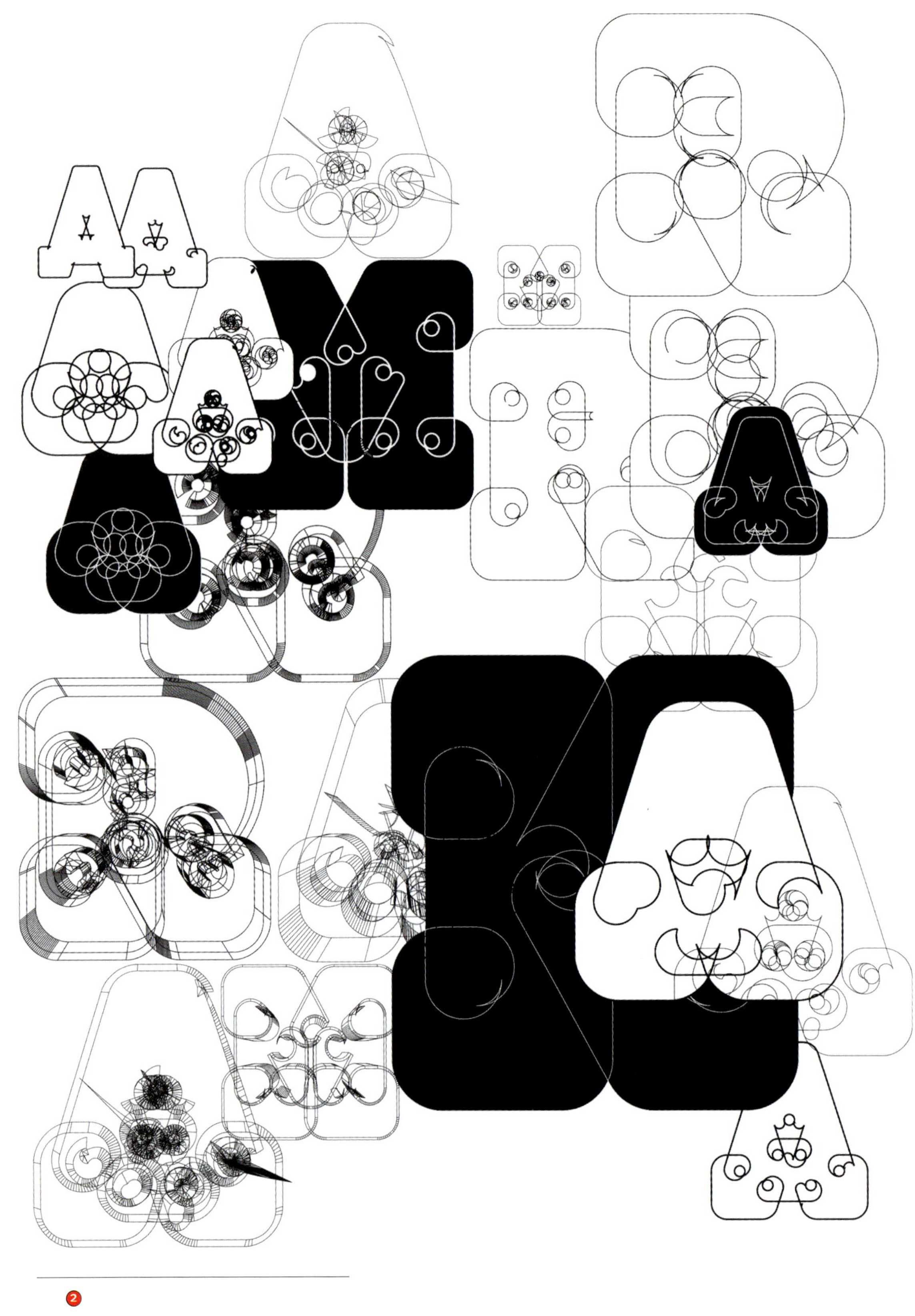

2

2 ✖ Cyberkitch
■ Geoff Kaplan
▲ General Working Group

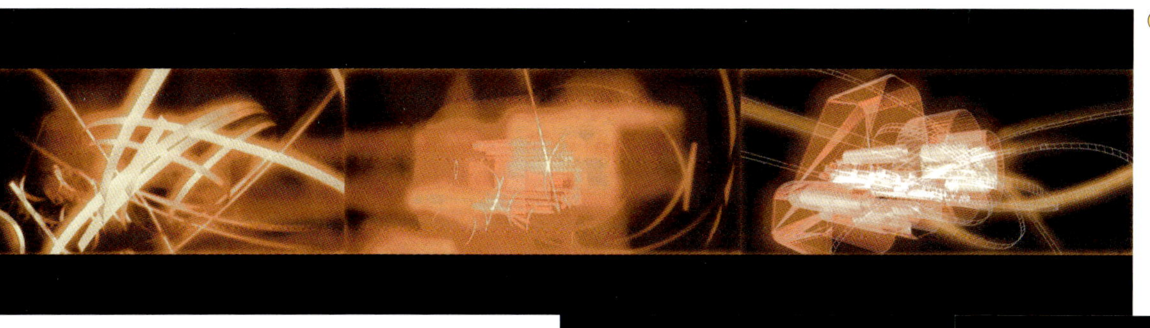

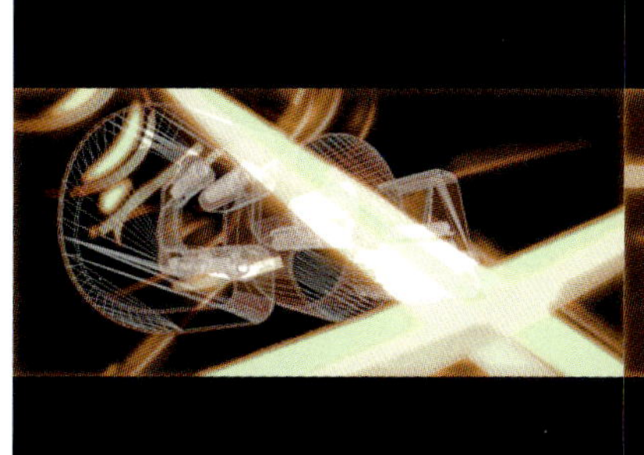

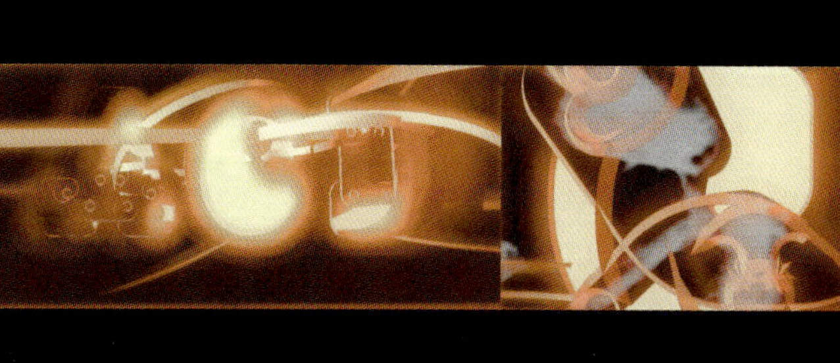

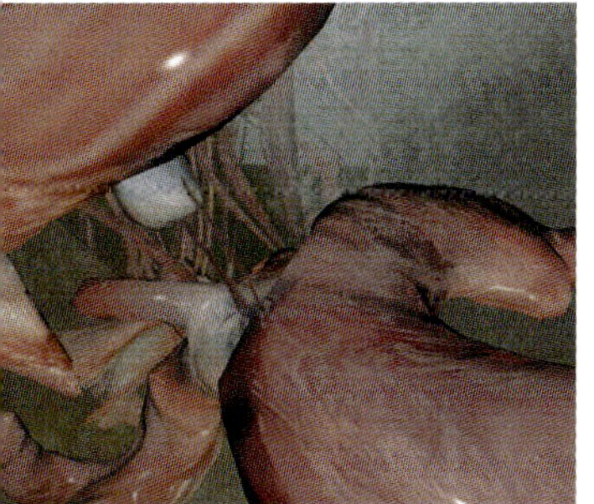

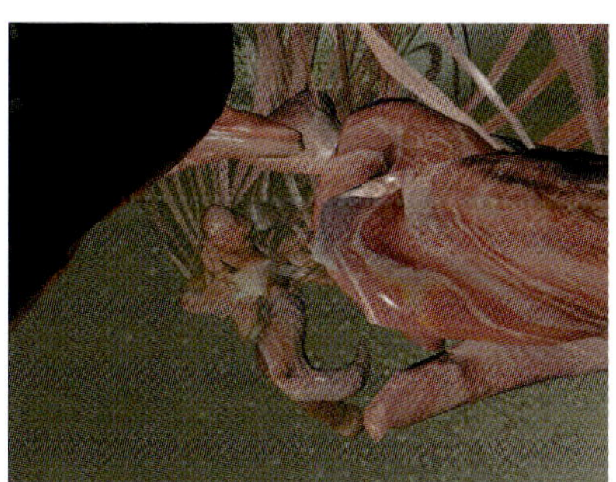

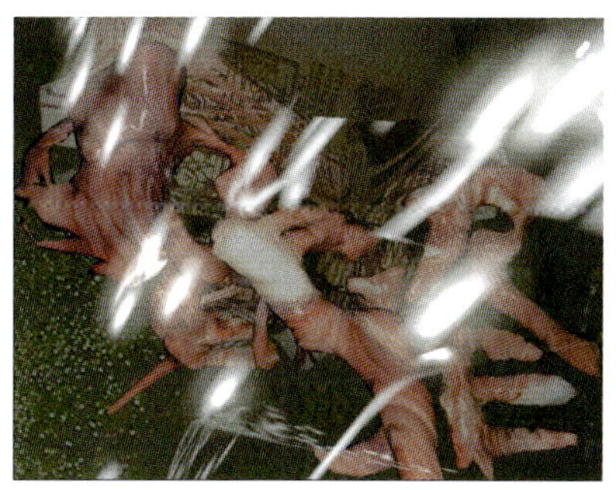

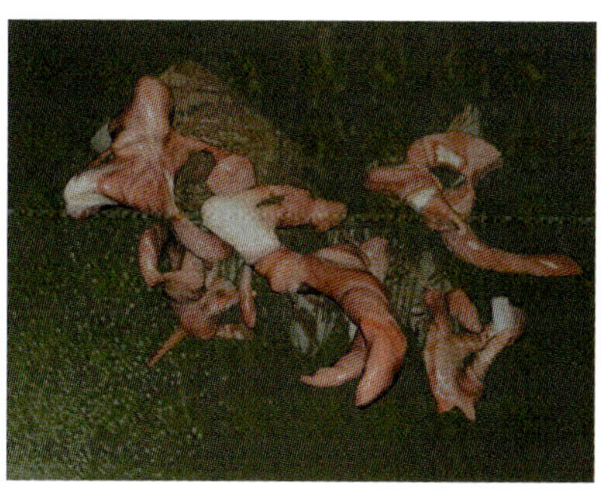

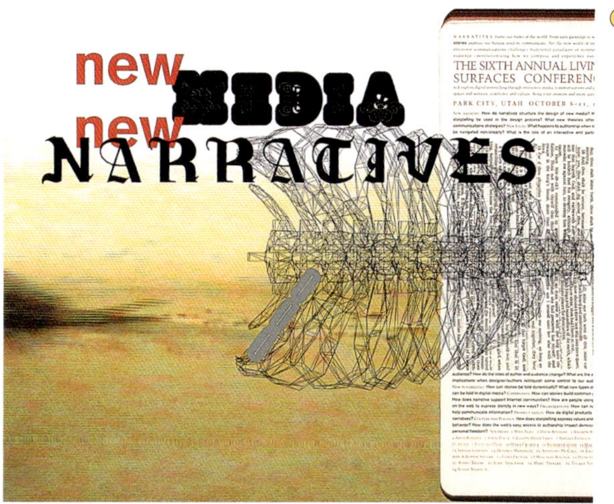

2 ● Video
■ Paul Seymour / Geoff Kaplan, General Working Group
✖ Sucker, but / Cyberkitch
★ American Center for Design

3 ● Hypnerotomachia Poliphili (Video)
■ Paul Seymour / Diane Gromala / Geoff Kaplan, General Working Group
✖ Hypnerotomachia Poliphili (designed by Paul Seymour / Geoff Kaplan)
★ Paul Seymour / Diane Gromala / Geoff Kaplan

4 ● Living Surfaces Six Conference
■ Geoff Kaplan
✖ Sucker, but / Cyberkitch
★ The American Center for Design

3

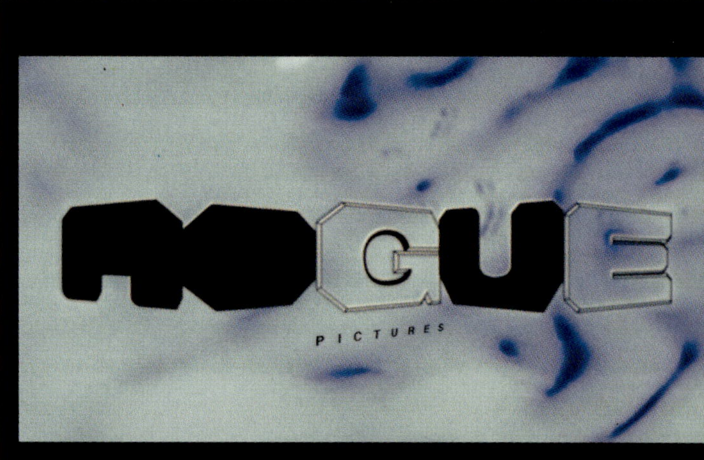

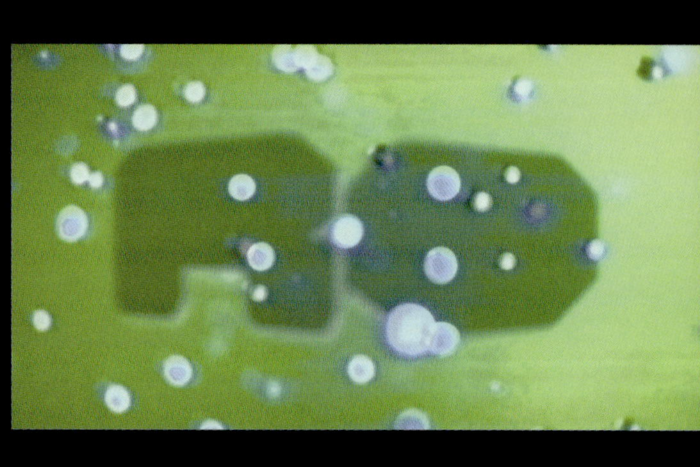

4 ✖ Car Washer
■ Geoff Kaplan
▲ General Working Group

5

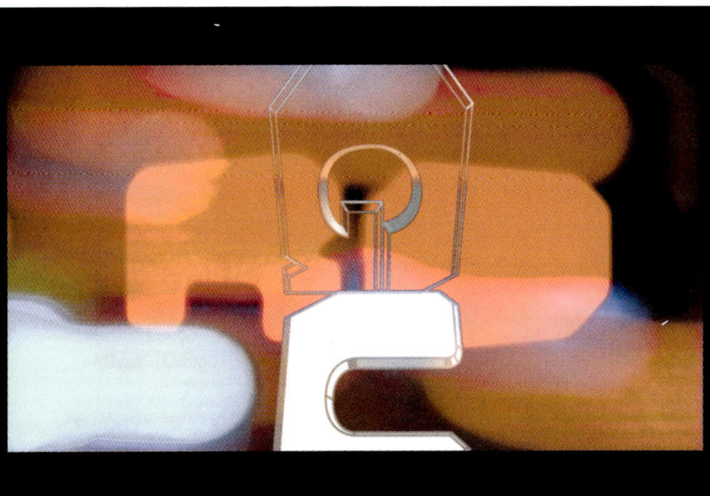

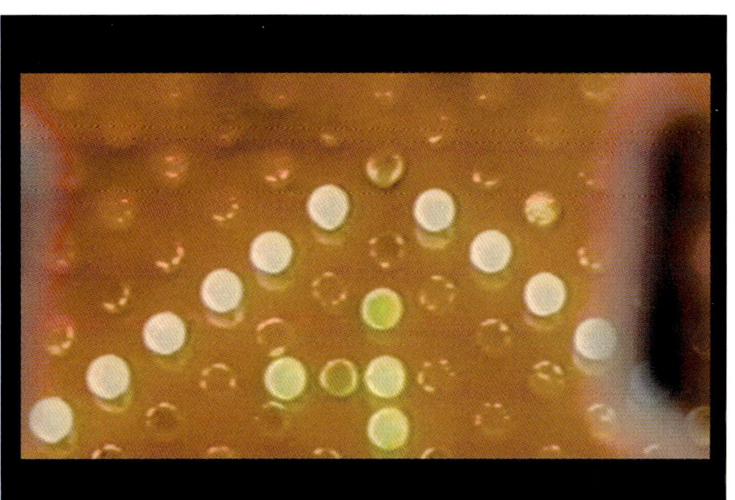

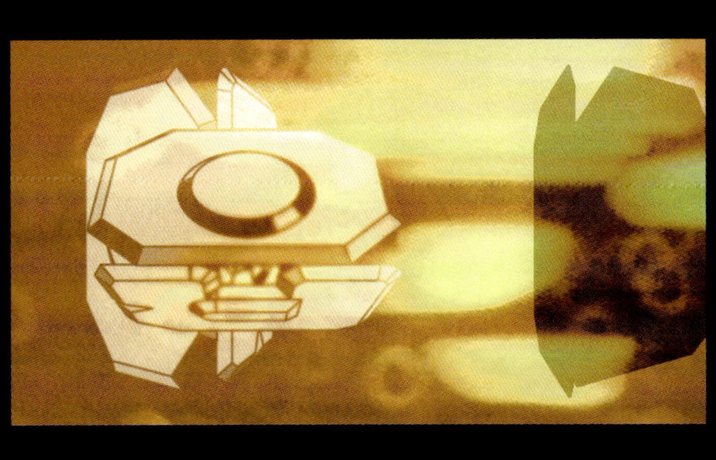

6

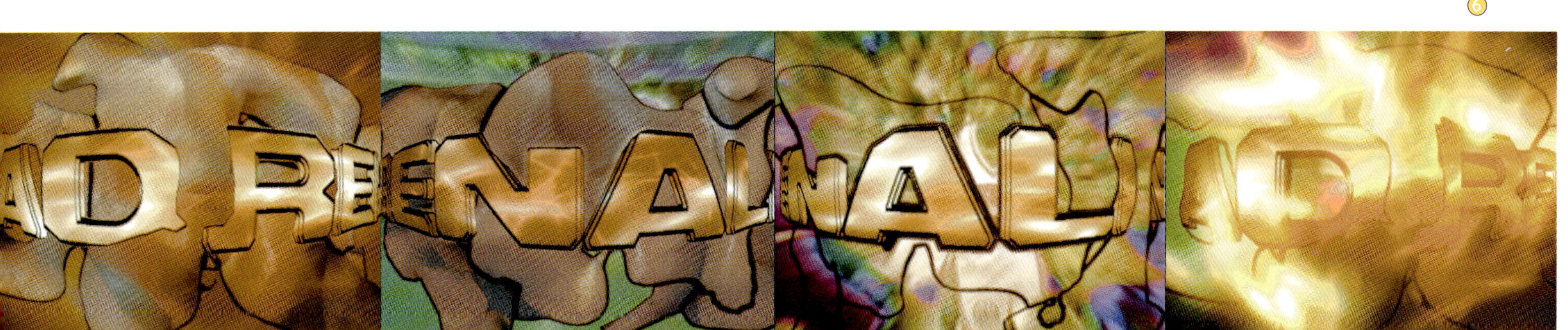

5 ● Rogue (Key Frames)
■ Alex Tylevich / Geogg Kaplan, General Working Group
✖ Car Washer
★ Rogue Pictures

6 ● Adrenaline (Video)
■ Paul Seymour / Geoff Kaplan, General Working Group
✖ Car Washer
★ Channel One

1

ABCDEFGHI
JKLMNOPQR
STUVWXYZab
cdefghijklmnop
qrstuvwxyz012
3456789&@€

ABCDEFGH
IJKLMNOP
QRSTUVW
XYZ01234
56789

2

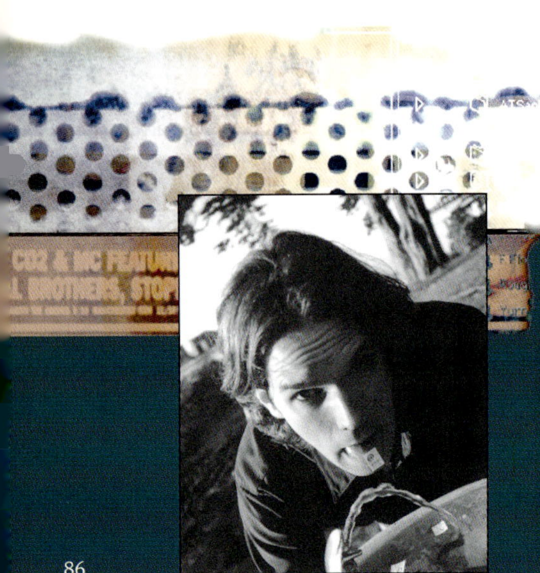

delve withrington

Delve Media Arts

I don't subscribe to the idea that letterforms created on a computer must emulate those created in another medium. A brush applying paint to canvas doesn't create letterforms like a hammer and chisel struck into stone or pen put to paper. A computer, while it can approximate those tools with a certain degree of accuracy, will never replace them. The computer's just another tool (albeit a complicated one). However, like no other tool before it, the computer allows us not only an ever-increasing speed and efficiency, but also a creative freedom seemingly limited only by the capacity of our own imagination. So when told a particular letterform with digital origins couldn't be created by hand, I have to ask: what tool do you use to create what your bare hands cannot?

Originally from Asheville, NC, Delve Withrington attended The Savannah College of Art and Design in Savannah, Georgia, where he majored in Graphic Design and Illustration. After a move to Boston in 1992, Withrington opened a private fine art studio in Boston's Fort Point and exhibited throughout New England. During this period, his interest and skill in type design grew from everyday exposure to typography in his position at an architectural signage company. Withrington now lives in San Francisco and operates the independent studio, Delve Media Arts (www.delvemediarts.com). This combines his knowledge of design, typography, art, and business in an energetic, creative manner. The studio publishes "Type Books for the well-read typographer" (www.typebooks.org) and specializes in typographic design for digital media and the Web. Work for clients include Ziff-Davis, Starbucks, Microsoft, and Hewlett-Packard.

3

ABCDEFGHIJKLM
NOPQRSTUVWXYZ
abcdefghijklmn
opqrstuvwxyz
0123456789BQ

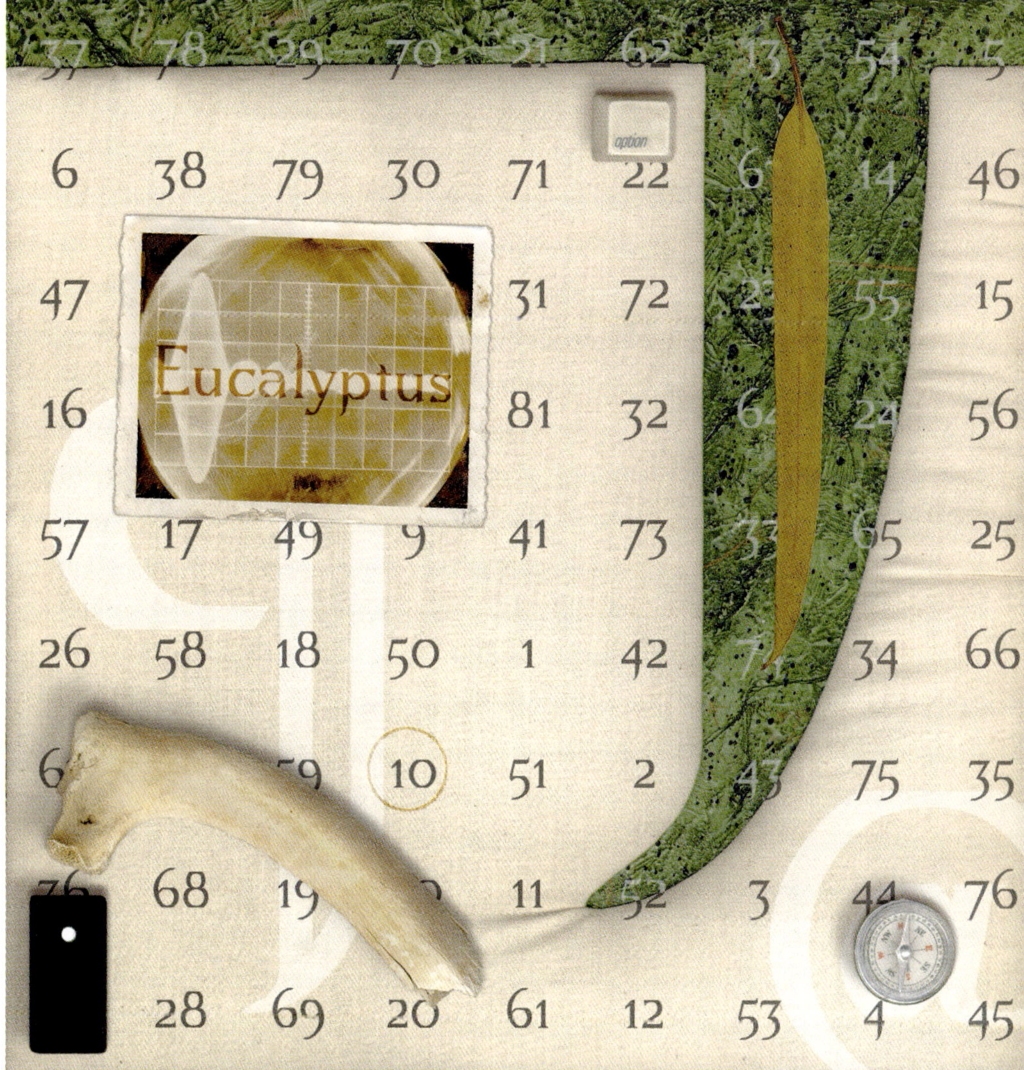

1

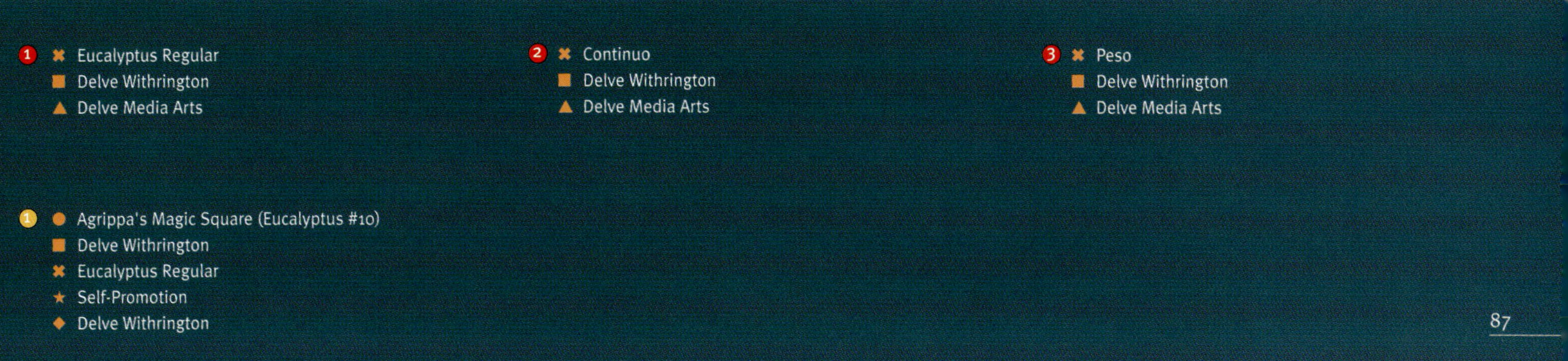

1 Eucalyptus Regular
Delve Withrington
Delve Media Arts

2 Continuo
Delve Withrington
Delve Media Arts

3 Peso
Delve Withrington
Delve Media Arts

1 Agrippa's Magic Square (Eucalyptus #10)
Delve Withrington
Eucalyptus Regular
Self-Promotion
Delve Withrington

ABCDEFGHIJKLM
NOPQRSTUVWXYZ
abcdefghijklm
nopqrstuvwxyz
0123456789
@®©¢ÁÈ*$%&?

1

ABCDEFGHIJKLM
NOPQRSTUVWXYZ
0123456789
@ YES NO ¢ $ % & ?

1

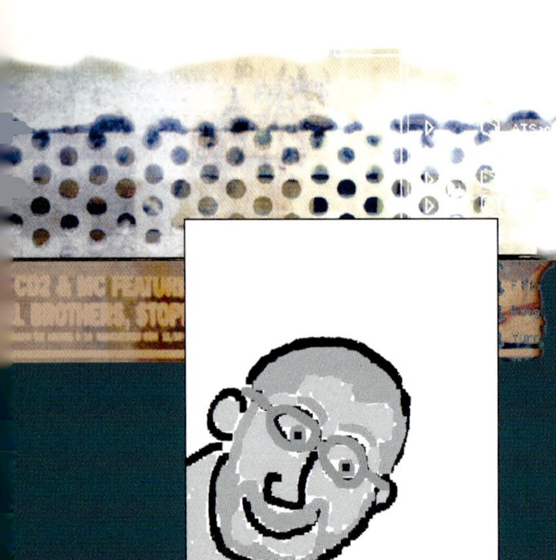

chester

Thirstype

When I have an idea for a typeface, I find it best to let it escape, set it free. Most typefaces start as sketches – pencil on paper. Some of those are scanned and retraced in a drawing program, others are recreated on screen using the sketches as visual guides. Some types are constructed directly on the machine. And some never escape the sketchbook at all. Of those type ideas sketched, only a fraction are ever completed, and a fraction of those are published.
My Philosophy of Type Design, then, is: Design many, publish few (and be damned).

Born in Montréal in 1971, Chester became interested in type at the age of nine, and taught himself calligraphy. He received his first commission the following year, at primary school: to write his classmates' names in italic script on their report cards.
A few years later, Chester studied graphic design at Collège Dawson, and then worked as a freelance designer, toiling nights at a typesetting bureau.
After a year in Montréal, he went to London in 1993 to work as a designer for Newell and Sorrell, and was posted to their Netherlands office a year later, where he spent an additional year.
In 1994, Chester's first published typeface, Schmelvetica, was released by FontShop International.
In 1995 Chester moved to Chicago to work as a designer for Thirst alongside his longstanding hero, Rick Valicenti. He has continued to design typefaces, now exclusively for Thirstype — including Rheostat, HateNote, LoveNote, and Virgil.

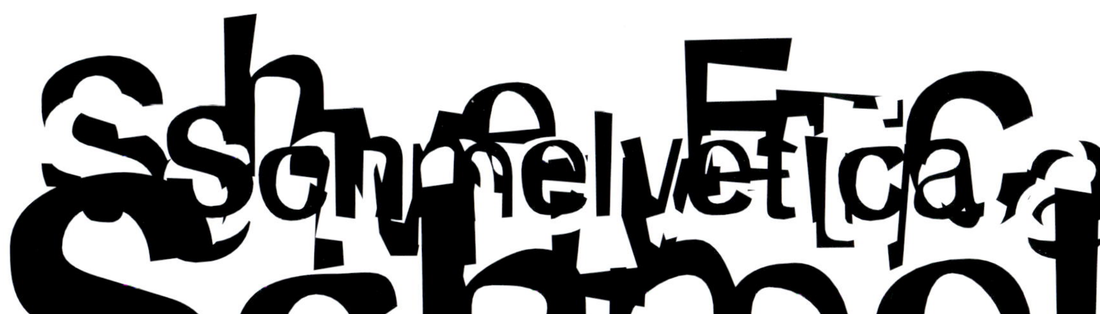

Schmel

The typeface with more kerning pairs than sense.

vetica

A dirty face and grubby behind the ears.

C'est vraiment un festival

1234567890(.,:;'?!)¢£@$&[]©®™

Et encore plus...

XYZabcdefghijklmnopqrstuvwxyz

ABCDEFGHIJKLMNOPQRSTUVW

Les caractéres caractéristiques:

¡É, toé, gadouç!

({[Looks wonky even in teeny-weeny sizes.]})

Zany fjord mugs whilst vexing quick bop. Five waxy cherubim jostle queer dozing kelp. Juvenile xenophobes quiz yards of mock twigs. Chintzy boxed fowl jump quivering arks. Zebras quit wavering from jacked xylophones.

1 Schmelvetica
Chester
Font Shop International

2 Psyche
Chester
unreleased

1 "It's a dirty old face"
Chester
Schmelvetica
Font Shop International

2

ABCDEFGHIJKLMNOPQRSTUVWXYZ
abcdefghijklmnopqrstuvwxyz
0123456789

3

ABCDEFGHIJKLMNOPQRSTUVWXYZ
abcdefghijklmnopqrstuvwxyz
0123456789

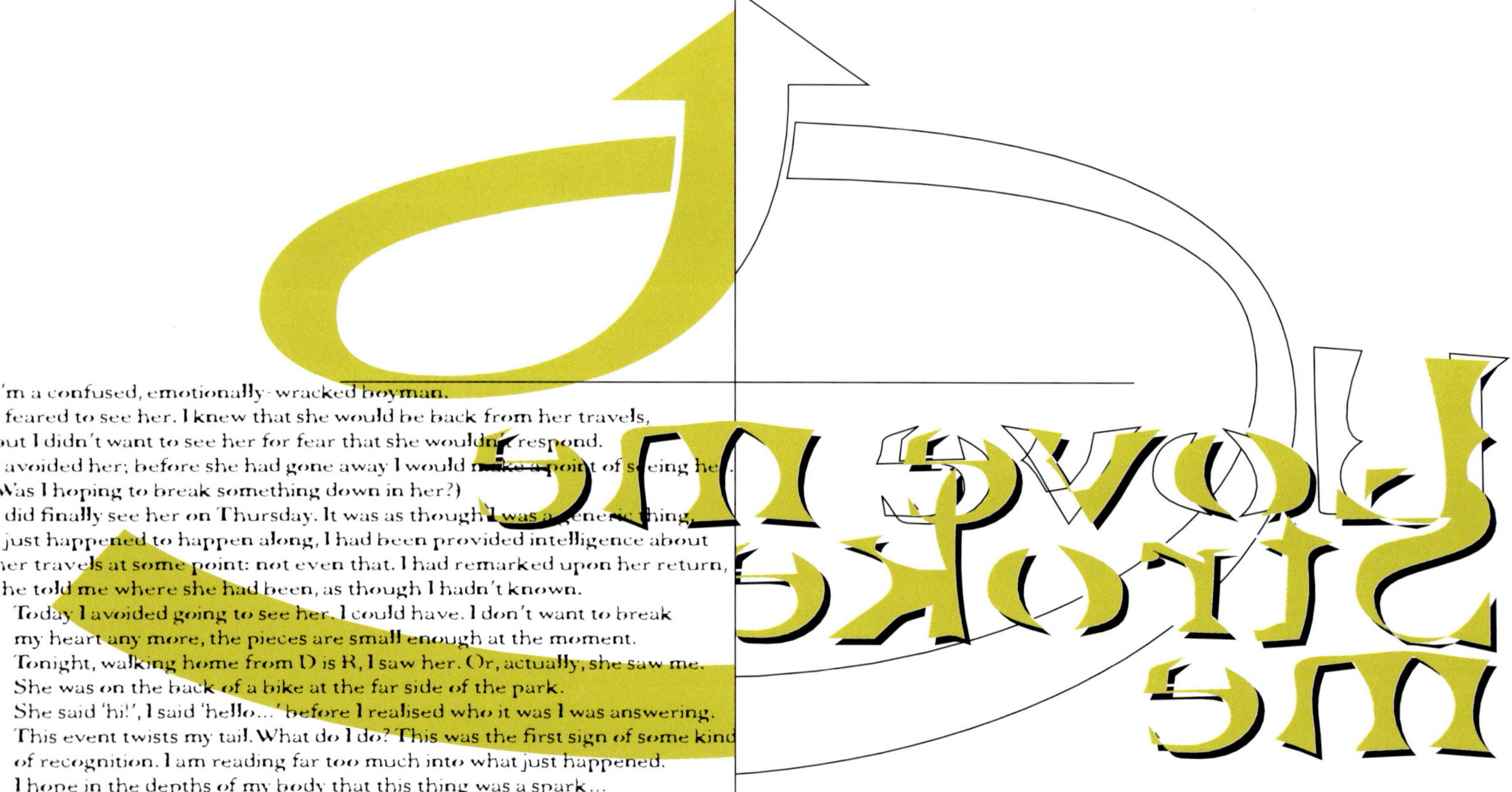

2 ✖ Love Note Regular (a 2 weight family)
■ Chester
▲ Thirstype

3 ✖ Hate Note Regular (a 7 weight family)
■ Chester
▲ Thirstype

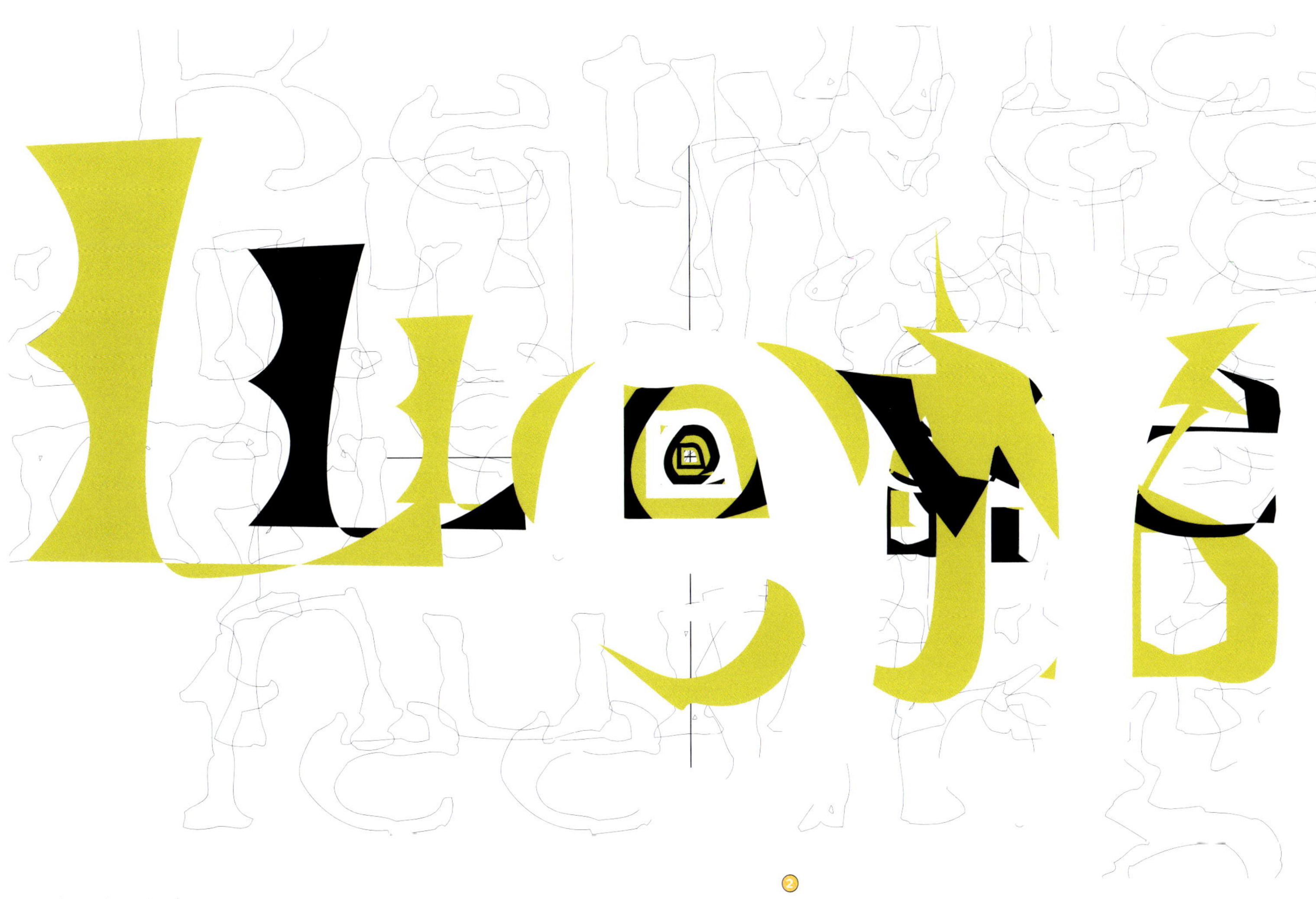

- Love and Hate (spreads)
- Rick Valicenti / Chester
- Love Note family / Hate Note family
- Thirstype

Pages from a book designed to create interest in the typefaces Love Note and Hate Note. The piece was printed on translucent stock. The back sides were designed by Frank Ford, using his typeface Stroke, now part of the collection of the National Design Museum.

ABCDEFGHIJKLMN
OPQRSTUVWXYZ
abcdefghijklmn
opqrstuvwxyz
0123456789

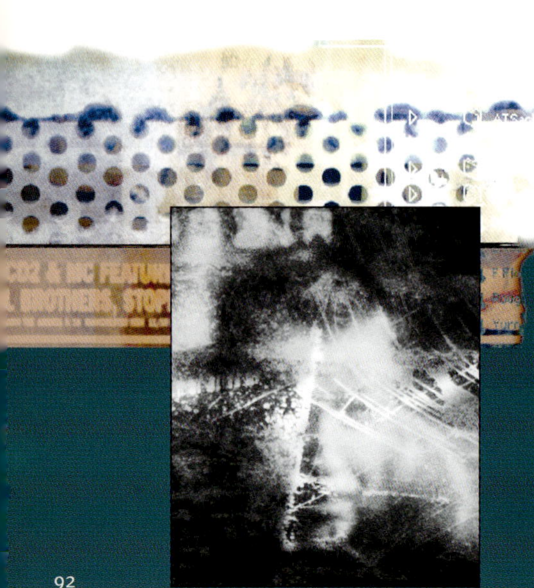

halvor bodin

Superlow, Union Design, Function

I am maybe too lazy and not explicitly talented at creating the primal shapes and geometry needed for good graphic design and illustration. My force lies in seeing clearly, combining and composing diverse elements into a fulfilling whole. I move between embracing the new groovy shapes and turn to the classical style and to hating every font in the fucking world... Does it mean anything at all, basically? Squarish fonts are kind of tired and overused right now, but everything is, isn´t it? So my philosophy on creating fonts and consuming them is: "Do what you wilt, that's the whole of the law..." Trends suck, but we live in the middle of the flow and we have to move with it, that´s the only sane thing to do... Believe in yourself and do what you feel and you will reach the eternal Kerning-Nirvana. Maybe we all will be reincarnated as Helvetica Narrow...

Born 1964 Lillehammer, Norway
University of Oslo, 1984-1986, studies in political science
1986-1989, freelance filmworker Favola Film,
1989-1993, producer/production manager, partner
Oslo International Filmfestival, 1991, co-founder
Subtopia, 1991-1994, graphic designer, founder
Megafon Design, 1994-1995, graphic designer
Union Design, 1995-, senior graphic designer, partner
Function, 1997-, experimental design guerilla group
Superlow, 1998-, personal fine-arts projects

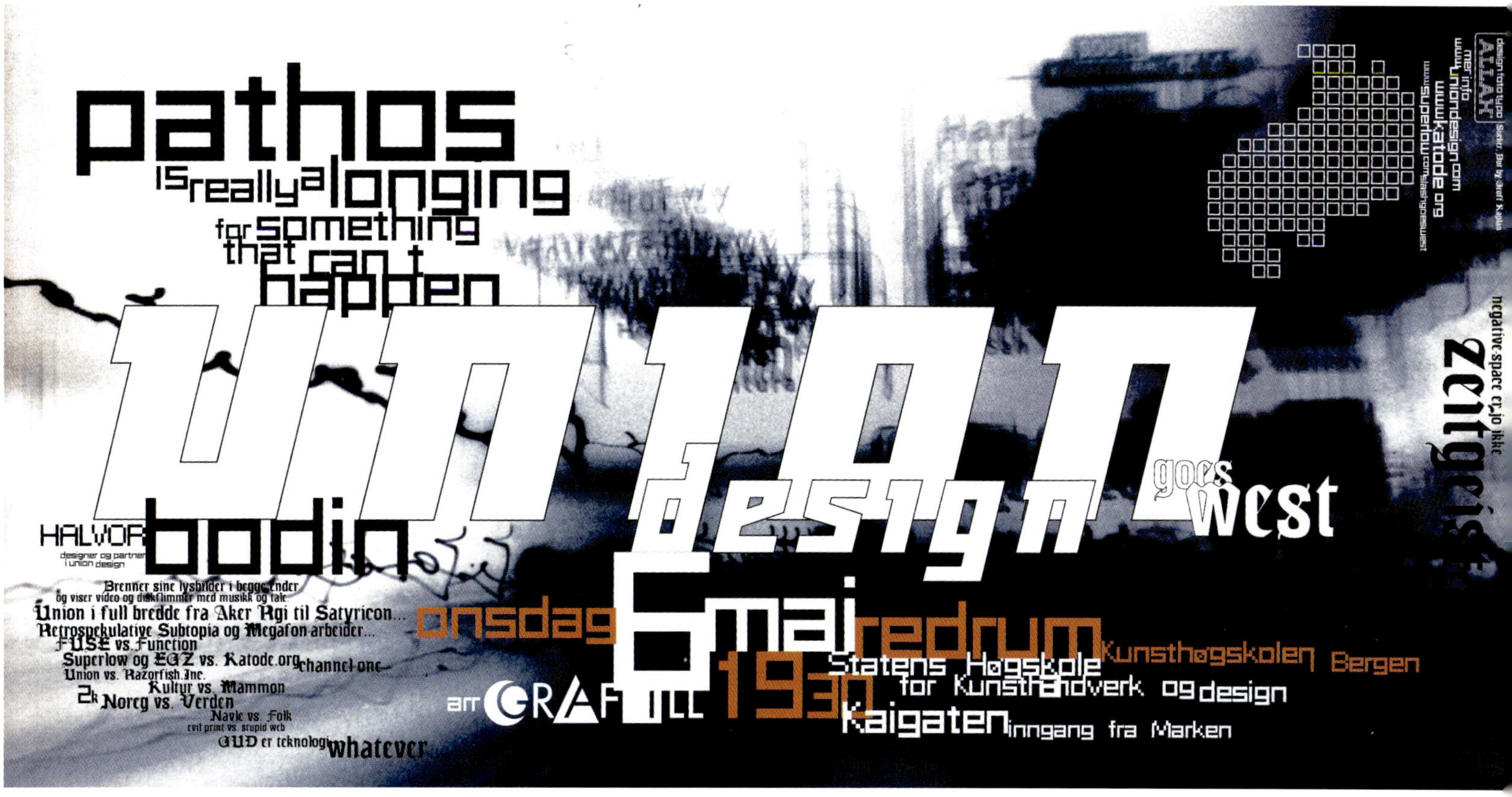

1

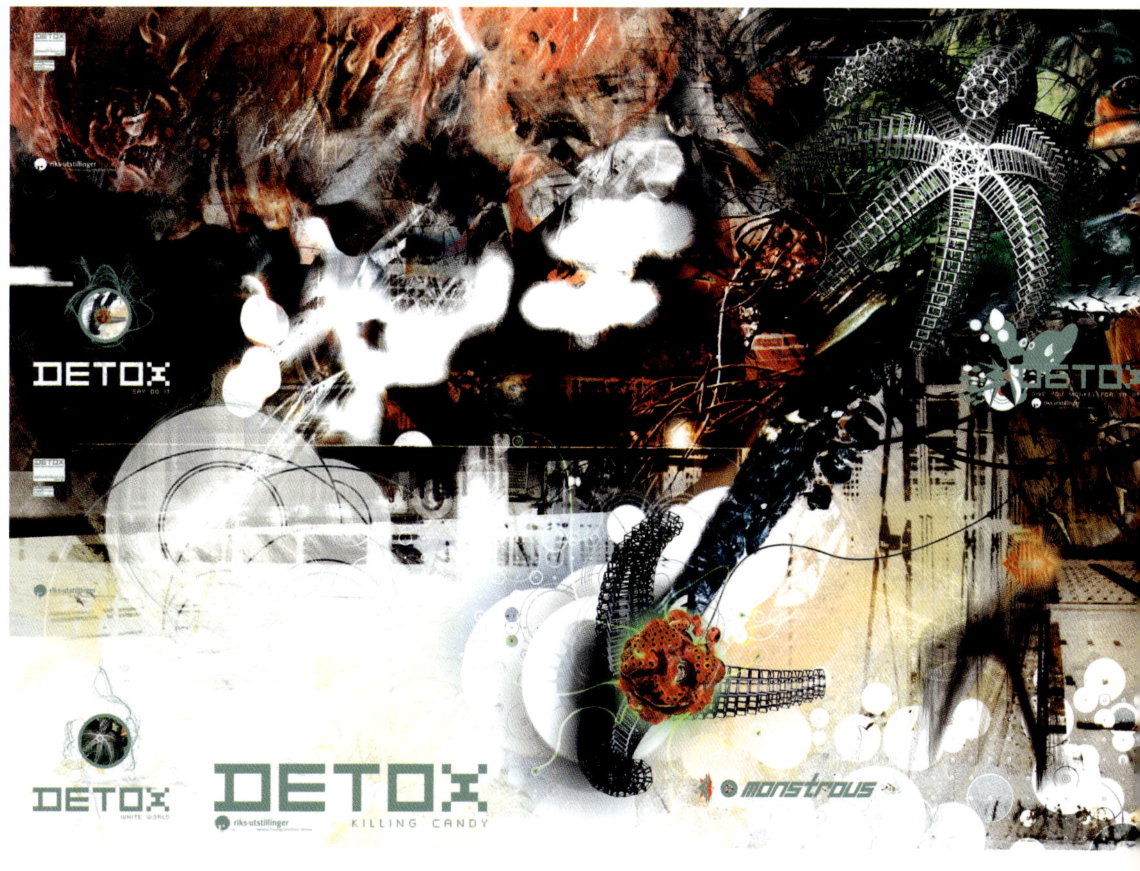

2

1
- Amp
- Halvor Bodin (Based on the mp3-player MacAmp)
- Superlow

1
- Union Goes West (flyer for a speech in Bergen)
- Halvor Bodin, Union Design
- Amp (Halvor Bodin), Sucker, But (Geoff Kaplan)
- Grafill, Kunsthøgskolen Bergen
- Halvor Bodin

2
- Detox poster (art exhibition)
- Halvor Bodin, Marius Watz
- Amp (Halvor Bodin), Protozoan (Marius Watz), Interstate (Tobias Frere-Jones)
- National Touring Exhibitions, Norway
- Halvor Bodin/Marius Watz

2

ABCDEFGHIJKLMNOPQRSTUVWXYZ

0123456789

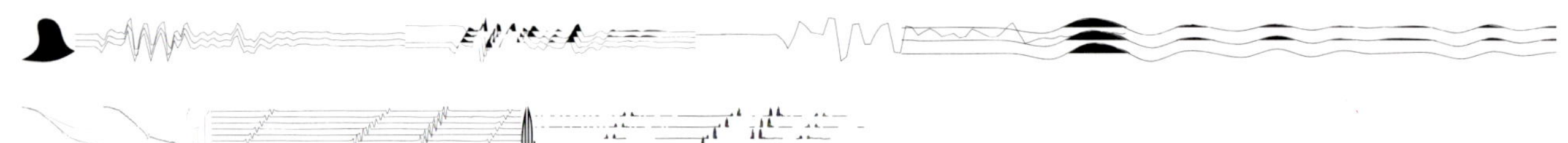

2.39SHOT.TRCTIME (SECS)

3

4

F This Is Where The Dog Is Buried + bonusfont F Shinjuku.

Look to Norway: We are rich and we are proud. We have oil and we have mobile phones. We hunt whales. We invented the cheese slicer and the paper clip. We ate our dogs to reach the South Pole. We trust our government. We have social security. We have less discrimination of women than most other countries. We have government support of the arts. We are approaching the millennium in a state of gluttony.

This Is Where The Dog Is Buried is a two-weight comment on Norwegian culture, as perceived by Norwegians themselves as well as by the world outside. The first weight (Bottom Of The Sea) is a literal interpretation of the Echo theme, scavenging shapes from the output of seismological readings of the ocean floor in search of black gold. The second weight (Top Of The Mountain) is a collection of Norwegian symbolic heritage from Vidkun Quisling and his nazi troopers to nostalgic Norwegicana.

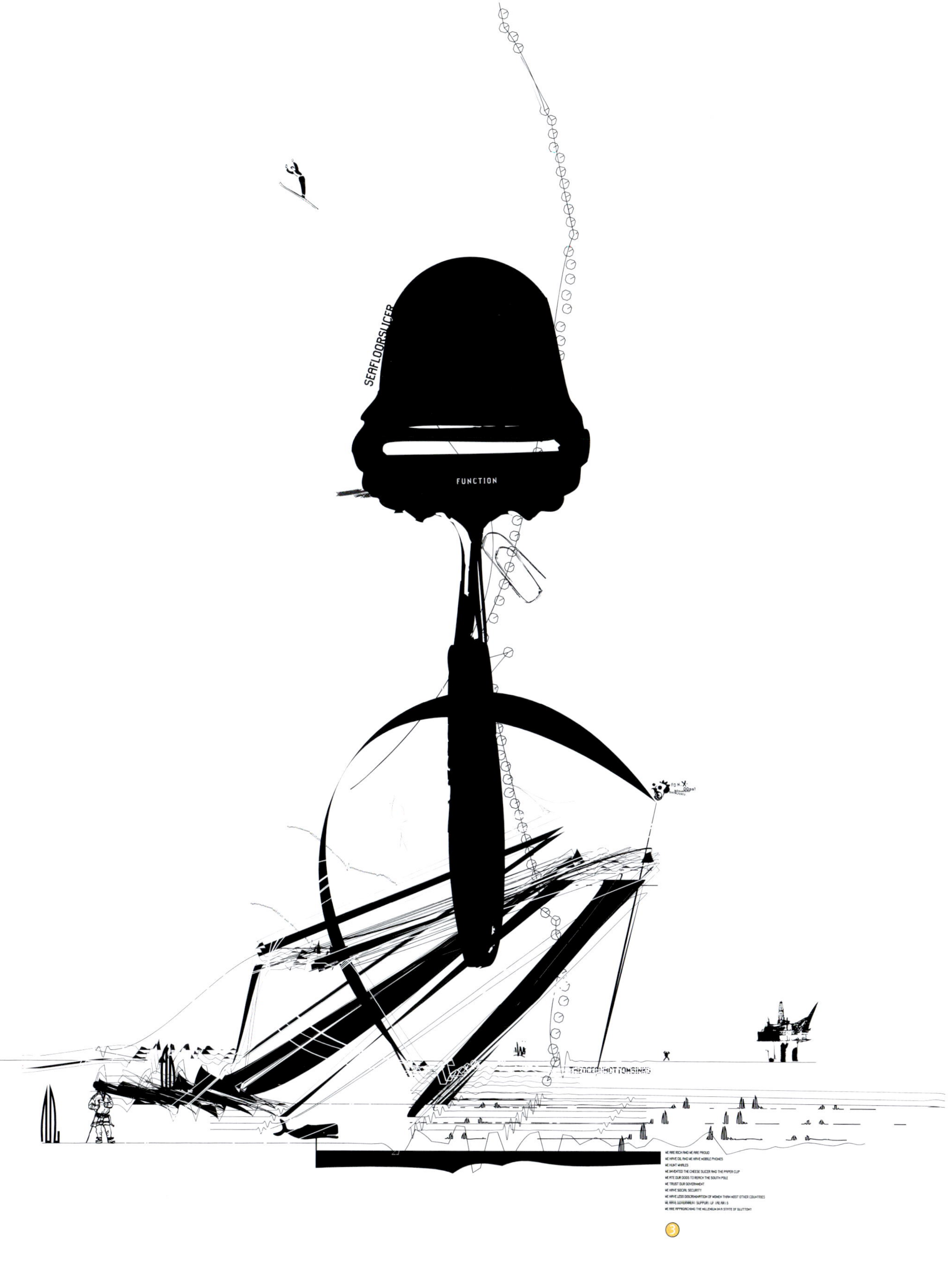

3

2 ✖ BurieDog Seabottom
■ Halvor Bodin (Function)
▲ FUSE 17, Fontshop International

3 ✖ BurieDog Mountaintop
■ Kim Hiorthøy, Marius Watz, Halvor Bodin (Function)
▲ FUSE 17, Fontshop International

4 ✖ Shinjuku
■ Kim Hiorthøy (Function)
▲ FUSE 17, Fontshop International

3 ● FUSE 17 poster
■ Marius Watz, Kim Hiorthøy, Halvor Bodin (Function)
✖ This is where the dog is buried (at the mountain top / This is where the dog is buried (at the bottom of the sea) / Shinjuku
★ Fontshop International

1 ABCDEFGHIJKLMNOPQRSTUVWXYZ
abcdefghijklmnopqrstuvwxyz
0123456789 (®©¢@*$%&?)

2 ABCDEFGHIJKLMNOPQRSTUVWXYZ
abcdefghijklmnopqrstuvwxyz
0123456789 (®©¢@*$%&?)

3 ABCDEFGHIJKLMNOPQRSTUVWXYZ
abcdefghijklmnopqrstuvwxyz
0123456789 (®©¢@*$%&?)

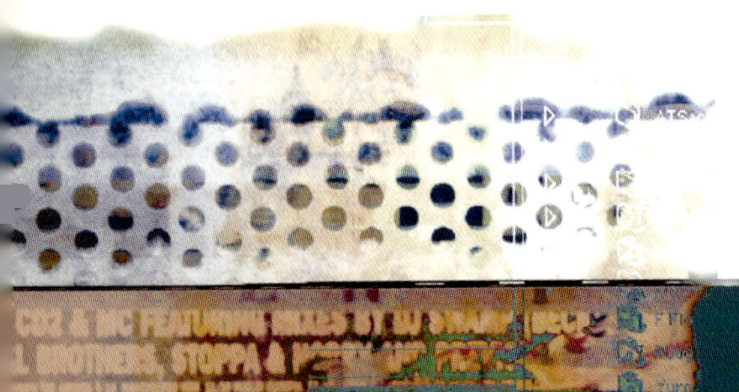

alias

Gareth Hague

Alias typefaces attempt to marry the attributes the computer has: perfect geometry, the copy and paste ethic, with a sense of craft and imagination in application. Therefore, how the initial theme or concept for a design is developed into a typeface can have as much to do with the devising and utilising of a system, or grid, onto which character shapes can be hung as it can drawing ability. Letterforms need not have the attributes attached to the physical act of writing (the stresses and serifs that derive from writing with a pen or chiselling in stone) or typographic convention (particularly if it is based on an outmoded technology). Instead, each letter can be treated as an individual graphic element within the parameters of a set grid – however loosely, or imaginatively, those parameters are applied. This is an aesthetic based purely on the look of the graphic form and not whether it meets a particular rule.

David James and Gareth Hague have been working together at David James Associates since 1990, mainly for clients in the music industry (including Boy George, Soul II Soul, System 7, Inner City and Wynton Marsalis) and fashion (Levi's, Koji Tatsuno, and David James is Art Director for Prada). They formed Alias to operate as a sister company alongside David James Associates at the beginning of 1996 to design and market their own typefaces and produce typographic-based design. They have produced custom typefaces for corportate clients and for *The Sunday Times Magazine (London)*. Other work includes an identity for Ad agency HHCL & P, a prospectus for a UK university and a photo library catalog for Pictor. Alias typefaces are distributed through Fontworks UK over the Internet, at www.type.co.uk, and through [T-26] and International TypeFounders.

(1)

it's not
what
this is
that's
impor-
tant,
it's what
it could
or might
be

1 ✖ Klute Black (a 2 weight family)
■ Gareth Hague
▲ Alias

2 ✖ August Medium (a 5 weight family)
■ Gareth Hague
▲ Alias

3 ✖ Harbour Medium (a 3 weight family)
■ Gareth Hague
▲ Alias

(1) ● Klute poster
■ Gareth Hague
✖ Klute Black
★ Fontworks UK

2

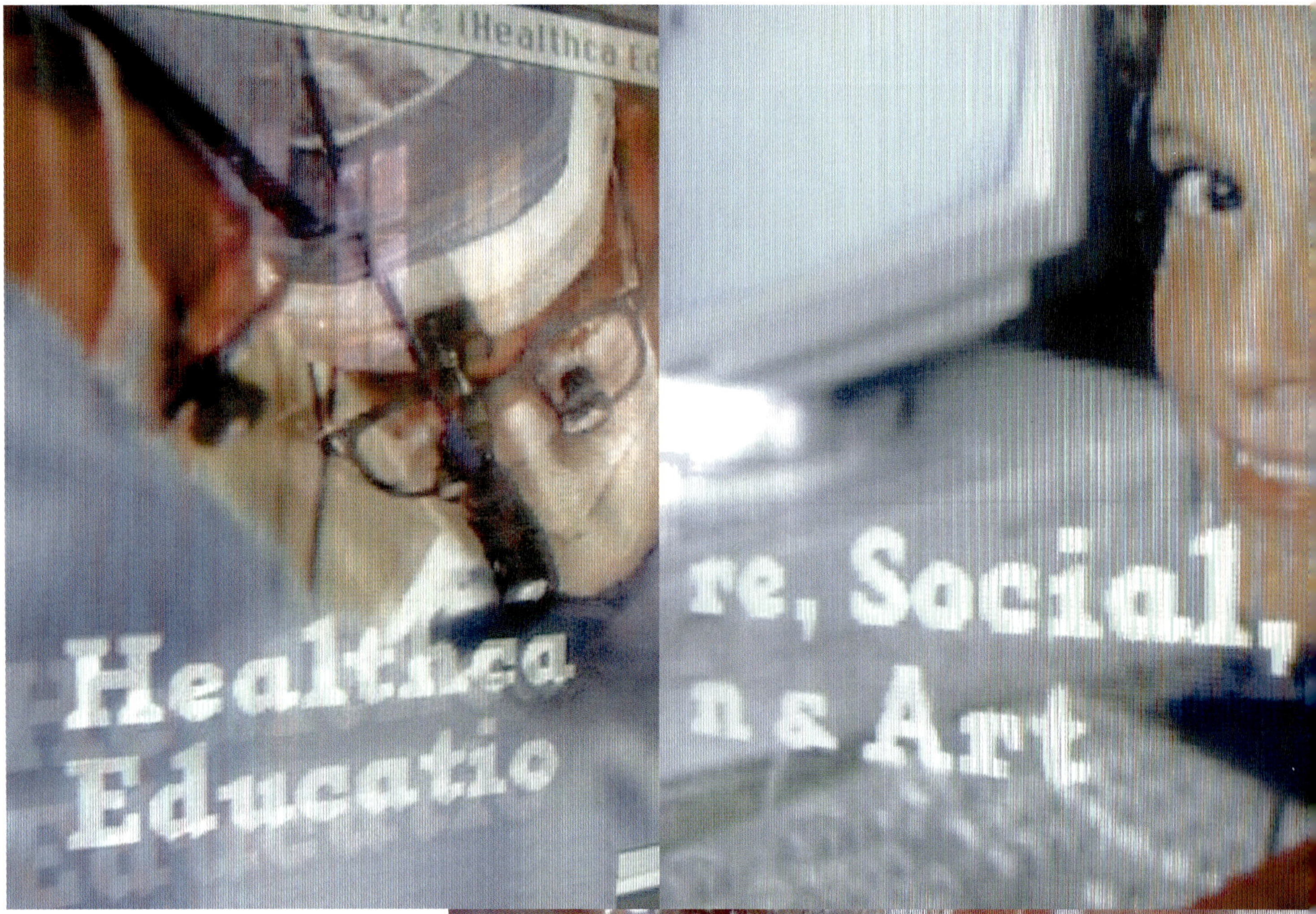

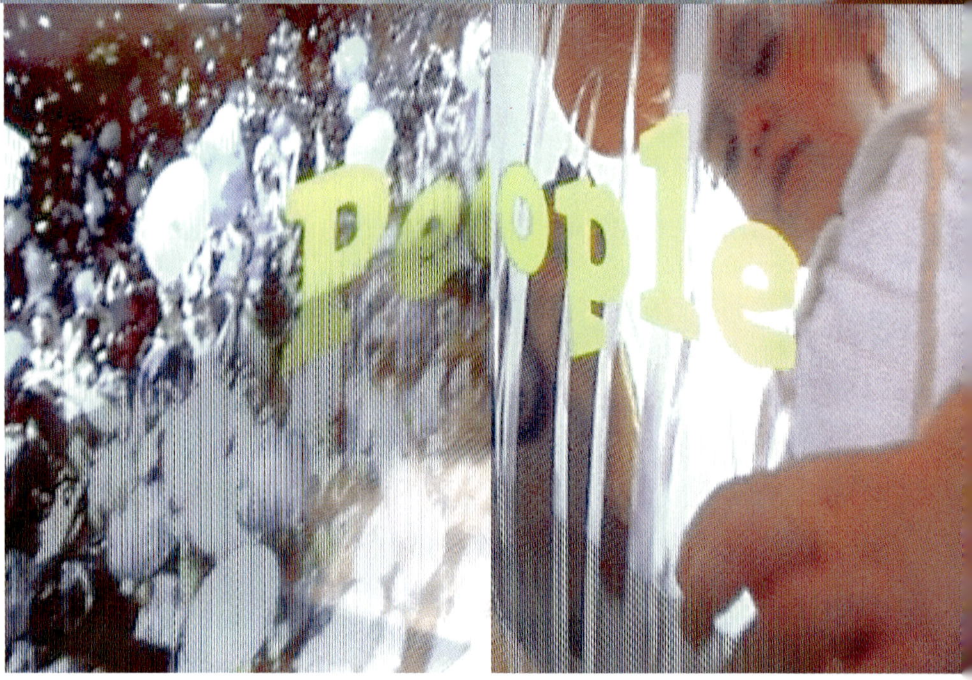

3

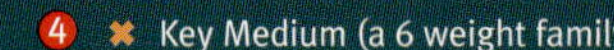

4 Key Medium (a 6 weight family)
Gareth Hague
Alias

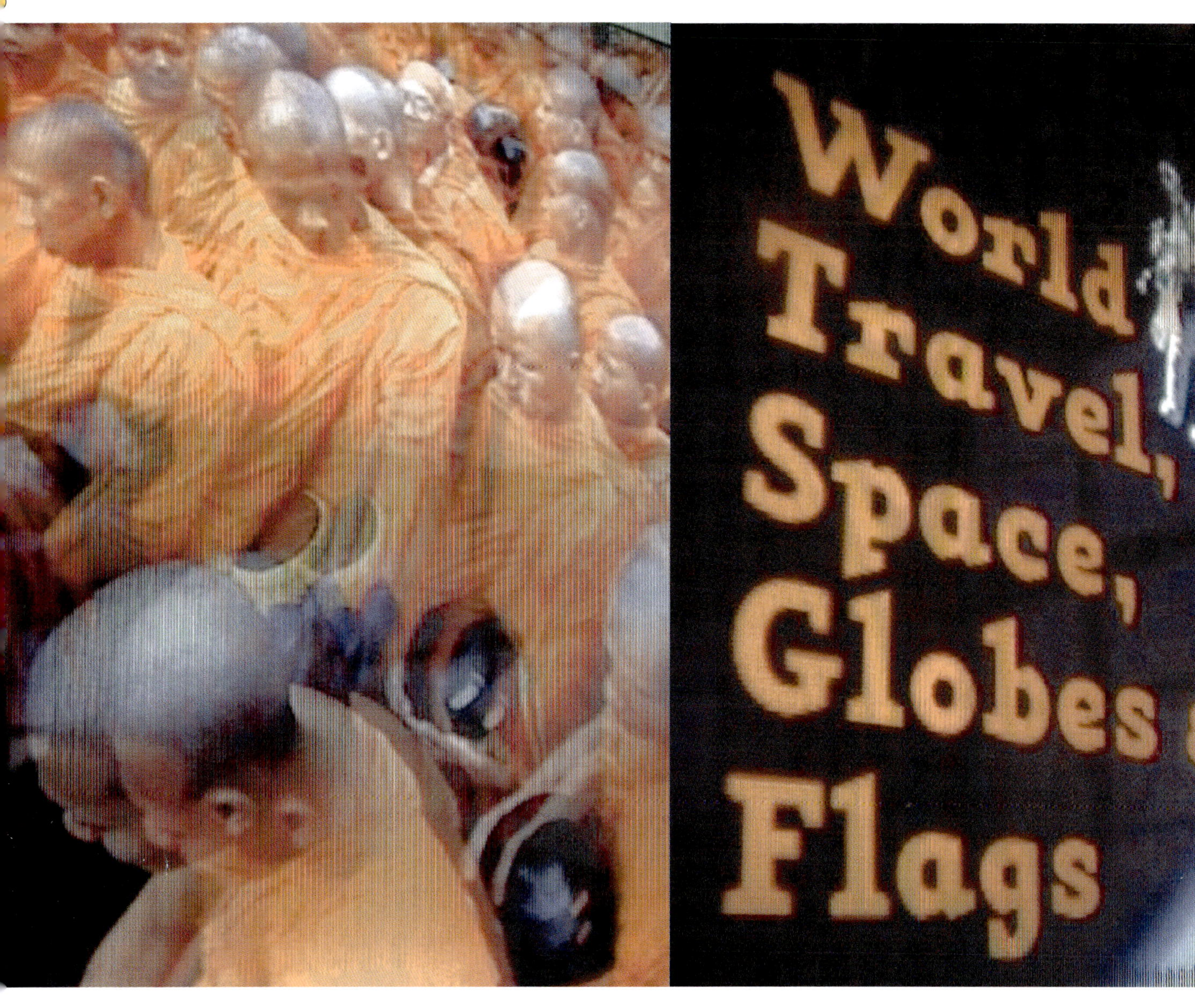

ABCDEFGHIJKLMNOPQRSTUVWXYZ
abcdefghijklmnopqrstuvwxyz
0123456789
(®©¢@*$%&?)

4

2
- Pictor Volume II section divider, double page spread Healthcare
- Gareth Hague / Malcolm Webb
- Key Bold
- Pictor International ltd
- Malcolm Webb

3
- Pictor Volume II section divider, double page spread People
- Gareth Hague / Malcolm Webb
- Key Bold
- Pictor International ltd
- Malcolm Webb

4
- Pictor Volume II section divider, double page spread World Travel
- Gareth Hague / Malcolm Webb
- Key Bold
- Pictor International ltd
- Malcolm Webb

5

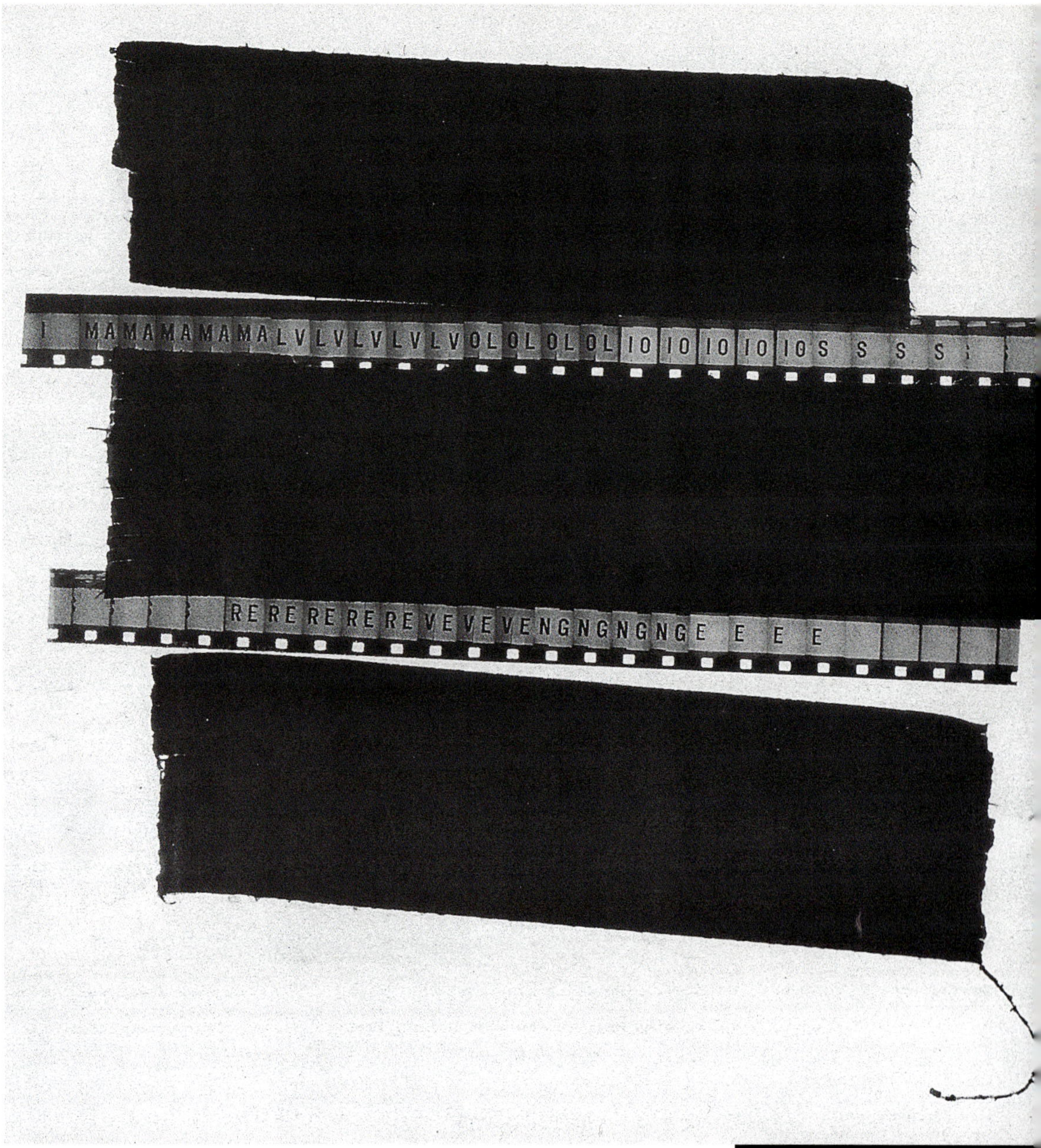

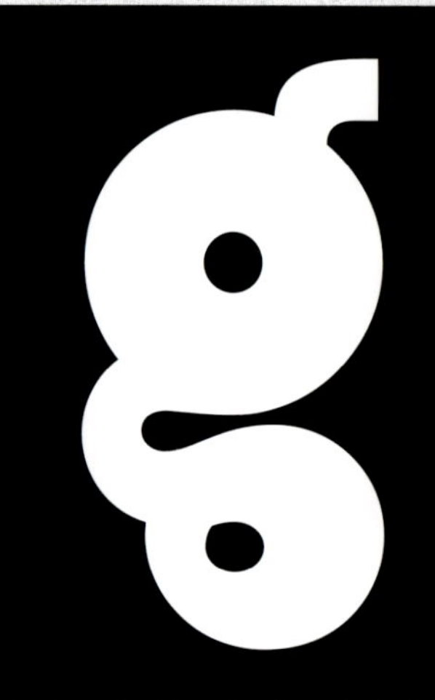

6

5 Elephant Medium (a 6 weight family)
Gareth Hague
Alias

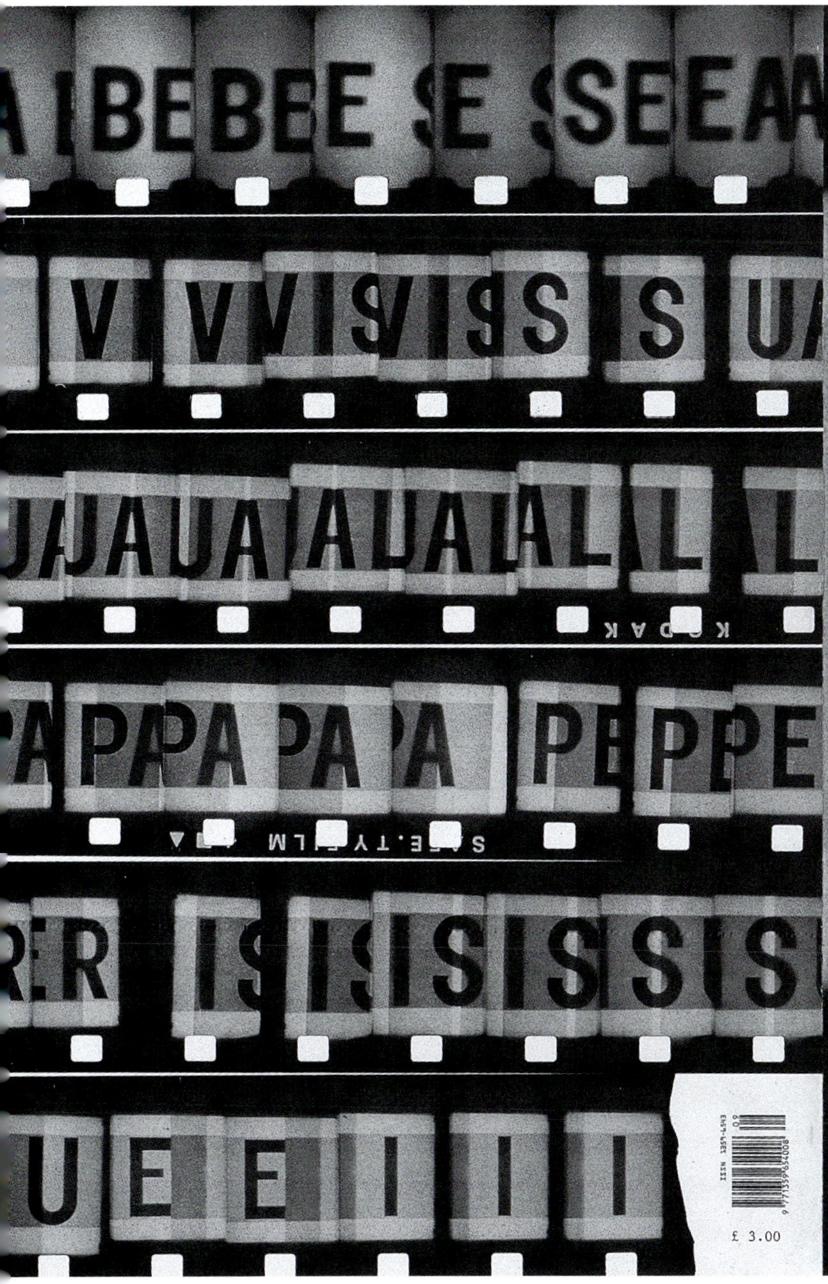

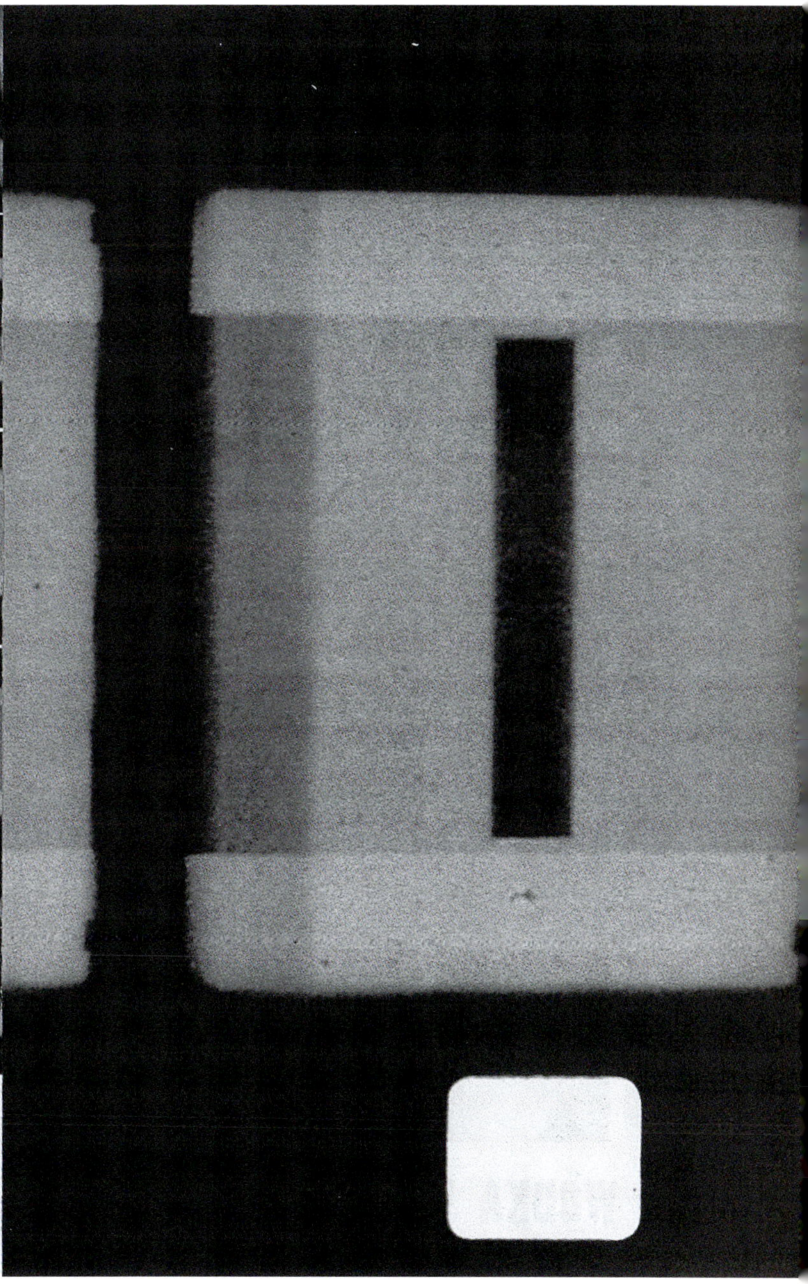

ABCDEFGHIJKLMNOPQRSTUVWXYZ
abcdefghijklmnopqrstuvwxyz
0123456789
(®©¢@*$%&?)

5
- A Be Sea "Issue i"
- David Tames
- Elephant Medium
- Sebastian Boyle
- Toby McFarlan Pond

6
- A Be Sea "Issue g" (cover)
- David Tames / Gareth Hague
- Elephant Black
- Sebastian Boyle

7
- A Be Sea "Issue i" (cover)
- David Tames
- Elephant Medium
- Sebastian Boyle
- Toby McFarlan Pond

1

abcdefghijklmnopq
rstuvwxyz
0123456789 (@¢$#÷%&)

abcdefghijklmnop
qrstuvwxyz
0123456789(@¢$÷%)

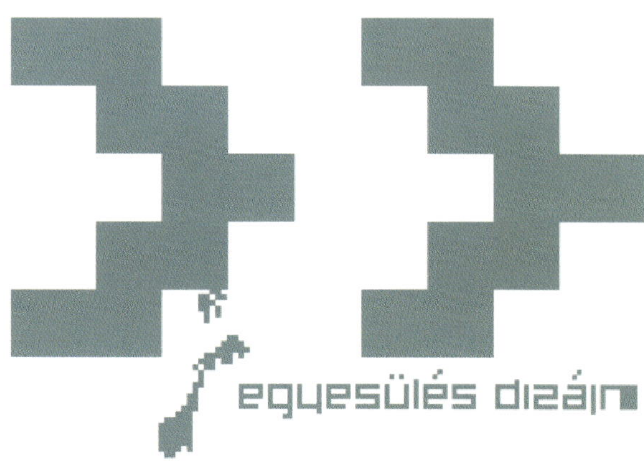

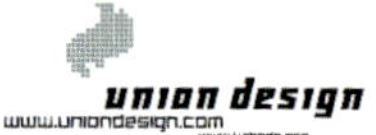

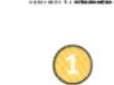

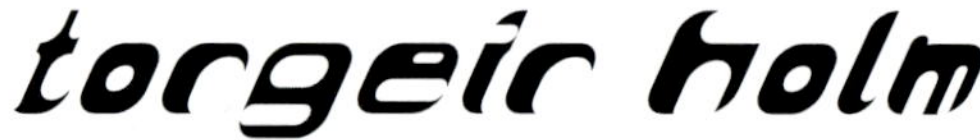

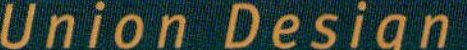

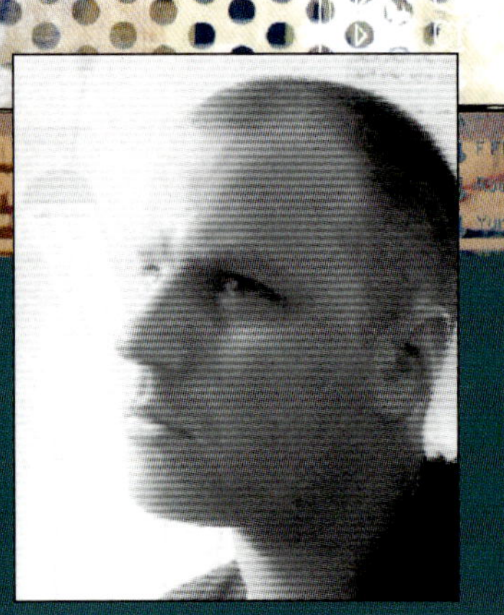

Anything goes, as long at it looks good, that is... Though an understanding of basic, classic typography is always helpful, even if you're creating or working with fonts that look nothing like a Garamond or Helvetica.

Torgeir Holm (egz, union design)
Born 1973, Sarpsborg, Norway. Grew up with his eyes glued to a C64 screen, now programs, designs, animates and creates on all types of media, in both CMYK and RGB colorspace at Union Design in Oslo, Norway.

Invaders
The font started out as a few letters in the bold weight done for a logo, and evolved into a complete font some weeks later. I aimed to create a font based on a strict 5x5 "pixel" grid, while still giving it enough character to prevent it from disappearing into the huge number of other "pixel"-based fonts cropping up. The light weight was added later, when the need arose while doing the Union Design Inspiration book. Inspiration for the font was both the blockiness of old video games, and the boldness and power of old USSR propaganda poster typography.

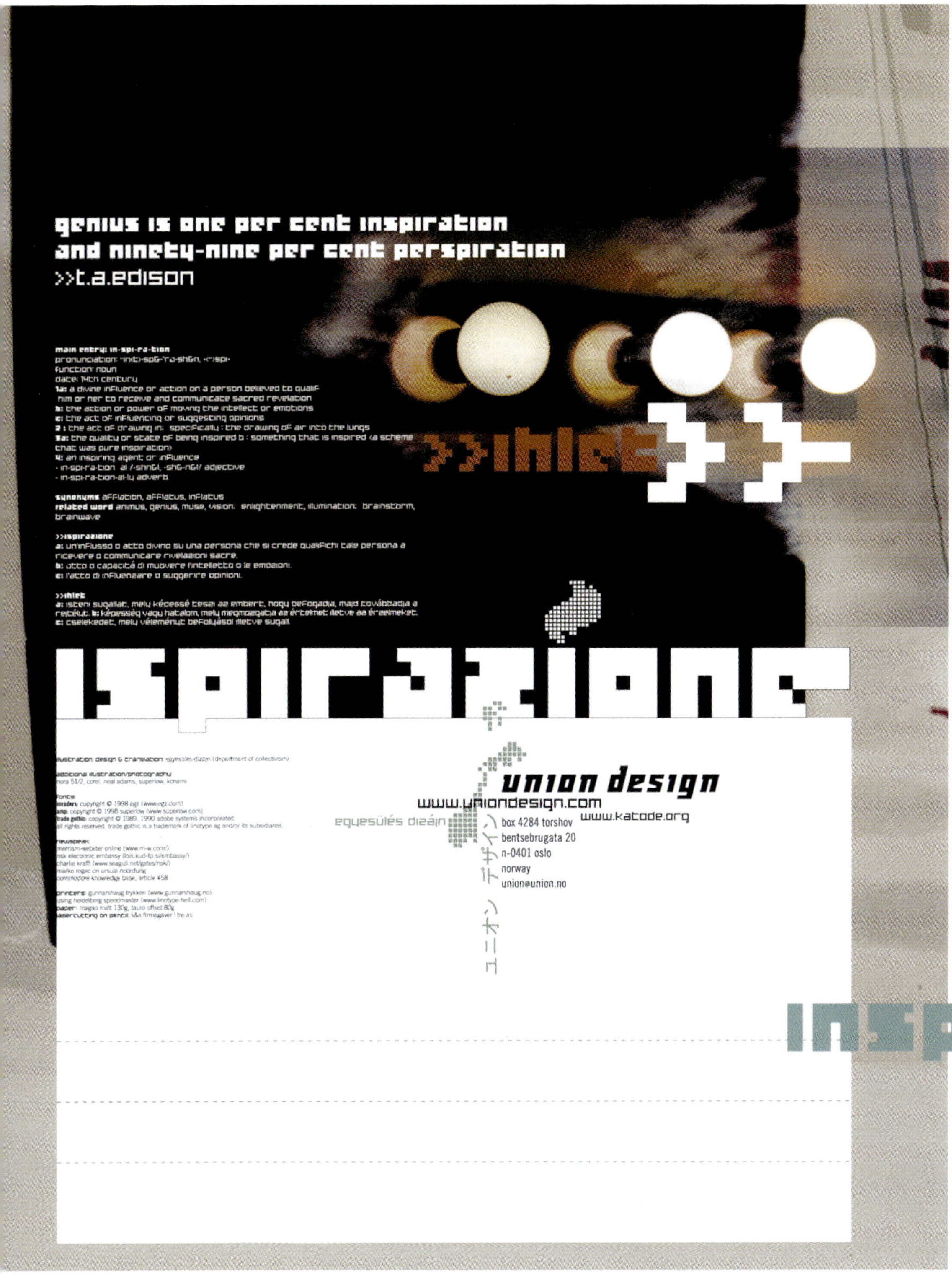

genius is one per cent inspiration
and ninety-nine per cent perspiration
>>t.a.edison

main entry: in-spi-ra-tion
pronunciation: ˌin(t)-spə-ˈrā-shən, -(ˌ)spi-
function: noun
date: 14th century
1a: a divine influence or action on a person believed to qualif
him or her to receive and communicate sacred revelation
b: the action or power of moving the intellect or emotions
c: the act of influencing or suggesting opinions
2 : the act of drawing in: specifically : the drawing of air into the lungs
3a: the quality or state of being inspired b : something that is inspired <a scheme that was pure inspiration>
4: an inspiring agent or influence
- in-spi-ra-tion al /-shnəl, -shə-nəl/ adjective
- in-spi-ra-tion-al-ly adverb

synonyms afflation, afflatus, inflatus
related word animus, genius, muse, vision; enlightenment, illumination; brainstorm, brainwave

>>ispirazione
a: un'influsso o atto divino su una persona che si crede qualifichi tale persona a ricevere o communicare rivelazioni sacre.
b: atto o capacitá di muovere l'intelletto o le emozioni.
c: l'atto di influenzare o suggerire opinioni.

>>ihlet
a: isteni sugallat, mely képessé teszi az embert, hogy befogadja, majd továbbadja a rejtélyt. b: képesség vagy hatalom, mely megmozgatja az értelmet illetve az érzelmeket.
c: cselekedet, mely véleményt befolyásol illetve sugall.

>>ihlet>>

ispirazione

illustration, design & translation: egyesülés dizájn (department of collectivism)

additional illustration/photography
nora 51/2, corel, neal adams, superlow, konami

fonts:
invaders: copyright © 1998 egz (www.egz.com)
amp: copyright © 1998 superlow (www.superlow.com)
trade gothic: copyright © 1989, 1990 adobe systems incorporated.
all rights reserved. trade gothic is a trademark of linotype ag and/or its subsidiaries.

printers: gunnarshaug trykkeri (www.gunnarshaug.no)
using heidelberg speedmaster (www.linotype-hell.com)
paper: magno matt 130g, tauro offset 80g

union design
www.uniondesign.com
www.katode.org
egyesülés dizájn
ユニオン デザイン
box 4284 torshov
bentsebrugata 20
n-0401 oslo
norway
union@union.no

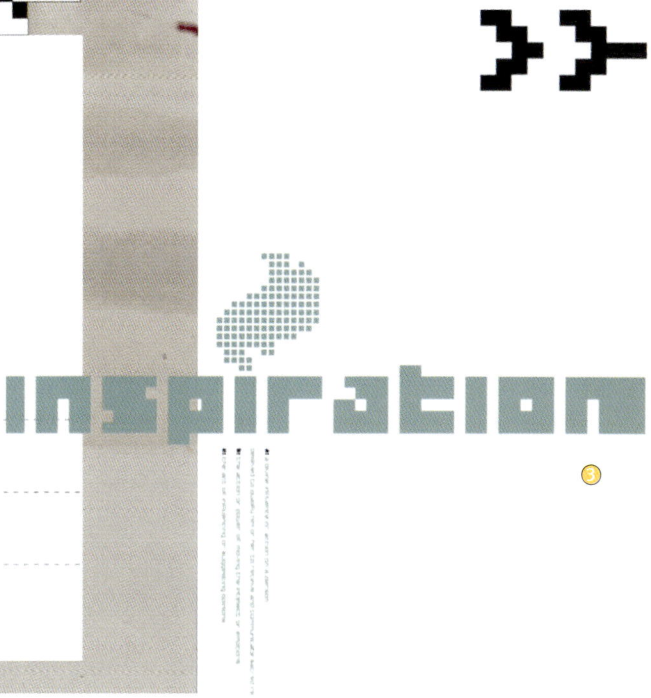

>>

inspiration

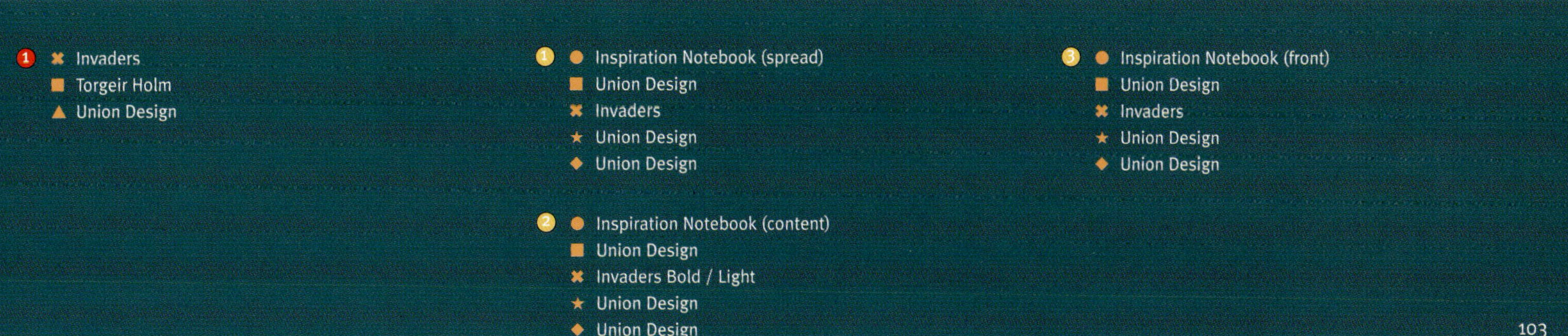

1
- Invaders
- Torgeir Holm
- Union Design

1
- Inspiration Notebook (spread)
- Union Design
- Invaders
- Union Design
- Union Design

2
- Inspiration Notebook (content)
- Union Design
- Invaders Bold / Light
- Union Design
- Union Design

3
- Inspiration Notebook (front)
- Union Design
- Invaders
- Union Design
- Union Design

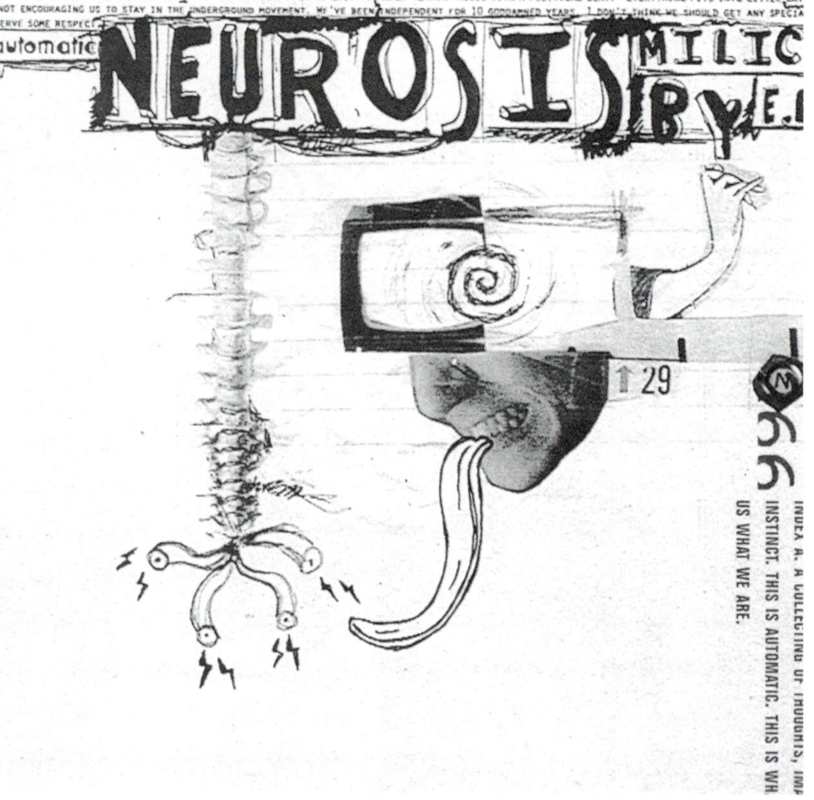

ABCDEFGHIJKLMNOPQRSTUVWXYZ

0123456789

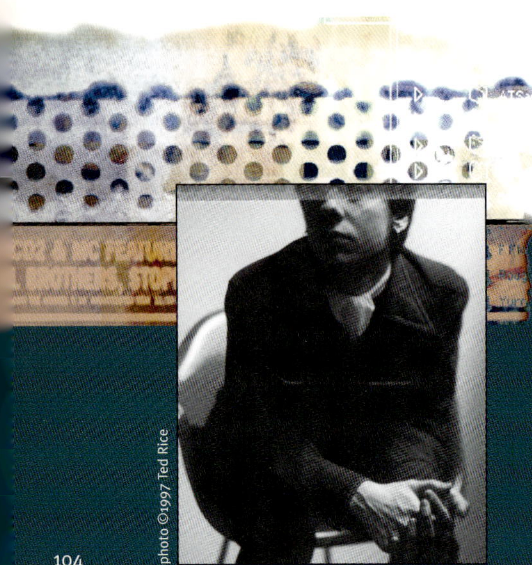

photo ©1997 Ted Rice

prototype experimental foundry

Charles Wilkin

Charles Wilkin created Automatic Art and Design in Columbus, Ohio, in 1994 as an outlet for conceptual graphic design, illustration, interactive media and fine art. The studio is in essence a collection of thoughts, images and instinct, or rather a process of assembly which informally connects art and human nature. This mixture of ideas, information and experiences blends both art and design, allowing Wilkin to create work which is strategic, personal and powerful. This process has attracted a wide range of clients, including: Coca-Cola, Capitol Records, Capricorn Records, Showtime Networks, Urban Outfitters and Columbia Sportswear. As an extension of Automatic's experimental process, Wilkin developed Prototype Experimental Foundry in 1994 as a means to transpose the organic nature of his work into typographic form. Currently Prototype has a diverse collection of over 50 fonts from designers such as Frank Ford, Robert Beck, John Wiese and Charles Wilkin. The collection spans from cyber pop-culture and hand painted letterforms to post modern blackletter. In 1996, several of Prototype's experimental typefaces were part of "Mixing Messages," an exhibition held at the Cooper-Hewitt National Design Museum in New York City which documented innovations in graphic design over the past 15 years. More recently, Prototype's font "Spin" was part of the exhibition "Blackletter: Type and National Identity" held at the Cooper Union School of Art in conjunction with the Herb Lubalin Study Center of Design and Typography. Wilkin's work with Automatic has also been featured in many books and magazines, including: *Communication Arts*, *Print* magazine, *How* magazine, *Idea* magazine, *Shift* magazine, Type Directors Club 19, AIGA 18, *Type in the Digital* by Steven Heller and *Alphabook* by Roger Walton.

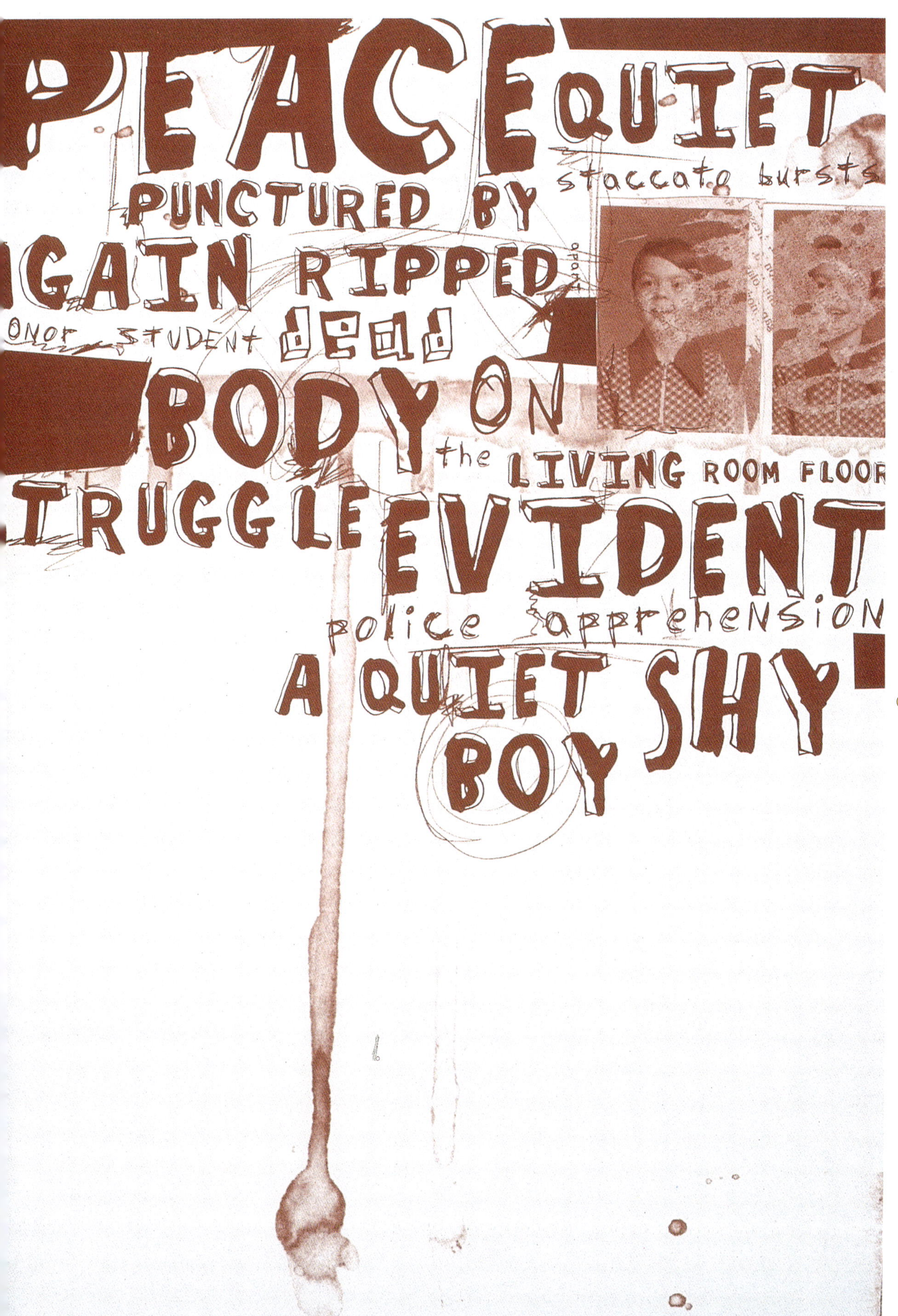

1 ✖ Superchunk
■ Charles Wilkin
▲ Prototype Experimental Foundry

1 ● Neurosis
■ Charles Wilkin
✖ Superchunk
★ Prototype Experimental Foundry
◆ Charles Wilkin

2 ● Creep and broken
■ Charles Wilkin
✖ Superchunk
★ Prototype Experimental Foundry
◆ Charles Wilkin

3

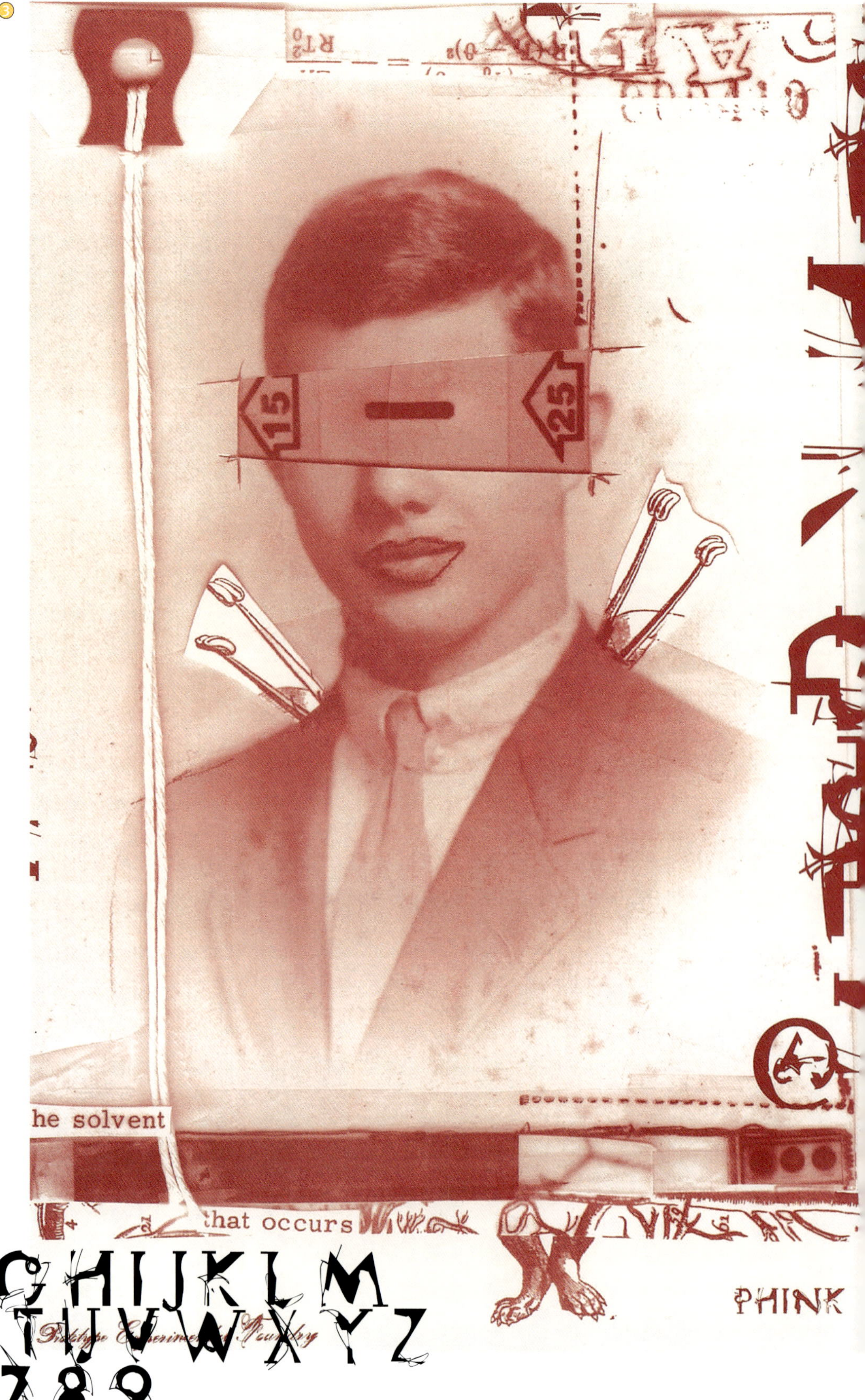

ABCDEFGHIJKLM
NOPQRSTUVWXYZ
0123456789

2

2 ✖ Phink
■ Charles Wilkin
▲ Prototype Experimental Foundry

3 ✖ Decline Light / Bold (a 4 weight family)
■ Charles Wilkin
▲ Prototype Experimental Foundry

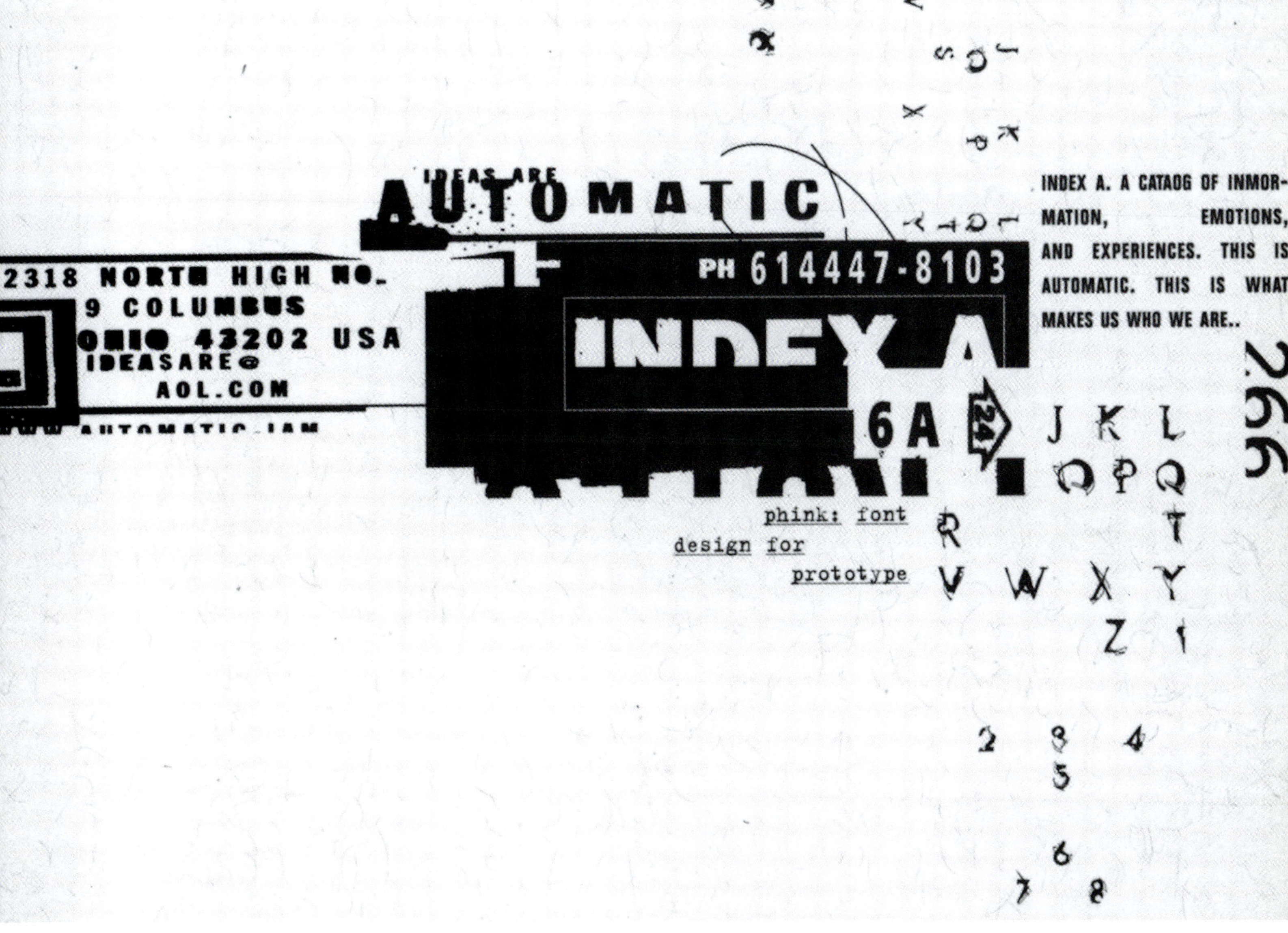

4

abcdefghijklmnopqrstuvwxyz
abcdefghijklmnopqrstuvwxyz
0123456789

abcdefghijklmnopqrstuvwxyz
abcdefghijklmnopqrstuvwxyz
0123456789

3

3
- Phink poster
- Charles Wilkin
- Phink
- Prototype Experimental Foundry
- Charles Wilkin

4
- Phink promotion card
- Charles Wilkin
- Phink
- Prototype Experimental Foundry
- Charles Wilkin

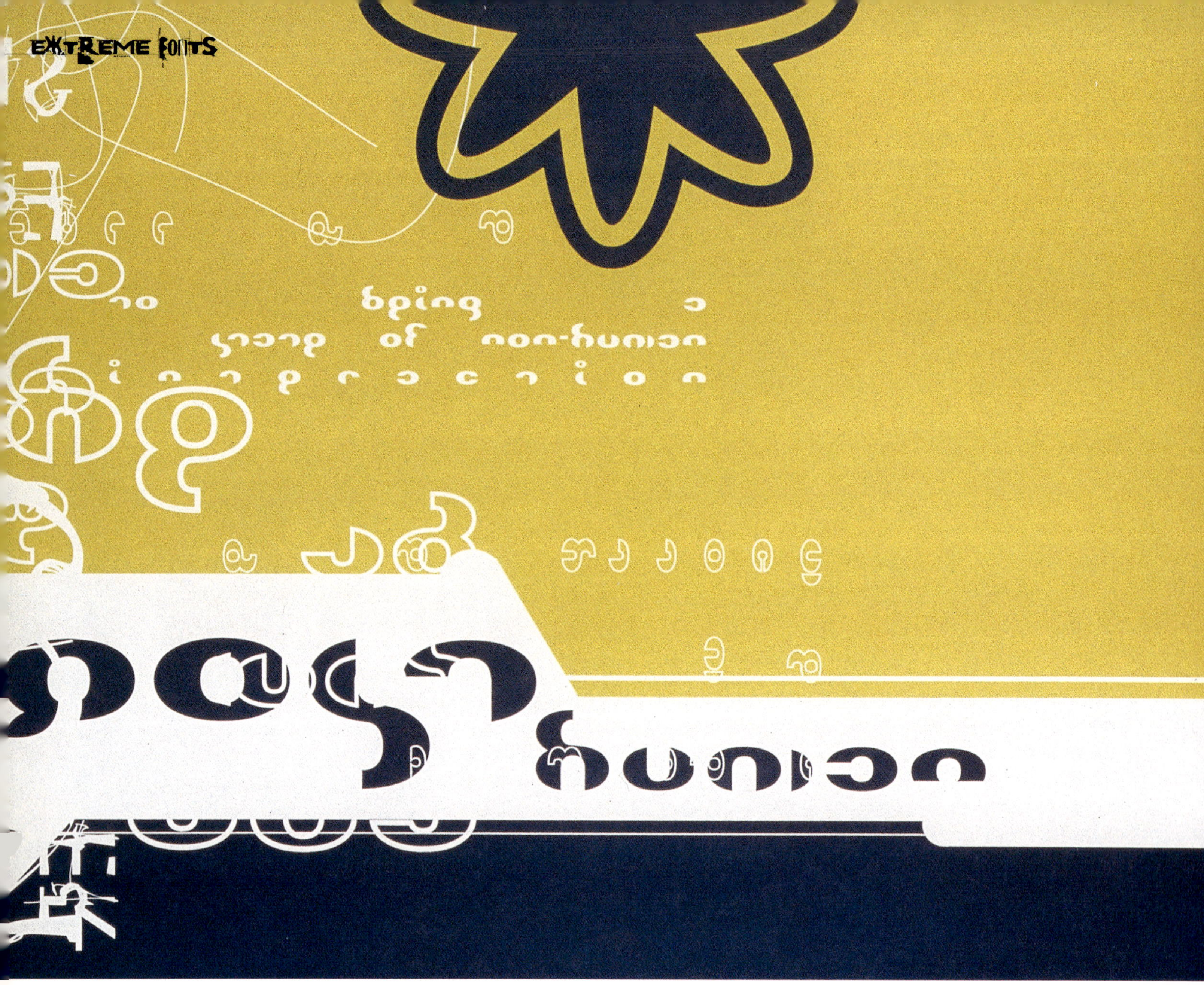

4

4 Spaceboy Regular / Outline (a 4 weight family)
Charles Wilkin
Prototype Experimental Foundry

5 Halo Regular / Outline (a 4 weight family)
John Weise
Prototype Experimental Foundry

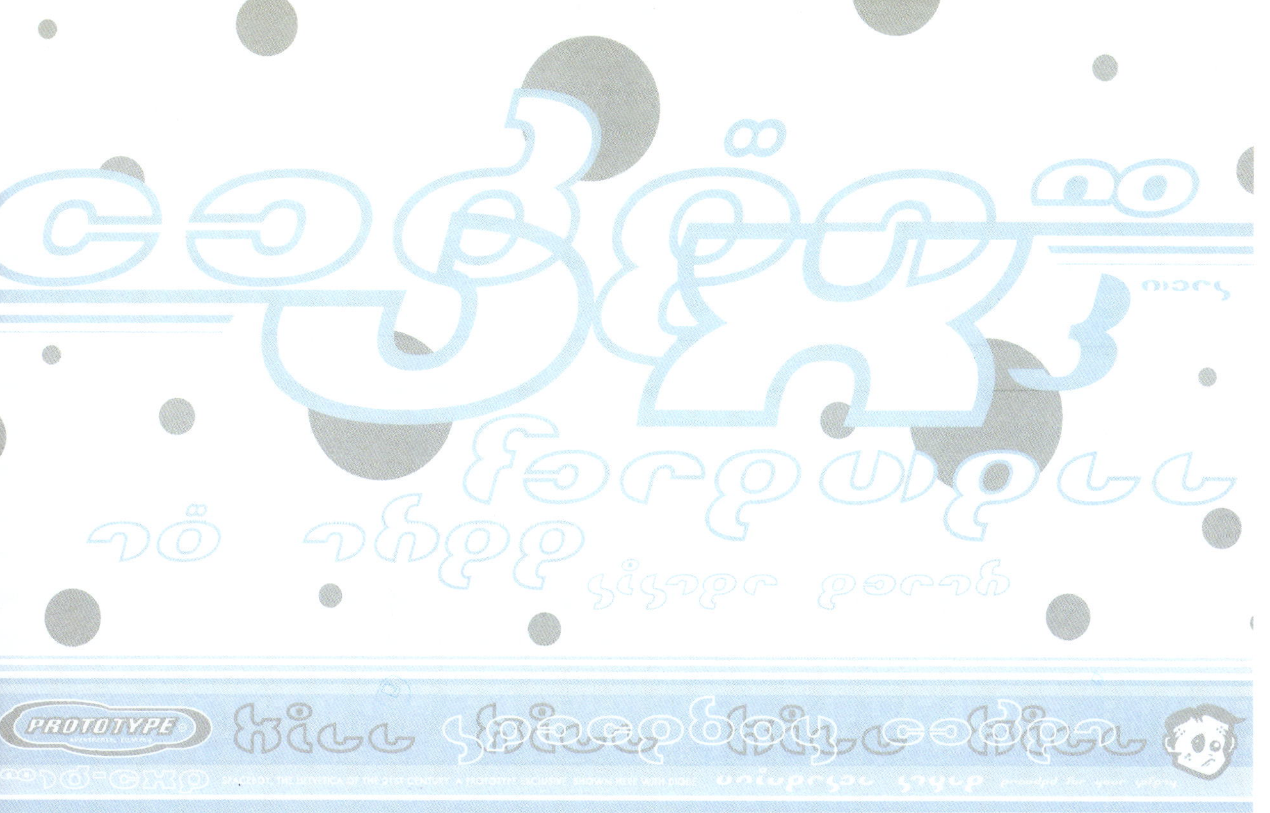

6

ABCDEFGHIJKLMNOPQ
RSTUVWXYZ
abcdefghijklmnopqr
stuvwxyz0123456789

ABCDEFGHIJKLMNOPQ
RSTUVWXYZ
abcdefghijklmnopqr
stuvwxyz0123456789

5

5
- ● Spaceboy promotion card
- ■ Charles Wilkin
- ✖ Spaceboy Regular / Outline
- ★ Prototype Experimental Foundry
- ◆ Charles Wilkin

6
- ● Spaceboy poster
- ■ Charles Wilkin
- ✖ Spaceboy Regular / Outline
- ★ Prototype Experimental Foundry

font

spumoni

there is nothing i
can do to make
this week

last a lifetime
and that's how
long i
need you

poem by

megan crawford

6 Ghetto Prince Regular (a 2 weight family)
Frank Ford
Prototype Experimental Foundry

7 Velvet Plush / Velour (a 3 weight family)
Charles Wilkin
Prototype Experimental Foundry

ABCDEFGHIJKLM
NOPQRSTUVWXYZ
a b c d e f g h i j k l m n o p q r s t u v w x y z
0 1 2 3 4 5 6 7 8 9

6

8

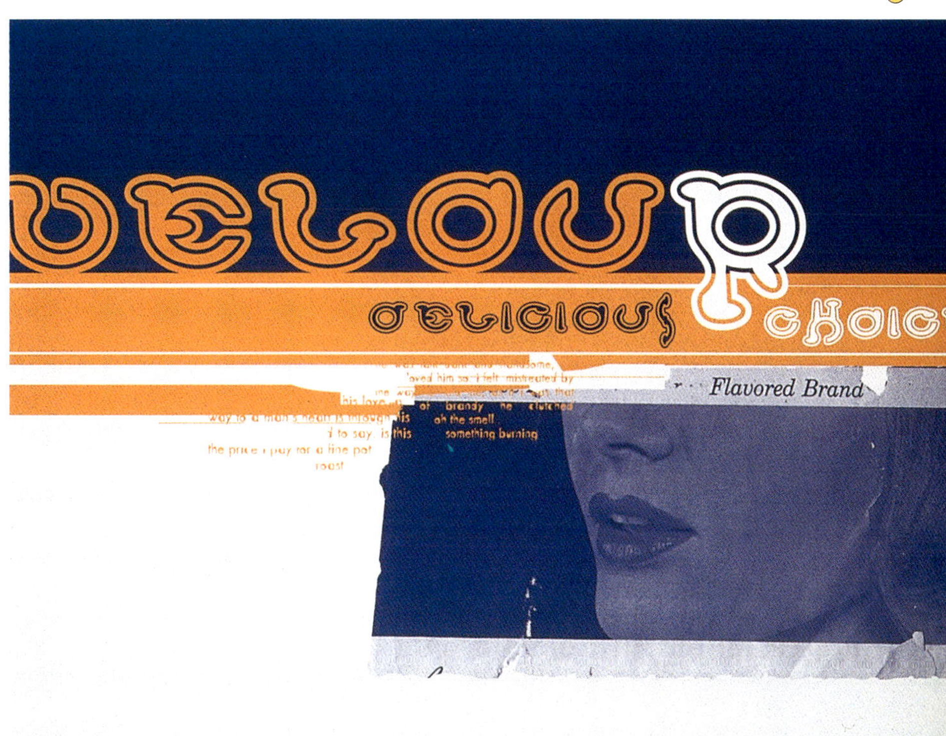

ABCDEFGHIJKLMNOPQRST
UVWXYZ
abcdefghijklmnopqrstuvwxyz
0123456789

7

ABCDEFGHIJKLMNOPQ
RSTUVWXYZ
abcdefghijklmnopqrstuv
wxyz 0123456789

7
- ● Ghetto Prince poster
- ■ Frank Ford
- ✖ Ghetto Prince
- ★ Prototype Experimental Foundry

8
- ● Velvet Velour promotion card
- ■ Charles Wilkin
- ✖ Velour Velour
- ★ Prototype Experimental Foundry

1

ABCDEFGHIJK
LMNOPQRSTUV
WXYZ
0123456789
<*+[]#¢$%&>

ABCDEFGHIJ
KLMNOPQRS
TUVWXYZ

2

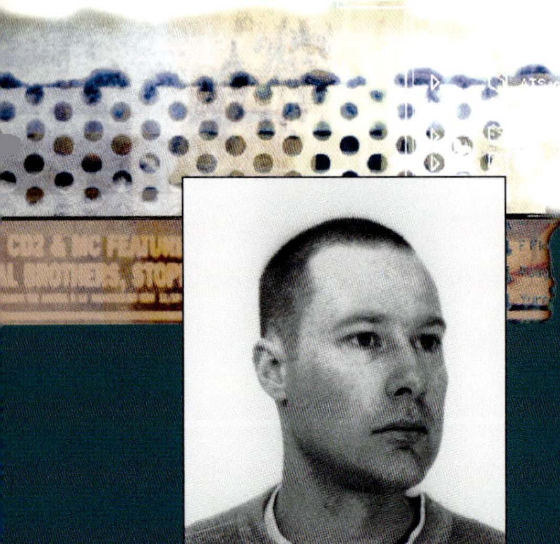

christian Küsters

Acme Fonts

Acme Fonts is a London-based foundry currently representing the work of nine type designers, including that of its founder, Christian Küsters. Küsters, who studied at the London College of Printing, and subsequently under Matthew Carter at Yale, has taken a highly conceptual approach to type design. In common with a number of young designers of the post-Fontographer era, Küsters believes that type, as a medium, can be pushed beyond its hitherto accepted role – can be consciously loaded with cultural signifiers which might then run in a visual parallel with verbal content; a type of commentary – perhaps emphasising, perhaps contradicting, perhaps in a surreal counterpoint. Of course type has been doing this in subtle ways since the 15th century: it is the very conscious manipulation and the degree of visual sophistication assumed in the audience which makes this approach emphatically contemporary. This is type as a way of exploring language and ideas, as well as a vehicle for transmitting them. "Perhaps the most valuable quality I learned from Matthew Carter was that of openness to ideas," says Küsters. The name of the foundry itself developed out of this preoccupation with the subtle mechanisms of language. "I like the word 'acme': the literal meaning, 'highest point or point of perfection,' is in complete contrast to its universal use to signify the opposite through a thousand-and-one 'Acme Laundry' vans and the like."

(Text by Ken Wilson, designer and writer, London)

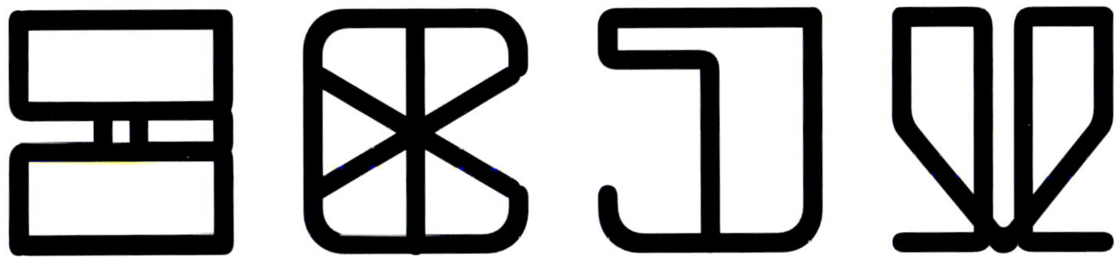

BEDFORD HILL GALLERY • 202 GREAT SUFFOLK STREET • LONDON SE1 1NY

NEW PAINTINGS BY PHIL ASHCROFT

DUEL

EXHIBITION 5–29 AUGUST 1998 • WED–FRI 11.00–5.00 SAT 12.00–5.00

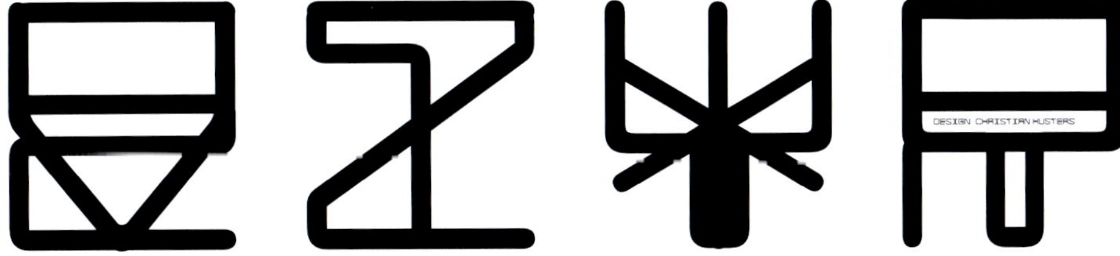

WWW.FOURSECONDMEMORY.DEMON.CO.UK/PHIL.HTM • WITH SPECIAL THANKS TO THE CORPORATION OF LONDON

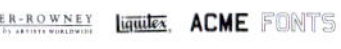

1

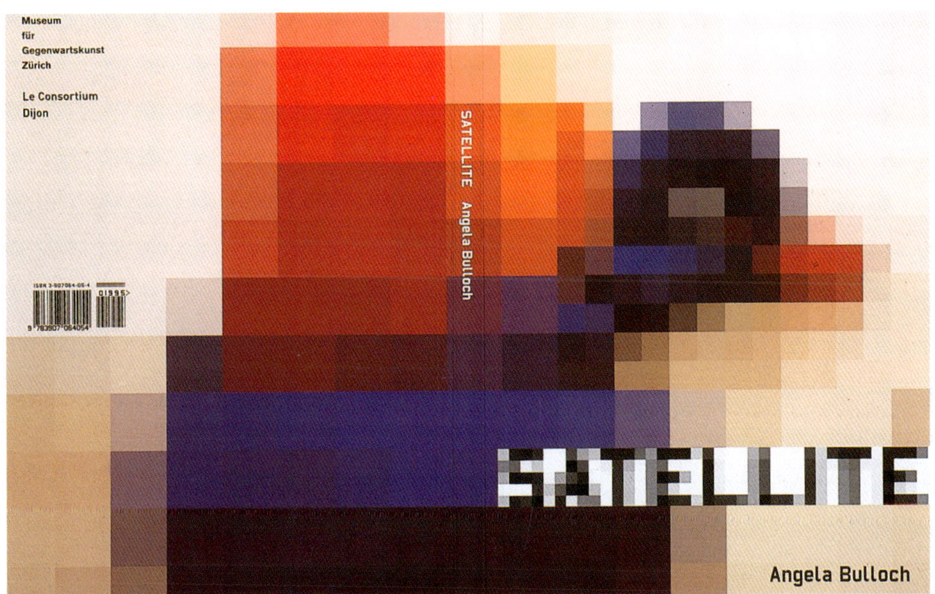

2

1 ✖ AF Angel
■ Christian Küsters
▲ Acme Fonts

1 ● Duel
■ Christian Küsters
✖ AF Angel
★ Phil Ashcroft/Bedford Hill Gallery, London

2 ✖ AF Satellite
■ Christian Küsters
▲ Acme Fonts

2 ● Satellite
■ Christian Küsters
✖ AF Satellite
★ Museum of Contemporary Art, Zürich

ABCDEFGHIJ
KLMNOPQRST
UVWXYZ
0123456789

3

ABCDEFGHIJKLMNO
PQRSTUVWXYZ
abcdefghijklmno
pqrstuvwxyz
0123456789 <+#¢$%&>

4

3 AF Video Wall
Anthony Burrill
Acme Fonts

4 AF Carplate Medium (a 2 weight family)
Sandy Suffield
Acme Fonts

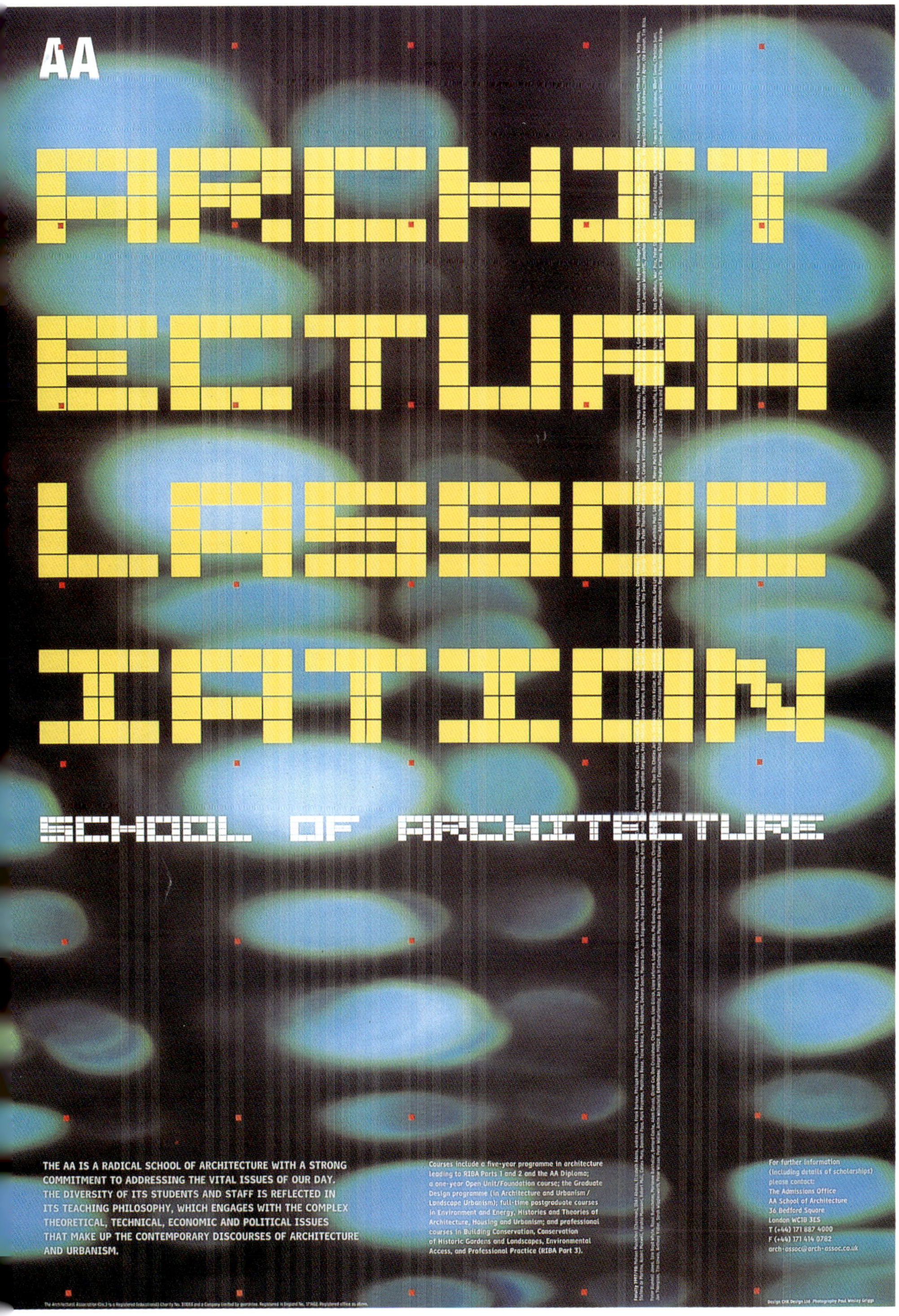

AA

ARCHITECTURAL ASSOCIATION

SCHOOL OF ARCHITECTURE

THE AA IS A RADICAL SCHOOL OF ARCHITECTURE WITH A STRONG COMMITMENT TO ADDRESSING THE VITAL ISSUES OF OUR DAY. THE DIVERSITY OF ITS STUDENTS AND STAFF IS REFLECTED IN ITS TEACHING PHILOSOPHY, WHICH ENGAGES WITH THE COMPLEX THEORETICAL, TECHNICAL, ECONOMIC AND POLITICAL ISSUES THAT MAKE UP THE CONTEMPORARY DISCOURSES OF ARCHITECTURE AND URBANISM.

Courses include a five-year programme in architecture leading to RIBA Parts 1 and 2 and the AA Diploma; a one-year Open Unit/Foundation course; the Graduate Design programme (in Architecture and Urbanism / Landscape Urbanism); full-time postgraduate courses in Environment and Energy, Histories and Theories of Architecture, Housing and Urbanism; and professional courses in Building Conservation, Conservation of Historic Gardens and Landscapes, Environmental Access, and Professional Practice (RIBA Part 3).

For further information (including details of scholarships) please contact:
The Admissions Office
AA School of Architecture
36 Bedford Square
London WC1B 3ES
T (+44) 171 887 4000
F (+44) 171 414 0782
arch-assoc@arch-assoc.co.uk

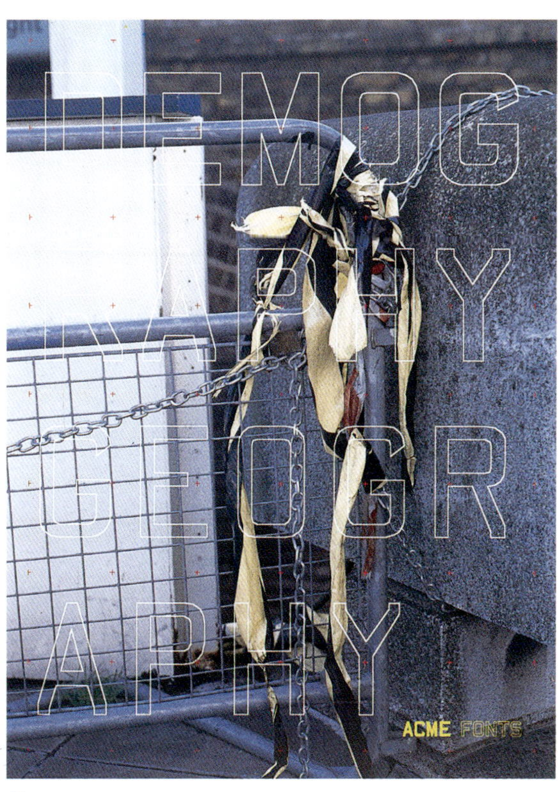

3
- ● Architectural Association poster
- ■ Christian Küsters
- ✖ AF Video Wall / AF Interface One and Two
- ★ Architectural Association, London
- ◆ Paul Wesley Griggs

4
- ● Demography Geography
- ■ Christian Küsters / Andy Long
- ✖ AF Carplate
- ★ Acme Fonts / Fontworks, London
- ◆ Christian Küsters

1

ABCDEFGHIJKLMNOPQRSTUVWX
YZabcdefghijklmnopqrstuvwxyz
0123456789 (@¢$#%&)

2

ABCDEFGHIJ
KLMNOPQRS
TUVWXYZabc
defghijklmno
pqrstuvwxyz
0123456789 (@¢$#%&)

3

abcdefGHIJ
KLMNOPQRST
UVWXYZabcd
eFGHIJKLMNO
PQRSTVWXYZ
0123456789
[@¢$#%&]

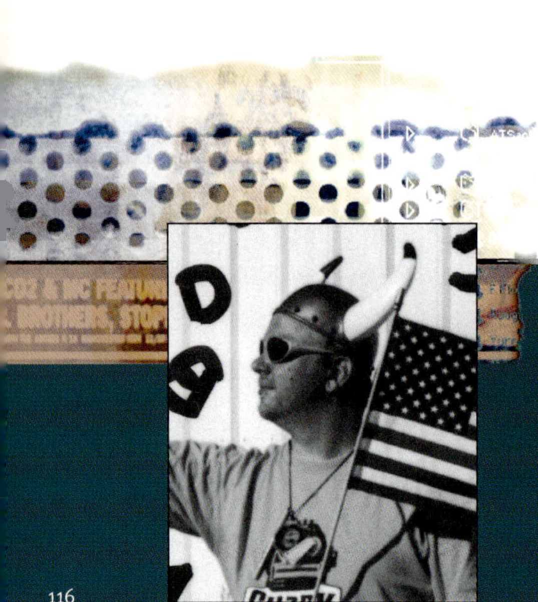

chank

The Chank Company

"My fonts are influenced by all the sparkly things that inspire me every day. Sesame Street, Dr. Seuss and Atari were my earliest influences. Then came Pop Tarts, Coffee, Cigarettes and an unending stream of loud rock music, and the Gulf Shore's Hotel Signage of Central Florida where I grew up, and the hand painted signs on the factories, laundromats and liqour stores of Northeast Minneapolis where I currently reside. All of these things work their way into my work. For me, fontmaking is a lot like playing a video game. I load up on sugar and coffee and stare at the computer screen for hours, hacking at the keyboard and wiggling my mousey joystick. All I have to do is draw a letter, then another, then another. Zap, zap, zap. Then I type words to see how it looks. Then I make changes to make it look prettier. The same damn alphabet, over and over again, and I try to make each one look special in its own unique way. The alphabet is the best brain puzzle I know of. Crowned by the press as "The Elvis of Fonts, "Chank Diesel has been drawing the alphabet since he was 5 years old. His fonts have been featured in the Smithsonian's Cooper Hewitt National Design Museum as an important example of contemporary typography. He was recently the first type designer to be profiled, complete with etching portrait, in *The Wall Street Journal.*

Diesel spends a lot of time in the cereal isle at grocery stores, hunting down his fonts on Honeycomb and Alphabets boxes. He also wantches a lot of TV and especially enjoys seeing his fonts star in commercials for Wrigley's Doublemint Gum, Frosted Mini-Wheats, and Hula Hair Barbie. Ocean Spray's "It's Your Zing" campaign featured Chevy Chase and Princess Fergie, as well as as a Chank font created for the juice company.

4

ABCDEFGHIJKLMNOPQRSTUVWX
YZabcdefghijklmnopqrstuvwxyz
0123456789 (@¢$#%&)

5

ABCDEFGH
IJKLMNOP
QRSTUVWX
YZabcdef
ghijklmn
opqrstuv
wxyz
0123456789
(@¢$#%&)

6

ABCDEFG
HIJKLMN
OPQRST
UVWXYZ

1 ✖ Crusti Wacky
■ Chank Diesel
▲ Chank!

2 ✖ Sister Frisky
■ Chank Diesel
▲ Chank!

3 ✖ Liquorstore Jazz
■ Chank Diesel
▲ Chank!

4 ✖ Orbital
■ Chank Diesel
▲ Chank!

5 ✖ Shakopee
■ Chank Diesel
▲ Chank!

6 ✖ Snipple
■ Chank Diesel
▲ Chank!

ABCDEFGHIJKLMNOPQRSTUVWXYZ
abcdefghijklmnopqrstuvwxyz
0123456789 (@¢$#%&)

ABCDEFGHIJKLMNOPQRSTUVWXYZ
abcdefghijklmnopqrstuvwxyz
0123456789 (@¢$#%&)

ABCDEFGHIJKLMNOPQRSTUVWXYZ
abcdefghijklmnopqrstuvwxyz
0123456789 (@¢$#%&)

1

abcdefghijklmnopqrstuvwxyz
0123456789 (@¢$#%&)

abcdefghijklmnopqrstuvwxyz
0123456789 (@¢$#%&)

2

abcdefghijklmnopqrstuvwxyz

3

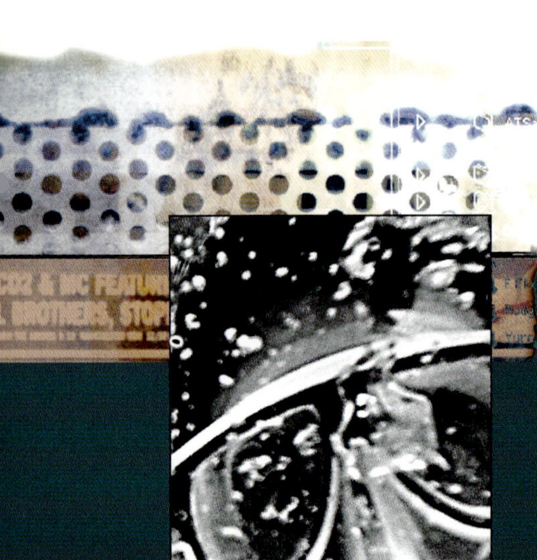

patrick giasson

Behaviour Design

I am interested in creating deceptively regular typefaces in which the individual elements, while appearing to conform to a rigid and regular system, show, upon closer scrutiny, signs of disruption by a secondary system, resulting in an imperfect yet harmonious whole.

A youth spent ingurgitating Alphabits daily could not be without consequences. From that early age, typomania slyly began germinating inside my body. It led me to devote my teenage years to the exploration of the whole gamut of balloon-letters-on-notebook, especially during math classes. After a period of semiological and practical exploration of four-letter words, I came upon the uqam (Université du Quebec a Montréal) combination which opened the doors to the enchanted world of type design where I since spend a (too) major part of my conscious existence.

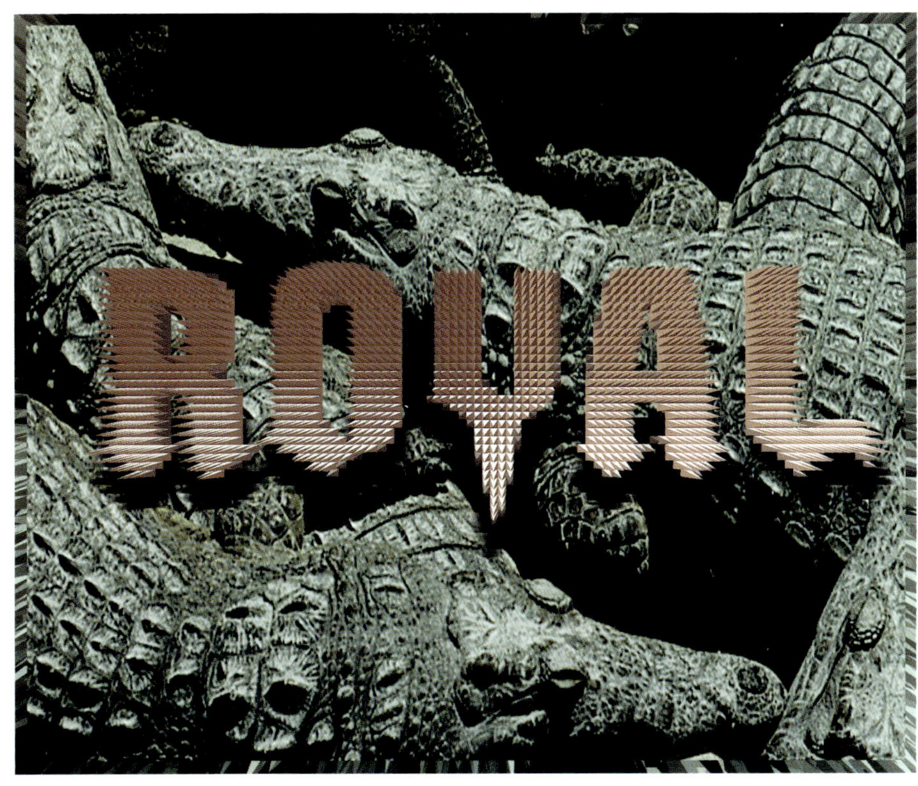

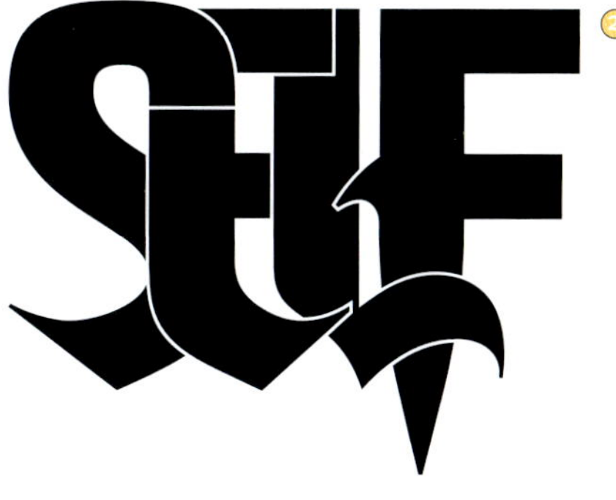

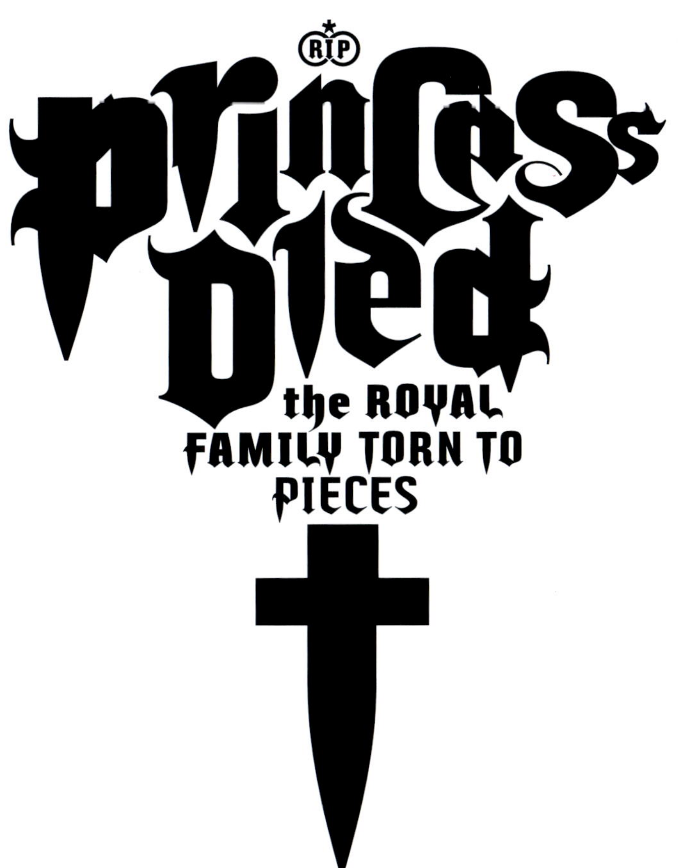

1 ✖ The Royal Family - Prince / Queen / King
■ Patrick Giasson
▲ Behaviour Design

2 ✖ Proton 1 / 2
■ Patrick Giasson
▲ Behaviour Design

3 ✖ Molotov
■ Patrick Giasson
▲ Behaviour Design

1 ● Royal life
■ Patrick Giasson
✖ The Royal Family
★ Personal project
◆ Patrick Giasson

2 ● Royal self
■ Patrick Giasson
✖ The Royal Family
★ Personal project

3 ● Obituary
■ Patrick Giasson
✖ The Royal Family
★ Personal project

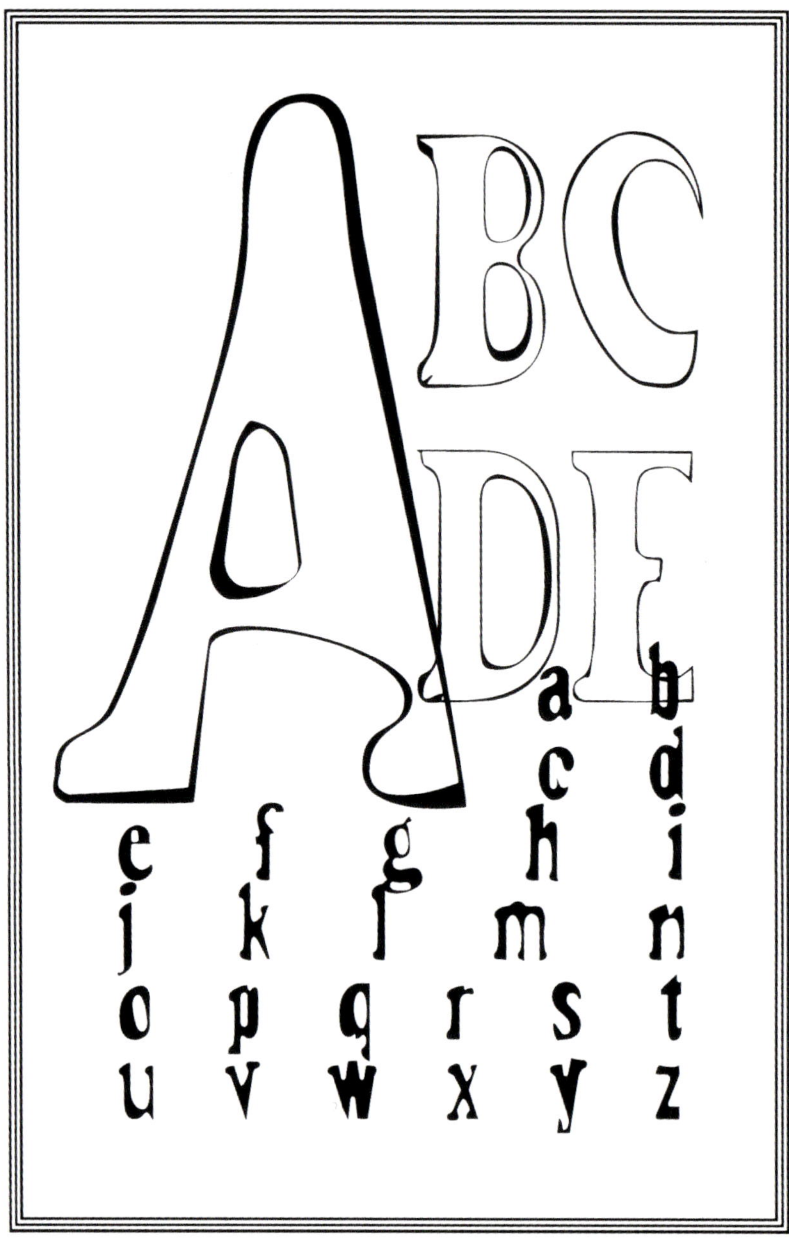

1

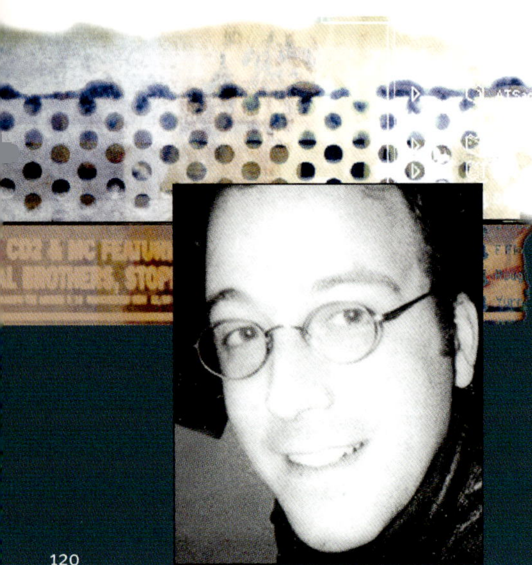

david shields

The only way out is through.

David Shields received his b.fa. in Printmaking and Graphic Design from the University of Memphis in 1991. While earning his Masters in design from Cranbrook Academy of Art, he spoke at the AIGA National Conference in Miami, was a visiting artist at Eastern Michigan University and appeared in various publications including *Emigre* and *Eye*. He went on to work at Concrete, in Chicago, and Studio Dumbar, in The Hague, and is now a design consultant in New York.

Shields's various clients include *Metropolis* magazine, Aveda, Yves Durif Salon, Little Brown & Co., Ideo, and Kirshenbaum Bond & Partners. In addition he has developed typefaces for USWest, *Speak* magazine, Allied Design Development, and Theater Zeebelt. He has lectured at the University of Illinois, Chicago, been published in Rethinking Design IV and AIGA's 50 Books/50 Covers, and exhibited work in Designer as Author: Voices and Visions, Northern Kentucky University. He currently works from his home studio in Brooklyn.

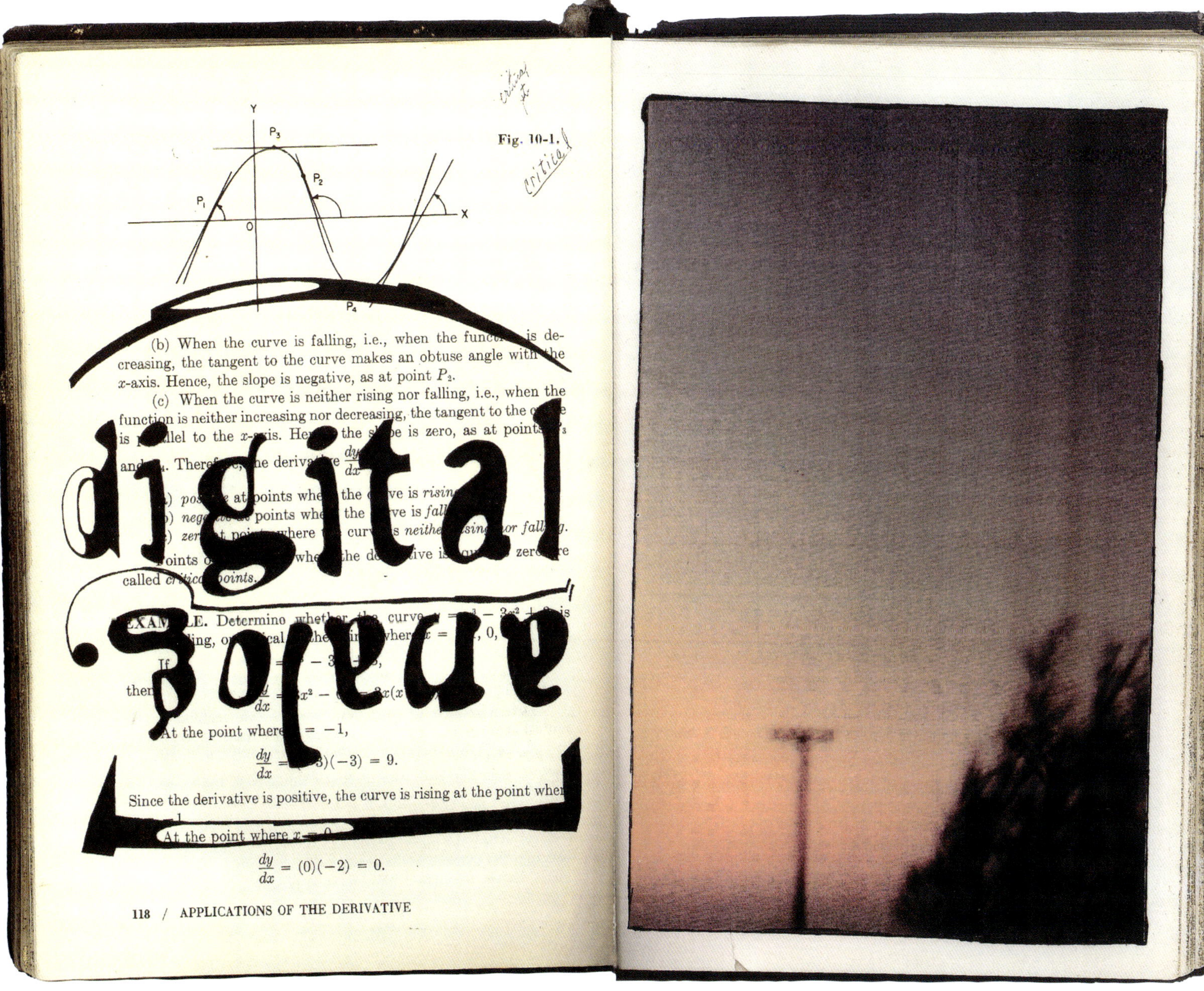

1 Goofypop
David Shields
David Shields

1 Spread (Sketchbook)
David Shields
Goofypop
Personal project
David Shields

A B C D E
F G H I J K
L M N O P
Q R S T U
V W X Y Z

a b c d e f g h i j k l m
n o p q r s t u v w x y z

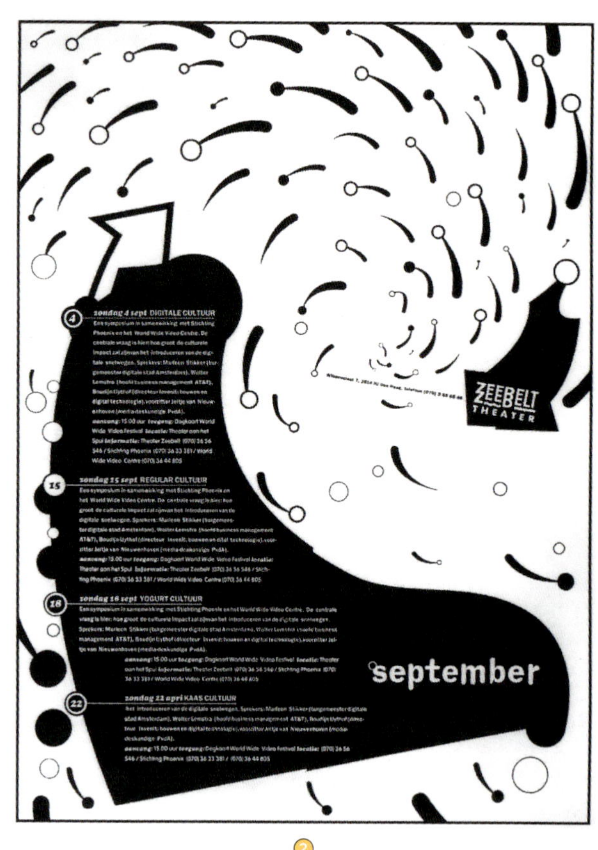

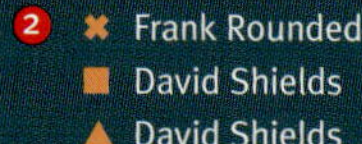

2 Frank Rounded
David Shields
David Shields

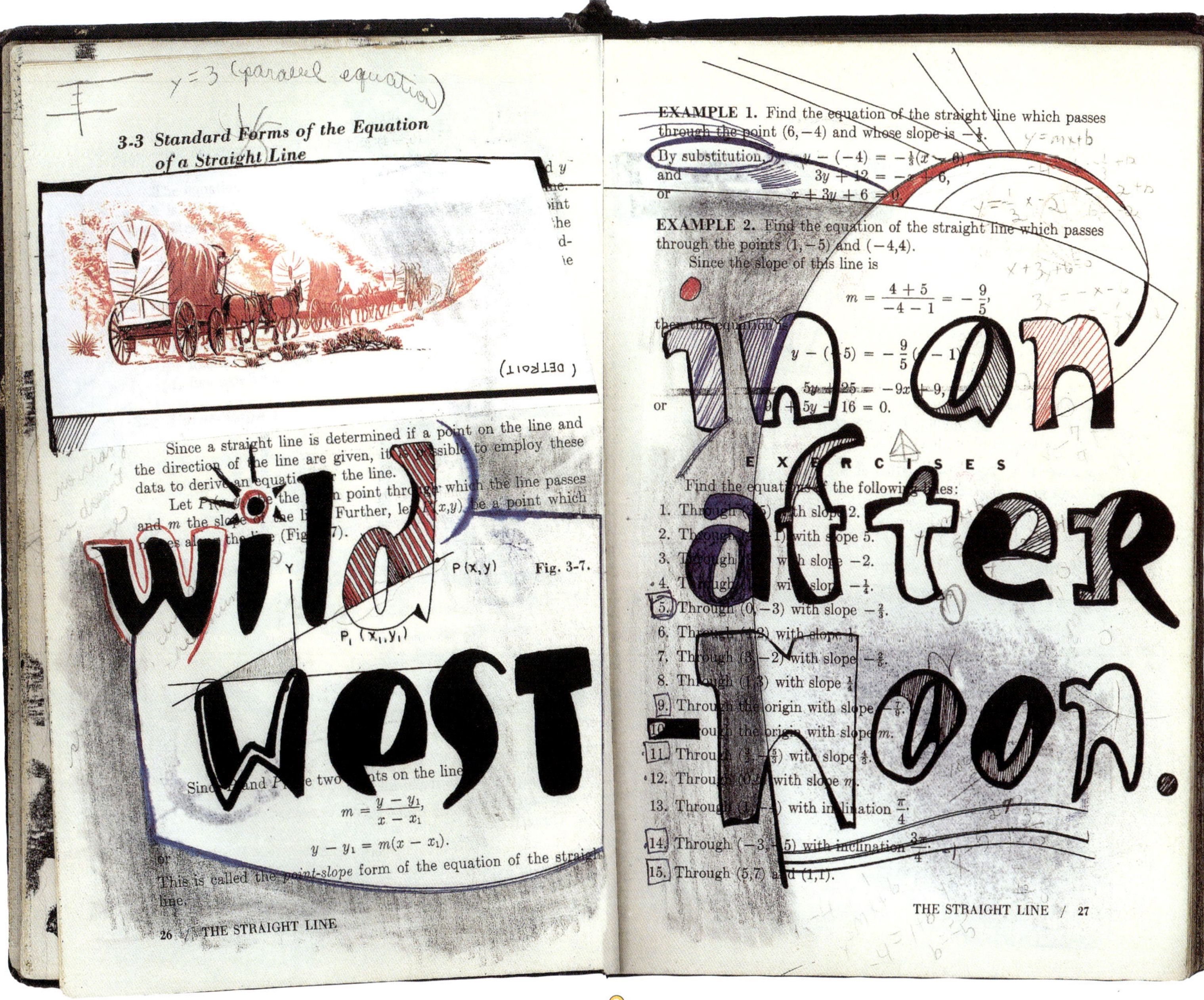

3

2
- Theater Zeebelt poster
- Studio Dumbar / David Shields
- Frank Rounded / Franklin Gothic
- Theater Zeebelt, Den Haag

3
- Spread (Sketchbook)
- David Shields
- Personal project
- David Shields

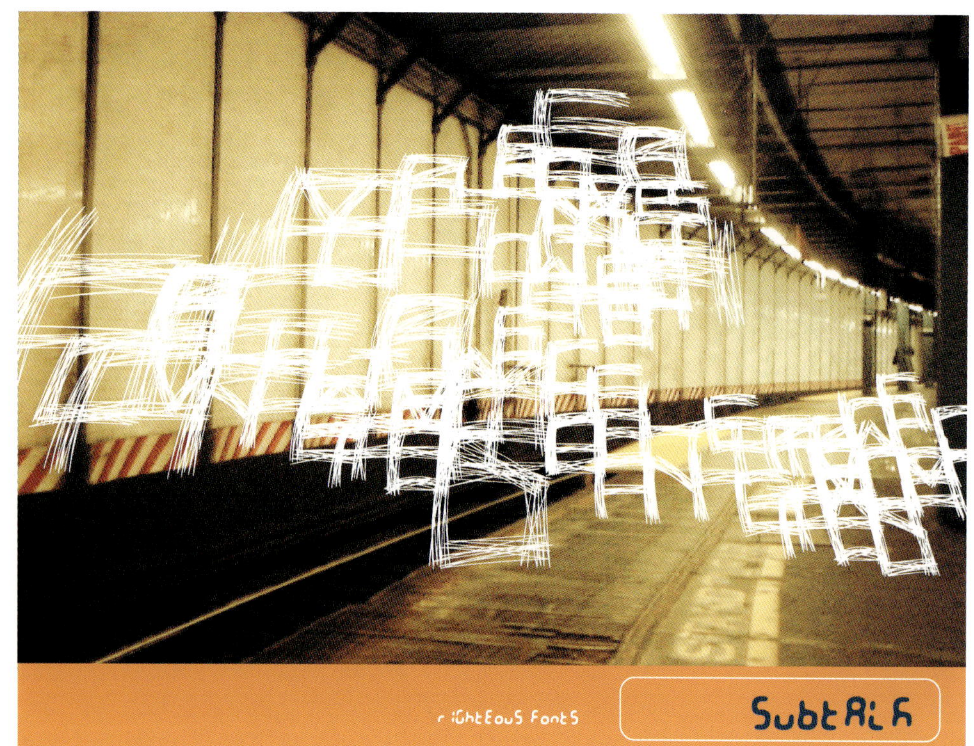

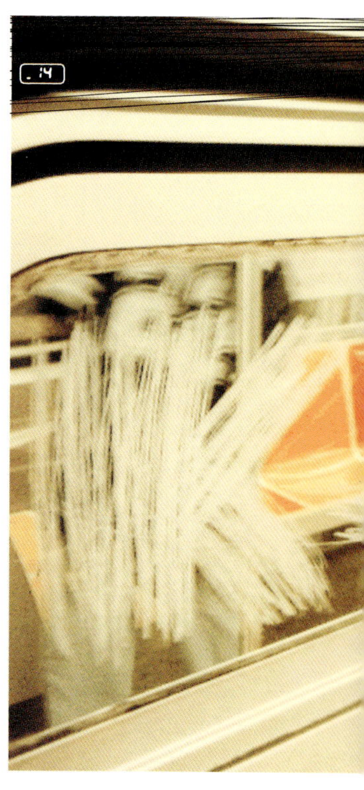

ABCDEF
GHIJKLM
NOPQRS
TUVWXY
abcedfghijklmn
opqrstuvwxyz
0123456789

1

AbcdEFGhi
jkLmnoPqr
StuvwxyZ
789
456
0 123

2

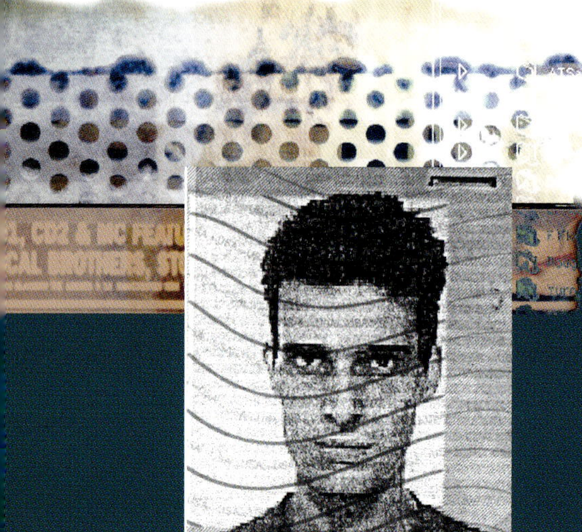

gill arno'

FLY/Righteous Fonts

Can a gesture that takes place in the real world keep its rabid power once vectorialized? This was the point for me while designing the font SubTalk, which is based on scratch tags found on New York City subways. On the other hand, Rec. comes out of an old LED display. Its defective light emission brought me the opportunity to explore the structure of a hyper-standardized man/machine interface.

After studying art and graphic design in Parma (Italy), Gill moved to Milan and broadened his experience at the graphic design firm Arcoquattro and video artists collective, Studio Azzurro. His first commissioned works were for cultural guerrilla units like Kipple Officina Libraria and the infamous comic book publisher Topolin Edizioni, as well as for institutional and corporate entities such as the City Municipality of Milan and Il Sole 24 Ore System.

Gill is primarily a music-propelled graphic designer, so he kept moving on in order to assemble his visions with the sounds he dug. He ended up in Brooklyn, and soon began collaborating with NYC's dub and electronica music scene. His visual shows, based on a flowing projection of slides, have been featured in the best chill out rooms like Soundlab's Abstrakt Future Lounge and with the live acts Byzar, Squelch and dj Spooky, among others. In addition to his performance activities, Gill teamed up with Swiss graphic designer Theres Wegmann and started up the design firm FLY, to carry on printed and Web-based design projects. They also established Righteous Fonts as a time-space continuum for experimenting with typography and alternative distribution strategies, the first installment being the production of a no-copyright digital booklet that incorporates the two fonts SubTalk and Rec.

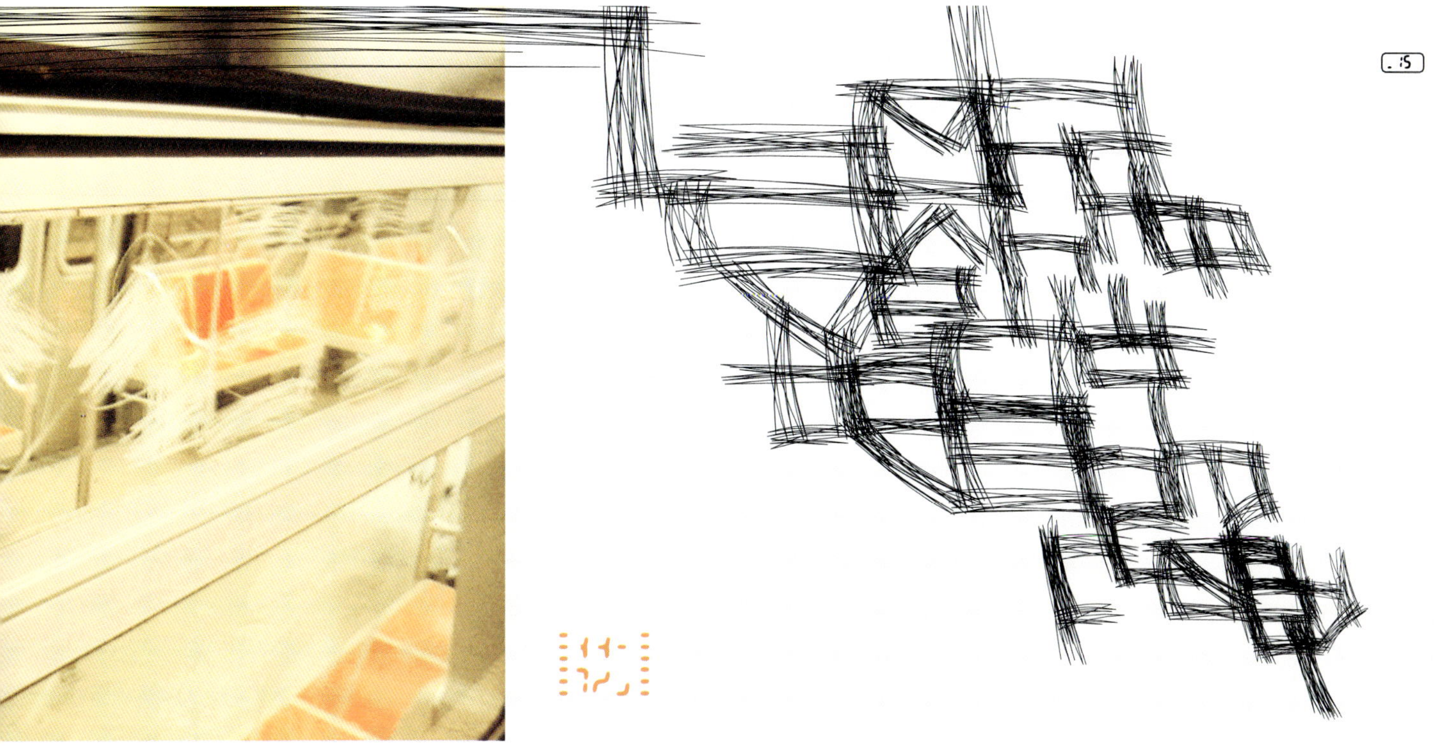

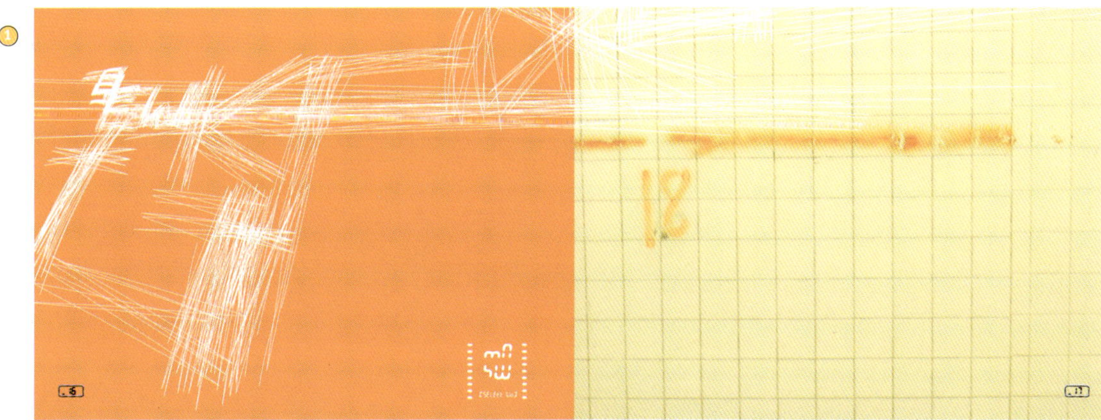

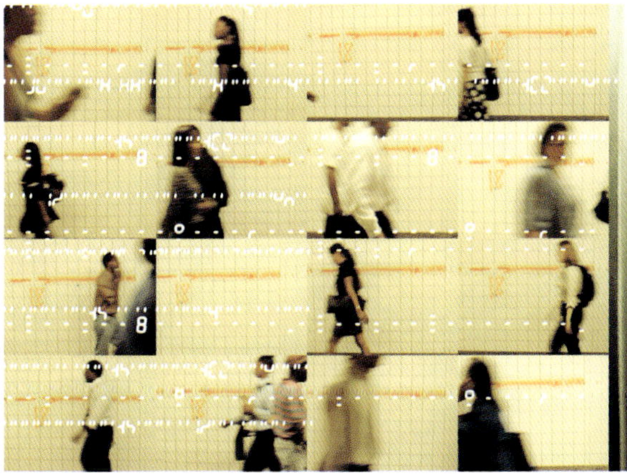

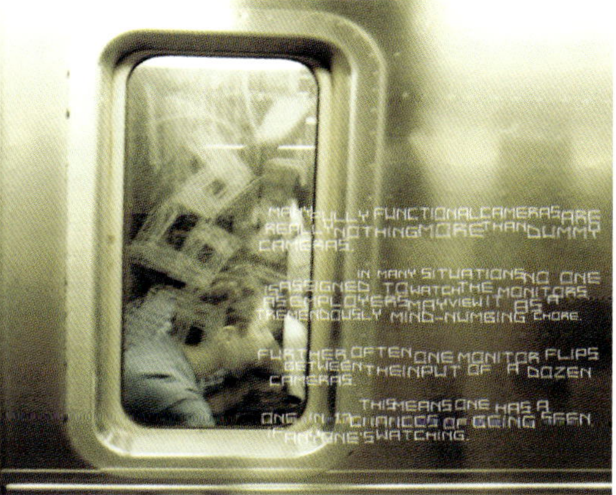

1
- ✖ SubTalk
- ■ Gill Arnò
- ▲ Righteous Fonts

2
- ✖ Rec.
- ■ Gill Arnò
- ▲ Righteous Fonts

1
- ● SubTalk booklet (cover and spreads).
- ■ Gill Arnò
- ▲ Righteous Fonts
- ★ FLY
- ◆ Gill Arnò/Theres Wegmann

ABCDEFGHIJKLMNOPQ
RSTUVWXYZ
abcdefghijklmn
opqrstuvwxyz
0123456789
‹@®©¢*$%&?›

1

2

ABCDEFGHIJKLMNOPQ
RSTUVWXYZ
abcdefghijklmno
pqrstuvwxyz
0123456789
‹@®©¢*$%&?›

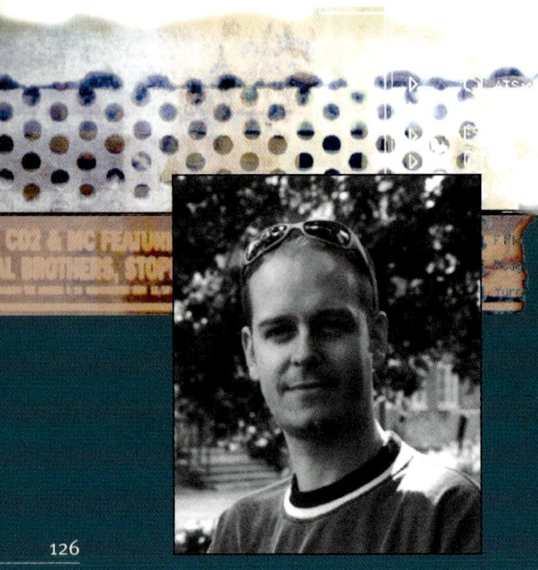

magnus rakeng

Millimeter Design

I regard Radio and my other fonts basically as advanced "Phone-doodling." Most of the characters for my fonts are scribbled down by hand in my sketchbook, or are worked out in my head before I go to sleep, just to define the general shapes. I never scan the sketches; I just use them as guides when I recreate them in Illustrator or Fontographer. Then I draw as many characters as I can in Illustrator just to see how they work together. When I'm pleased with the overall look, I import the files into Fontographer. Then I keep tweaking and refining till I get the shapes right. I spend a lot of time doing this, working hard for a few days/weeks. Then I leave it alone for a period of time. I find these breaks just as important as the working periods, and a lot of the problems are solved during this time. When I'm really sick of staring at the shapes, I start kerning. With the kerning almost done I start doing the additional weights, which should be quite easy to do, but I always end up re-drawing the whole font apart from a few characters.

Magnus was born in 1967 in Lillehammer, Norway. After attending two fine art courses and a woodcarving course (!) in Lillehammer he moved to Oslo in 1987 to go to Westerdals reklameskole (a two-year advertising course), and then undertook the graphic design course (BA) at the London College of Printing from 1989 – 1992. Back in Oslo he joined Megafon design ('93) as a graphic designer. In 1994 Rakeng started working on his first font, Pilot. Pilot was released by Thirstype the same year. Late 1995 Megafon design merged with another company and became Union design. Thirstype released his second font, Envy, in 1996. Magnus left Union to start working for Millimeter design in October 1996 where he still works as a senior designer with emphasis on CD covers. In 1998 Thirstype released his third and latest font, Radio

ENVY ™

{ ¥ ¢ £ ¤ }

HTTP://WWW.3ST.COM HTTP://WWW.MMPRESS.NO/~MAGNUS

ENVY ER EN FONT I FIRE VEKTER DESIGNET TIL ÆRE FOR OG I KRAFT AV REN MISUNNELSE.

ABCDEFGHIJKLMNOPQRSTUVWXYZÆÅØ
abcdefghijklmnopqrstuvwxyzæøå
1234567890.,!?&

"But if ye have bitter envying and strife in your hearts, glory not, and lie not against the truth...
For where envying and strife is, there is confusion and every evil work"

[James 3:14.16].

© P ®

RESENTMENT KILLS A FOOL, AND ENVY SLAYS THE SIMPLE

ENVY

Envy is distributed by Thirstype only. Soon to be sold through FontShop Germany and FontShop Norway

…PS IN FOUR WEIGHTS WITH COMPELETE INTERNATIONAL CHARATCER SETS FOR US$150. ENVY IS AVAILABLE FROM THIRSTYPE IN BOTH MAC AND PC FORMAT.

Pilot *The truth is out there*

In order to explore the solar system, coordinates must be developed to consistently identify the locations of the observer, of the natural objects in the solar system, and of any space-craft traversing interplanetary space or orbiting a planet.

Pilot is a five style Macintosh font sold exclusively through Thirstype

ABCDEFGHIJK

Pilot

MNOPQRSTUVWXY

Thirstype@aol.com

ABCDEFGHIJKLMNOPQRSTUVWXYZÆØA
abcdefghijklmnopqrstuvwxyzæøå
123456789

1
- Envy
- Magnus Rakeng
- Thirstype

1
- Envy
- Magnus Rakeng
- Envy
- Magnus Rakeng

2
- Pilot
- Magnus Rakeng
- Thirstype

2
- Pilot
- Magnus Rakeng
- Pilot
- Magnus Rakeng

1

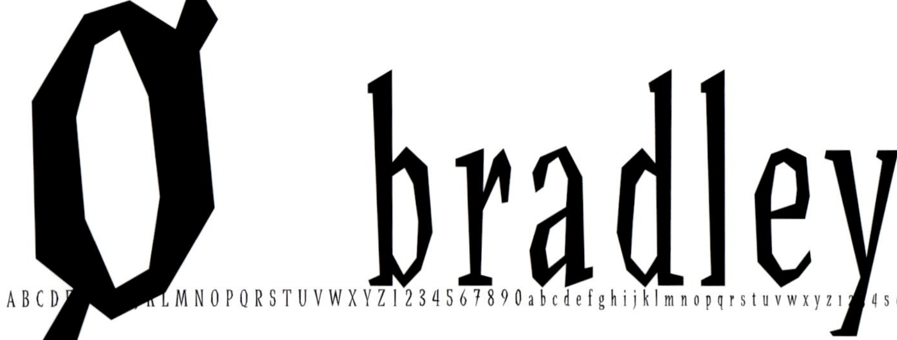

ABCDEFGHIJKLMNOPQRSTUVWXYZ1234567890abcdefghijklmnopqrstuvwxyz123456

7890ABCDEFGHIJKLMNOPQRSTUVWXYZ1234567890abcdefghijklmnopqrstuvwxyz1

234567890ABCDEFGHIJKLMNOPQ Inspired by the work of Czechoslovakian type designer Vjoteck Pressig, Bradley is a wood-cut style serif font with an additional set of old-style numerals.1234567890

1234567890abcdefghijklmnopqrstuvwxyz

2

abcdefghijklmnopqrstuvwxyz

PQRSTUVWXYZ1234567890abcdefghijklmnopqrstuvwxyz

?!@$%&ABCDEFGHIJKLMNO

envision

Inspired by mediaeval uncial manuscript characters, envision has an ancient, yet sensual, modern feeling. Designed by Margo Chase 1234567890!@#$%&?

3

evolution

abcdef Designed by Margo Chase

ghijklmnopqrstuvwxyz

ABCDEFGHIJKLMNOPQRSTUVWXYZ

1234567890

Inspired by the latest rash of alien abductions, the truth is out there and it's set in evolution.

margo chase design

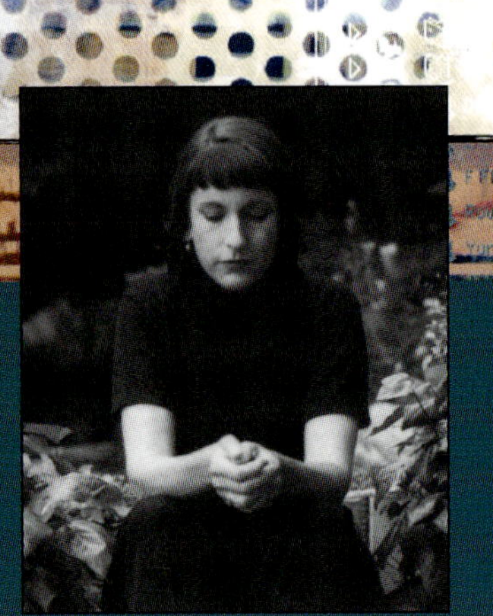

At Margo Chase Design we approach design as a systematic process. We consider the goals of the client first. Do they need to entertain, to inform, to educate or to sell something? Next we consider the audience the client wants to reach. Are they young or old, hobbyists or dedicated computer users? In most cases, the client and the audience will guide and determine the design approach and its application.

Each individual project has limitations and strengths. Designers must be prepared to adjust to the parameters of a project. This does not mean restricting your vision. Whether designing a print ad, a Website, or a font, the end result must be a compelling and functional solution.

Margo Chase is the owner/principle of Margo Chase Design, a Los Angeles-based graphic design studio specializing in print, Web and film. Committed to unique and effective communication, MCD draws upon diverse sources to stay on the cutting edge. Over the past 12 years, Margo Chase Design's landmark CD art for Madonna, Prince, Bonnie Raitt and many movie posters, including Francis Ford Coppola's "Dracula," have gained international recognition. Margo Chase Design was selected as one of *I.D. Magazine's* "I.D. Forty" for 1997 and featured in the January/February 1997 issue of *Graphis* magazine. Margo Chase Design continues to explore the cutting edge, creating distinctive visuals for film and the Web and unique typefaces for the newly launched digital foundry: Gravy Fonts, represented exclusively by Carlos Segura's [T-26].

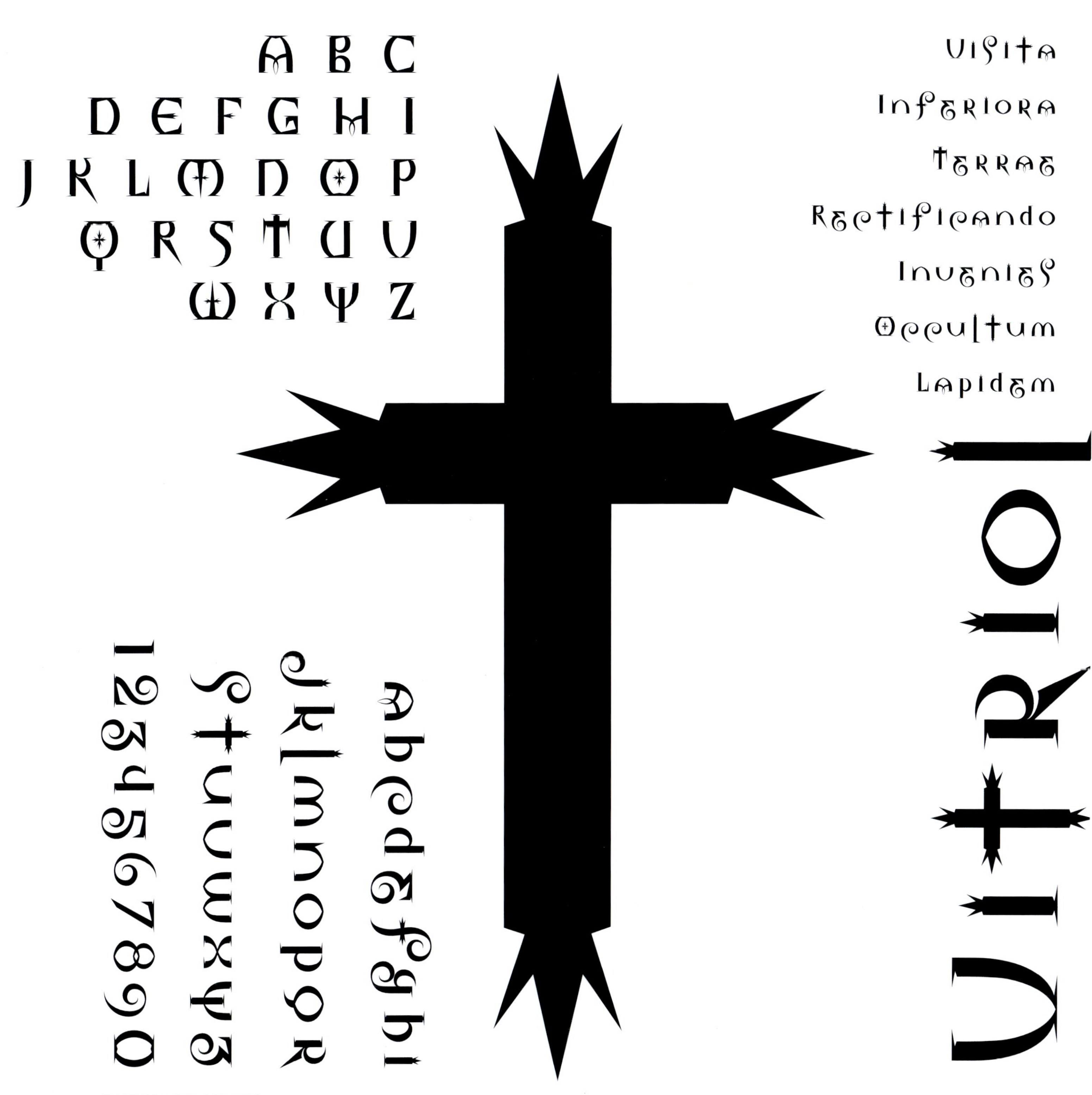

4

1 ✖ Bradley
■ Margo Chase
▲ Gravy Fonts

2 ✖ Envision
■ Margo Chase
▲ Gravy Fonts

3 ✖ Evolution
■ Margo Chase
▲ Gravy Fonts

4 ✖ Vitriol
■ Margo Chase
▲ Gravy Fonts

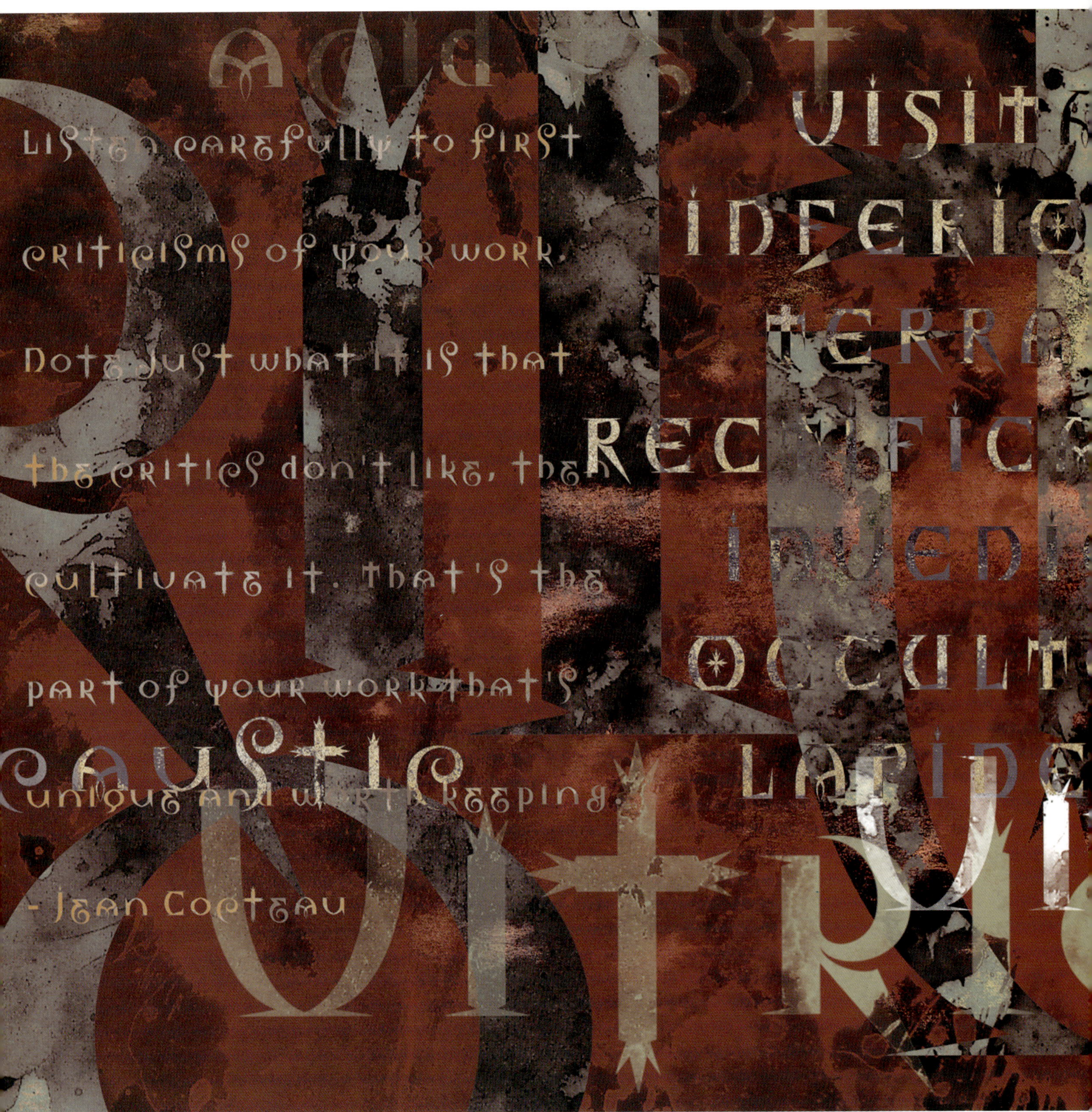

1

1
- Vitriol (poster)
- Margo Chase
- Vitriol
- Letter Arts Review
- Margo Chase

2
- Germs
- Margo Chase
- Bradley
- Germs lecture series
- Margo Chase

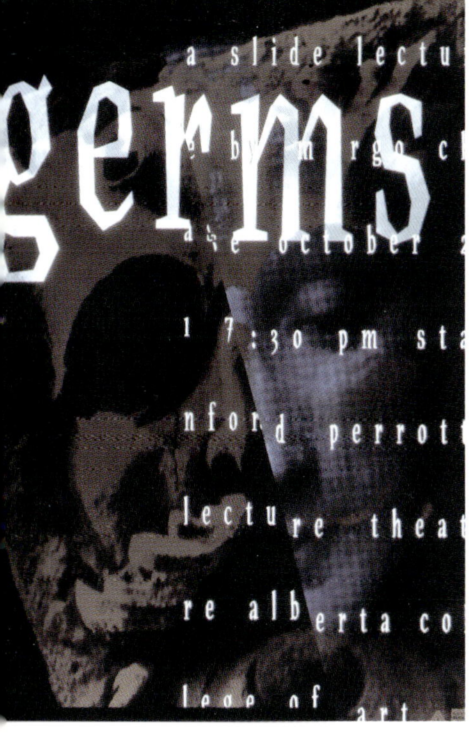

2

3

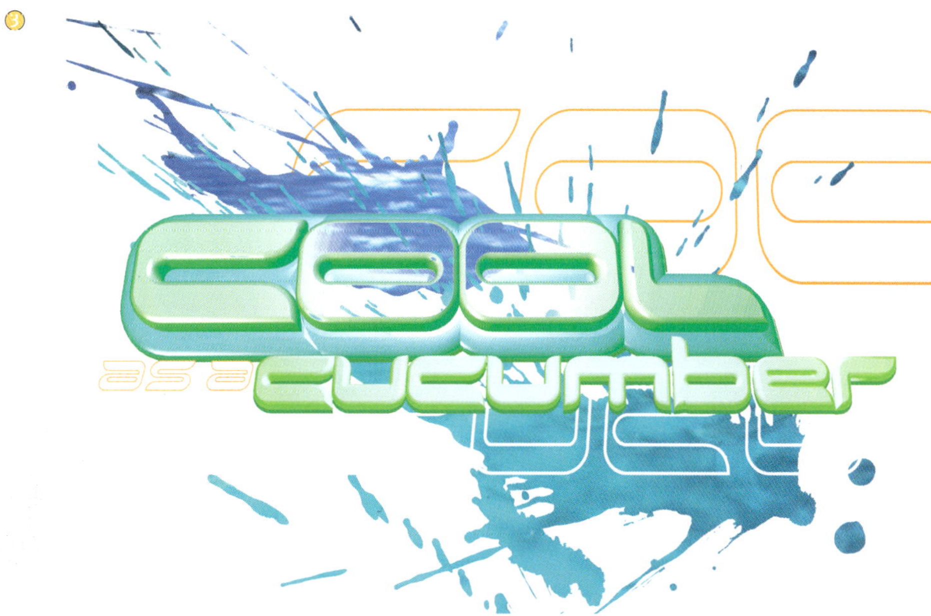

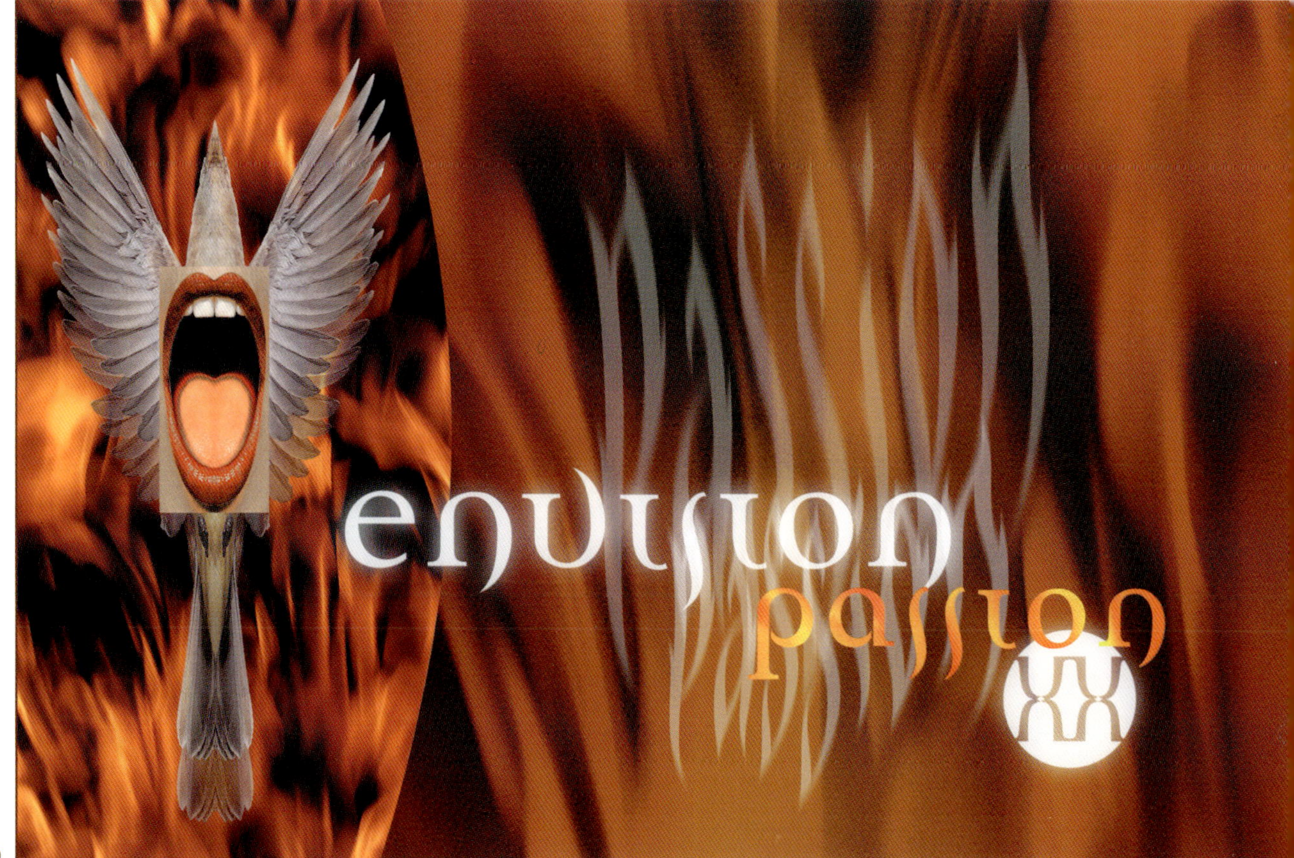

4

3
● Cool Cucumber
■ Margo Chase
✖ Evolution
★ Westland Graphics
◆ Margo Chase

4
● Envision
■ Margo Chase
✖ Envision
★ Envision Design Conference
◆ Margo Chase

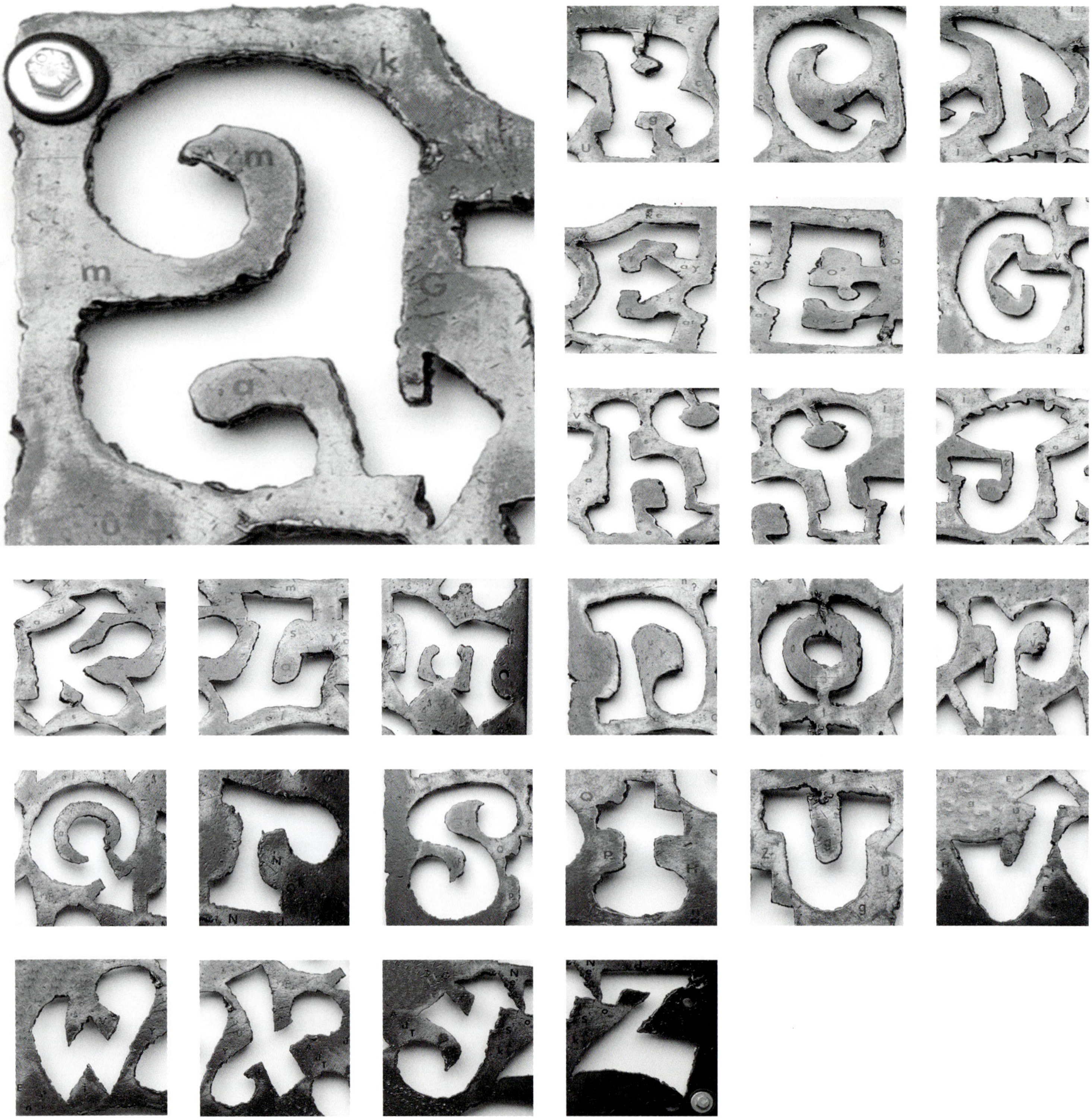

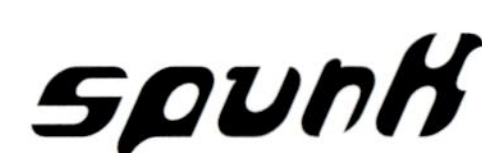

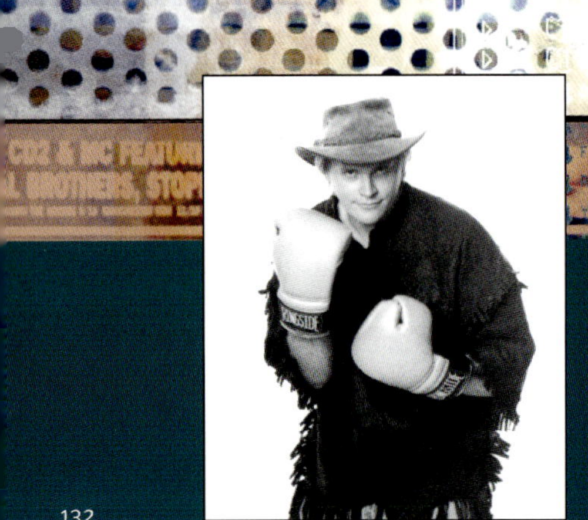

spunk

Jeff Johnson

Design is a baby of an industry. It is far from being resolved. We do good work; then we let it follow us around like an overeager kid brother.

Johnson is from Fargo. Johnson graduated from Moorhead State University in 1992 and then began working at Duffy Design in Minneapolis, MN, until 1998. He worked as a senior designer for Duffy from '94 to '98 on such clients as BMW, Nikon, Coca-Cola Lee Jeans, and the Kieth Haring Estate. Johnson's won virtually every national and internationally recognized design award. Johnson also has work featured in the Smithsonian Institute's permanent collection of 20th Century Design and the Cooper-Hewitt Design Museum in NYC. Johnson is also an accomplished Polka dancer. Some of the projects include the 1993 design and launch of the "then-alternative" beverage Frutopia™; the 1994 redesign of the Diet Coke™ brand; and the 1997 design of the Miller Lite "Dick" Campaign. As a result, he drinks a lot of sugary beverages and beer – sometimes even mixed. Johnson started Spunk in 1998 with his partners and promptly moved to New Zealand for a year (Go figure?). While there he invented and patented the World's First Puff Ink Coloring book "Handilines!" which is sold on www.handilines.com. He also ate a lot of Kiwi fruit. He also lauched www.spunknation.com in 1999 and continually sells his fonts at www.chank.com. Spunk is a design studio in Minneapolis doing new product design, service oriented design, and custom furniture design. Johnson was born the same year as the Moon Landing, the launch of the Big Mac, the release of Led Zepelin 2, and the launch of Sesame Street.

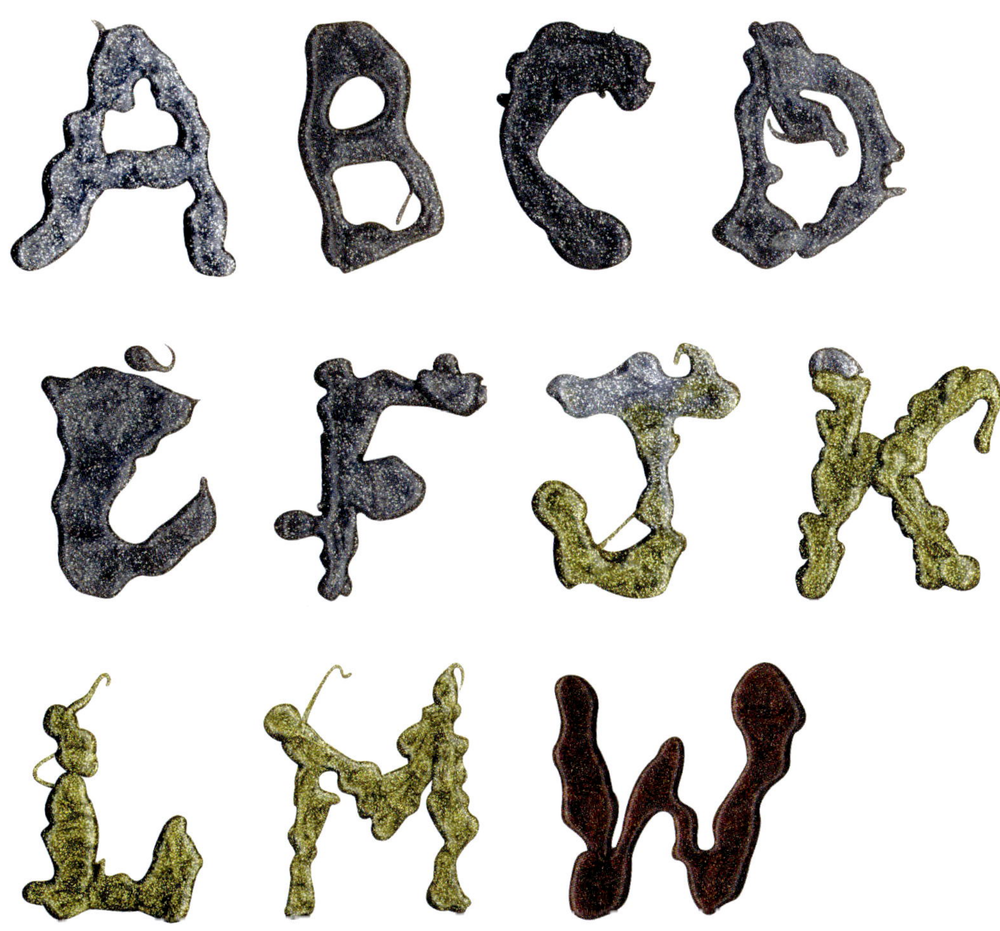

ABCDEFJKLMW
abcdefyxwuoz
01789
.,;:!?@

2

1 ✖ Blow Me
■ Jeff Johnson and John Morris
▲ Spunk

2 ✖ Gary's Kids
■ Jeff Johnson and John Morris
▲ Spunk

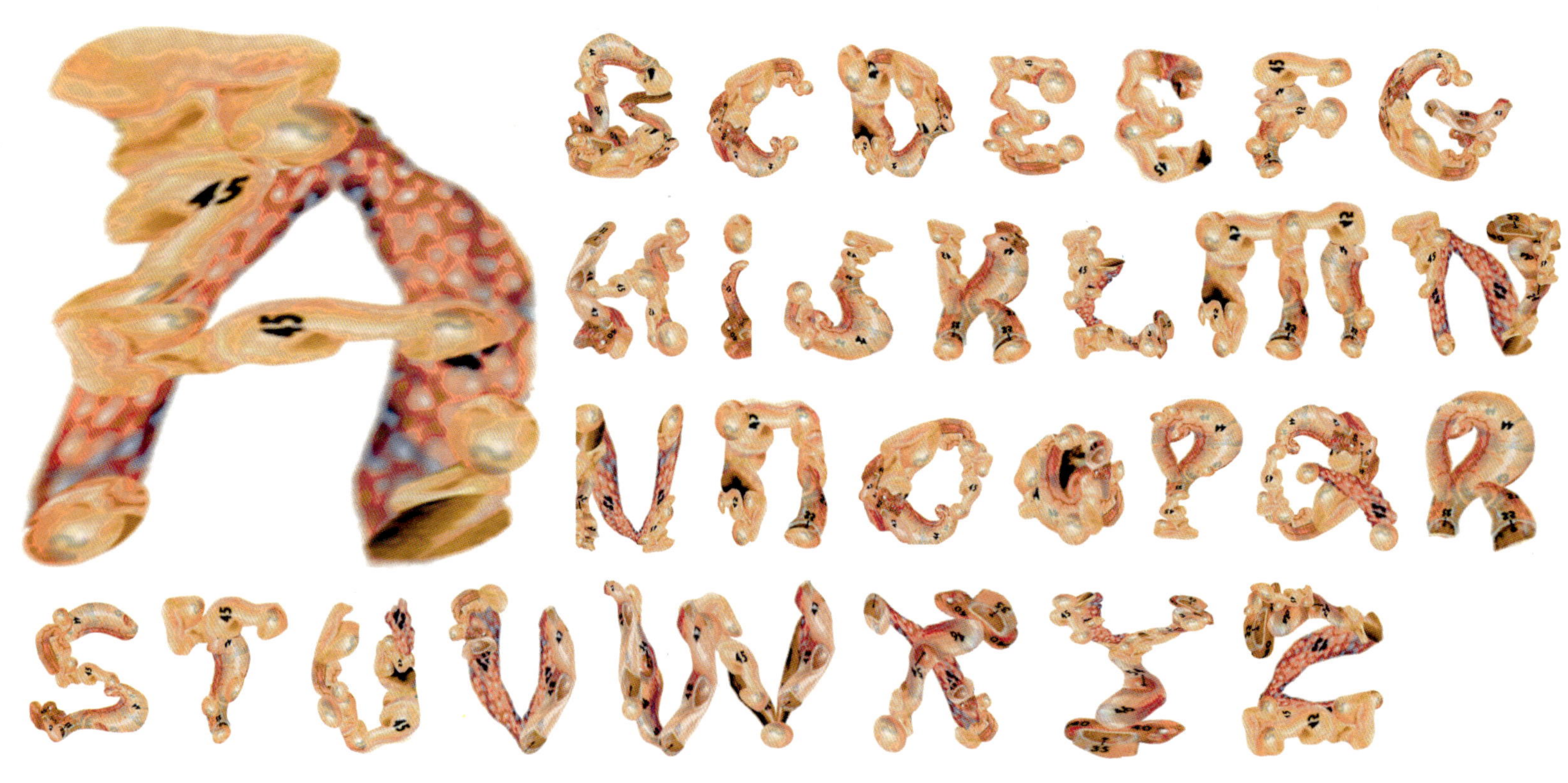

3

ABCDEFGHIJKLM
NOPQRSTUVWXYZ
0123456789
(@¢$#%&)

3 ✖ Guts
■ Jeff Johnson and John Morris
▲ Spunk

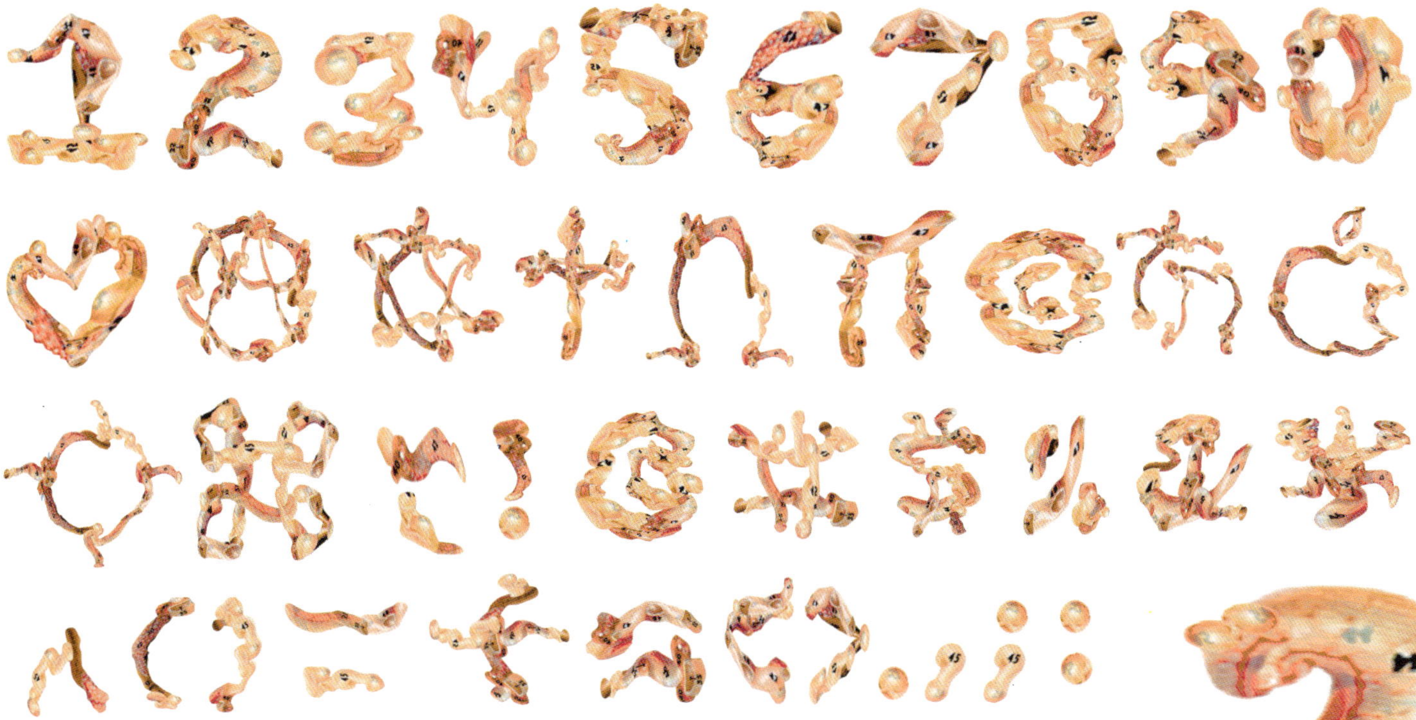

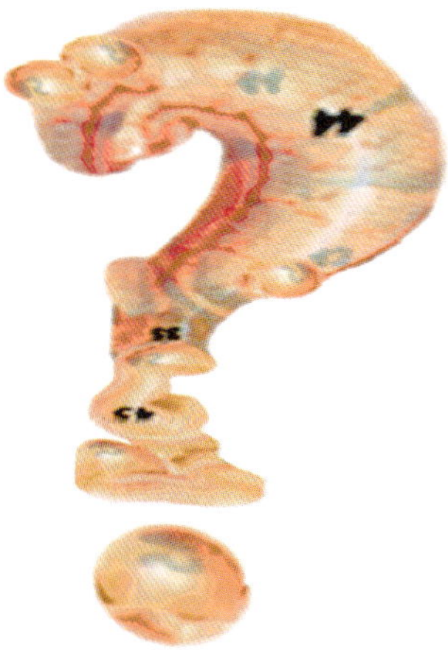

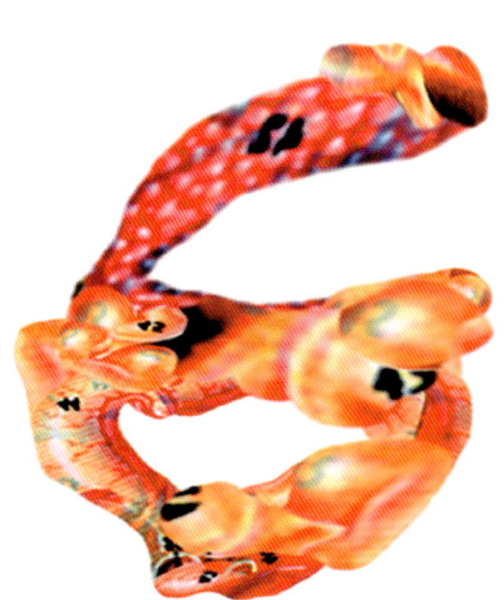

Abcdefghi
jklmnopqr
stuvwxyz

1

abcdefghijklm
nopqrstuvwxyz
?! 0123456789

2

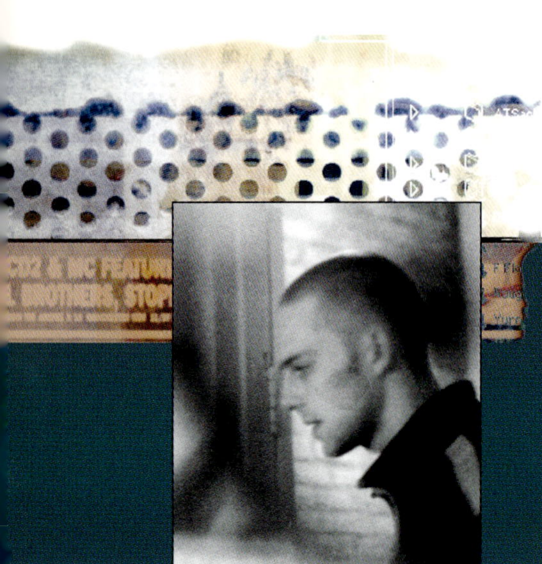

boyz and girls

Anselm Dästner

These days everyone is talking about samples – both sonic and visual – as a reflection of the environment, a cultural byte. Take a shape or typeface – it is only a question of constructing a technique to recompose these images, redefine them, and make them more apparent. BOYZandGIRLS specializes in design for club culture, a contemporary symbol of the redefinition of tradition and post-modernity. Everything in pop culture that has been done, has been done. Many are looking for a more abstract medium to diversify and break up this mainstream. Shapes are replacing people, and more graphic symbols are replacing communication. The typefaces of BOYZandGIRLS were designed to give way to the new rise of symbolic consciousness and break through the tradition of conventional type design. They were created to move people to dance, and explore more of the unconscious.

Anselm Dästner was born in Freiburg in Southern Germany. His parents, both musicians, encouraged him to lead a childhood filled with art and creativity. At 17, he interned at a photographer for 3 years. During this time he had also acquired a job at a local dance club and started to design a series of their nightclub flyers. In 1993 he moved to New York, where he completed his studies in graphic design. He freelanced with The New York Times, Prodigy and IO 3600, which in turn led him to start his own company, BOYZandGIRLS, Inc. Founded in 1994, it quickly became known as New York's foremost graphic design and club flyer republic. BOYZandGIRLS has produced design for MTV, Giant Step, Limelight, Billboard, Manga and many nightclubs, promoters and music labels. Presently BOYZandGIRLS hosts the design and production of Flyer NYC, a dance music culture guide, and consults the trend-setting European clothing label Pash.

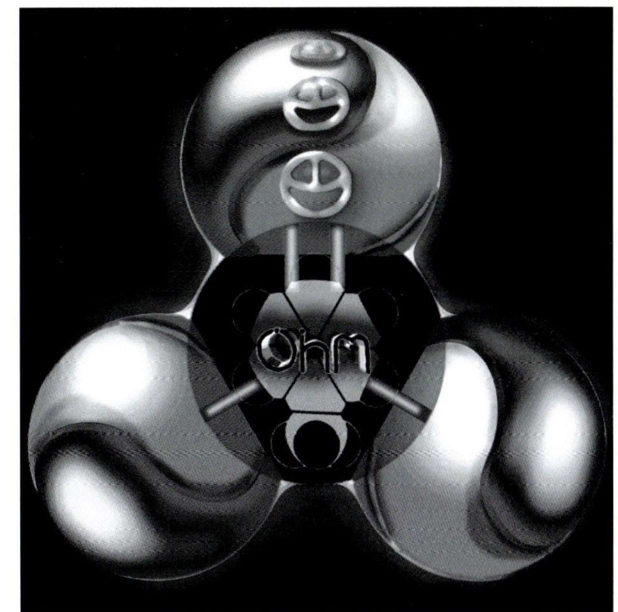

1

2

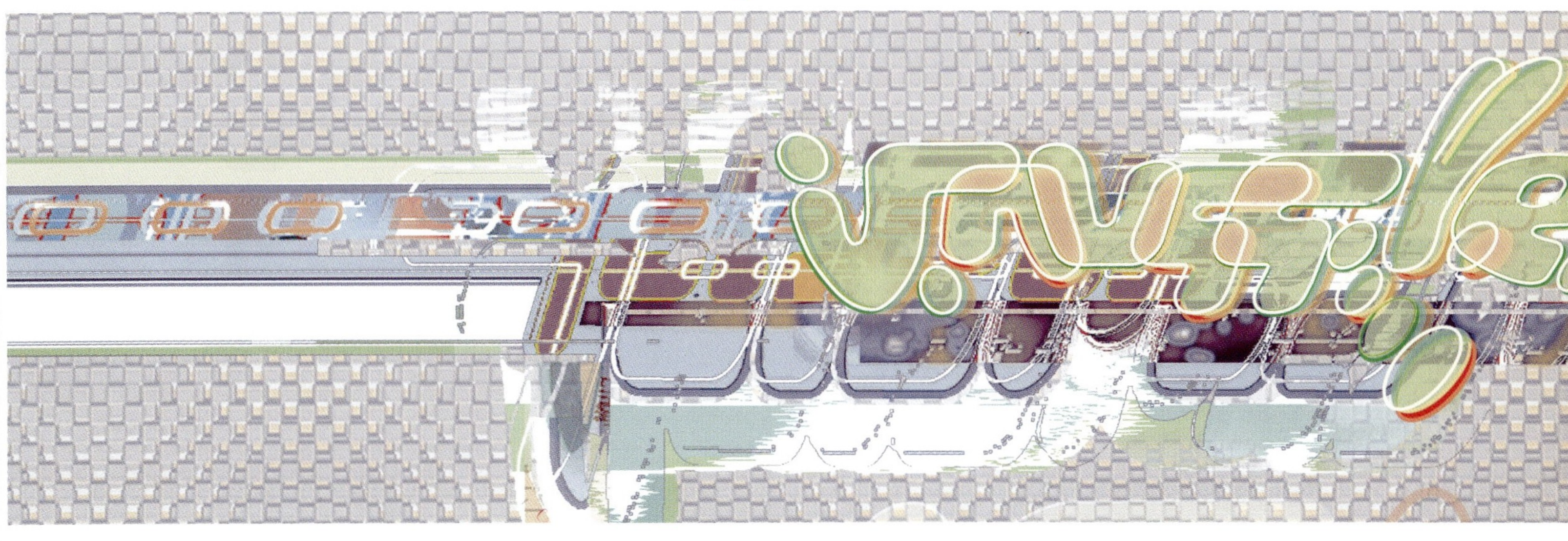

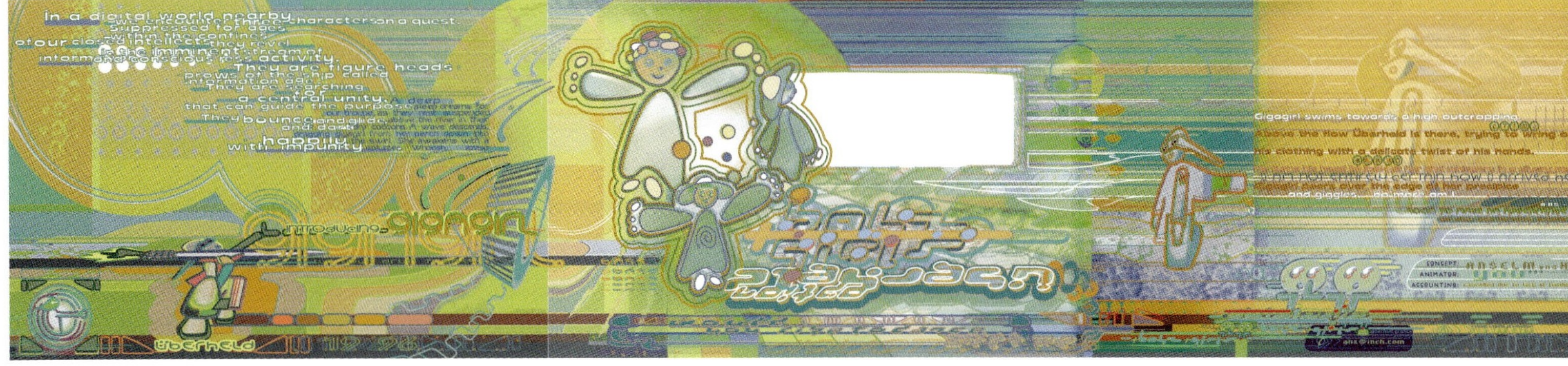

3

a b c d e f g h i
j k l m n o p q
r s t u v w x y z

3

4

a b c d e f f
g h i j k l m
n o p q r s t
u v w x y z z

4

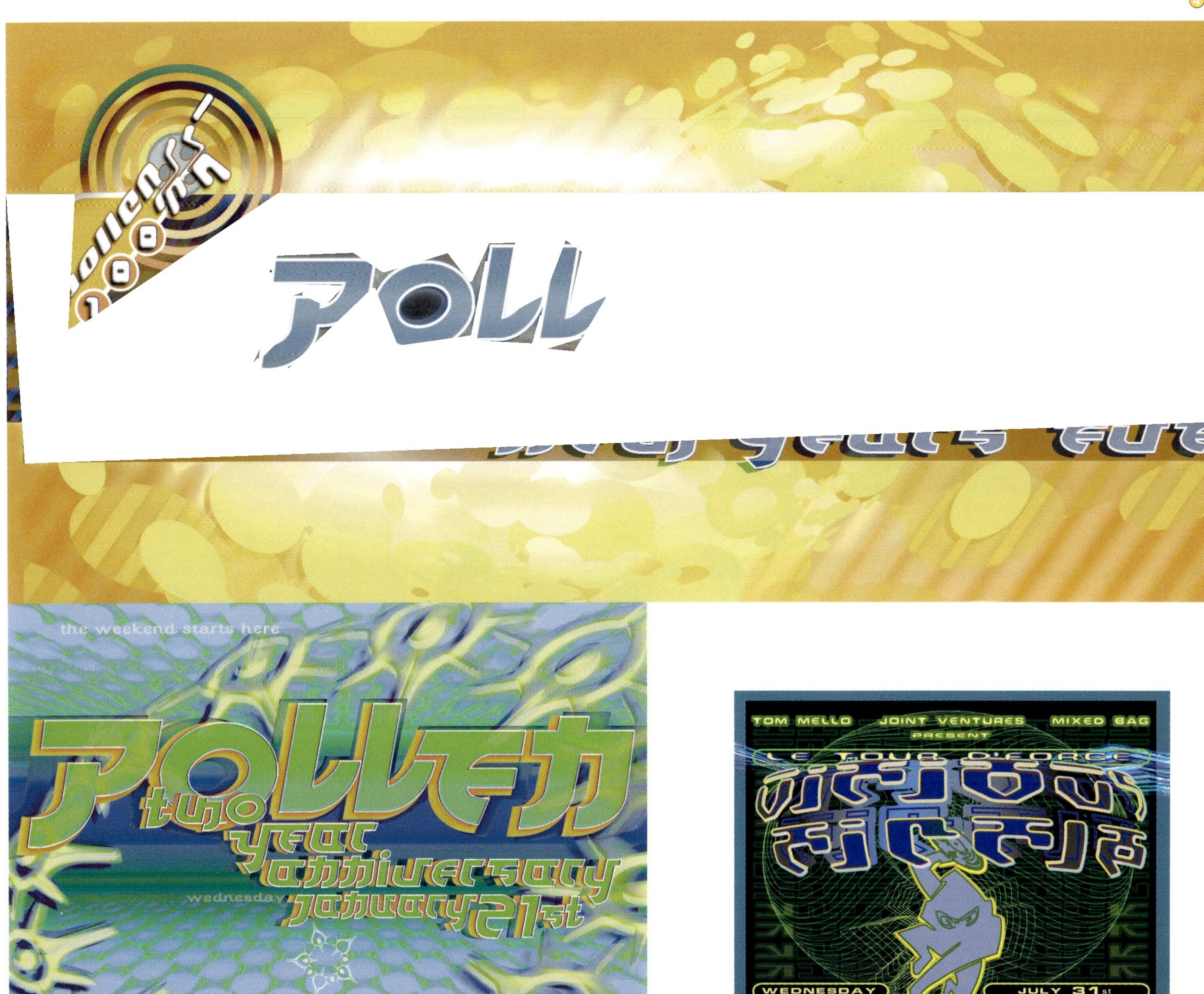

the weekend starts here
two year anniversary
wednesday january 21st
TOM MELLO JOINT VENTURES MIXED BAG
PRESENT
LE TOUR D'FORCE
WEDNESDAY
JULY 31st

5

6

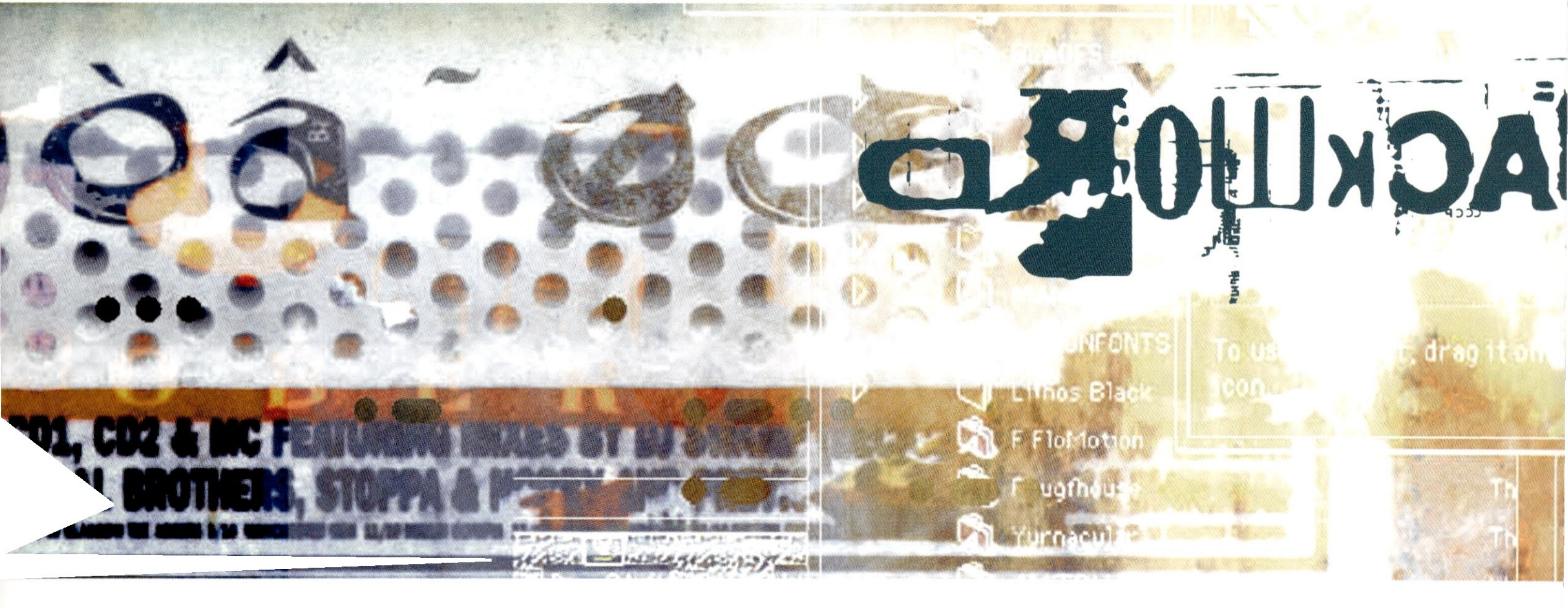

Typography? You cats floor me. Once again focusing on the wrong damn thing. Listen, The life, like some grand king of the roller derby, should lord over the manifestation of all forms of our expression. Let the life lived give rise to this shit. You can't buy it in a can, and you won't find it between the sheets of no book. Did species nautilus find the blueprints for his waxy armor in the bible? [Look, that corkscrew shell weren't no act of plagiarism, dig?] That mollusk had no choice. Nobody held a gun to his tiny head, he grew that shit from the depths of his soul and from the syncopated rhythm of his DNA. Can't say it more plainly. All this voodoo be nothin' but doo-doo, without a natural original-gangster-mac-daddy growth scheme.

I think the issue examined from the perspective of "Typography" is completely inane. Look in the mirror. See that mass of hair (or lack thereof) plastered to your head? That's typography. Yea, you can cut it, dye it, flop it, weave it, but all the mouse in the world ain't going to get you no Pantene™ endorsement deal, cause you ain't no Selma Heyak™. The point? The point would be don't let your left hand know what the hell your right had is doing. Live that shit. Breathe that shit, and let your ideas manifest themselves like some big-assed sea turtle laying mad eggs. A sea turtle rutting, grunting and kicking sand. Reject that flunky homo sapien simu-lectual posturing. Reject that australopithecus man proto-hunchback art brute shit. Be natural like little flowers growing wild in a summer field. Be natural, stupid like moss or skunks are stupid, dig? If we must discuss "Type," let's discuss it like the crows living high above our heads in the canopy. High above our earthbound feet, our un-feathered lives.

Elliott Peter Earls 4.21.99

Directory of Designers

Every effort has been made to ensure that this list was correct at time of going to press.

2Rebels
4623, Harvard
Montréal (Québec)
H4A 2X3 CANADA
P 514 481 0984
F 514 486 8657
info@2rebels.com
www.2rebels.com

Alias
Gareth Hague
23-25 Great Sutton St.
Clerkenwell
London ECIV OND, UK
P 0171 - 608 1967
F 0171 608 1969

Gill Arnò
506 Grand Street /#1
Brooklyn, NY 11211, USA
P 718 - 486 5391
F 718 - 599 7560
gill@interport.net
www.trans-form.net/fly

Jill Bell
428 First Street
Manhattan Beach, CA 90266, USA
P 310-322-5542
F 310 640-0819
jill@jillbell.com
www.jillbell.com

boyz and girls
Anselm Dästner
60 Avenue B / #2
New York, NY 10009, USA
P 212 - 260 8764
F 212 - 260 0716
ans@flyernyc.com

Halvor Bodin
Union Design
Box 4284 Torshov
N-0401 Oslo
Bentsebrugata 20, NORWAY
P +47 22040850
F +47 22715899
hal@union.no
www.uniondesign.com
www.katode.org

Marcus Burlile
Raw Types
P.O. Box 12131
Burke, VA 22009, USA
P 703 - 660 4982
F 703 - 361 4586

Margo Chase Design
2255 Bancroft Avenue
Los Angeles, CA 90039, USA
P 323 668 1055
F 323 668 2470

Chester
162 Buckley
Barrington Hills, IL 60010, USA
P 847 - 3816942
chestergim@aol.com

Chank
The Chank Company
P.O. Box 580736
Minneapolis, MN 55458, USA
P 612 - 782 2245
F 612 - 782 1958
www.chank.com

Elliott Peter Earls
The Apollo Program
82 East Elm Street
Greenwich, CT 06830, USA
P 203.861.7075
elliott@theapolloprogram.com
www.theapolloprogram.com

fontboy.com
Aufuldish & Warinner
Bob Aufuldish & Kathy Warinner
183 the Alameda
San Anselmo, CA 94960, USA
P 415 - 721 7921, 415 - 721 7920
F 415 - 721 7965
bobauf@well.com
www.fontboy.com

Patrick Giasson
Behaviour Design
10 rue Duke
Montréal (Québec)
CANADA H3C 2L7
P 514 - 879 3339
F 514 - 879 3362

Hale & Co
James Hale
180 NE 39th Street, Suite 221
Miami, FL 33137, USA
P 305 - 438 1805
F 305 - 438 1806
haleco@thenet.net

Torgeir Holm
Union Design
Box 4284 Torshov
N-0401 Oslo
Bentsebrugata 20, NORWAY
P +47 - 22 04 08 50
F + 47 - 22 71 58 99
torgeir@union.no
www.uniondesign.com
www.katode.org

Geoff Kaplan
General Working Group
3203 Glendale Boulevard
Los Angeles, CA 90039, USA
P 323 - 906 0063
F 323 - 906 0017
geoff@generalworkinggroup.com
www.generalworkinggroup.com

Christian Küsters
Acme Fonts
4 Regent House
109-111 Britannia Walk
London N1 7ND, UK
P +44 71 490 7877
F +44 71 490 8442
acmefonts@chkdesign.demon.co.uk

Pablo Medina
51 St. Marks Pl. /#11
New York, NY 10003, USA
P 212 - 254 2081

Javier Michalski
20 Clinton Street / #2E
New York, NY 10002, USA
P 212 - 473 0786
javier@bway.net

Plazm
Joshua Berger, Niko Courtelis, Pete McCracken
Box 2863
Portland, OR 97208, USA
P 503 - 222 6389
F 203 - 222 6356
editor@plazm.com
www.plazm.com

Prototype Experimental Foundry
Charles Wilkin
2318 North High #9
Columbus, OH 43202, USA
P 614 - 447 8103
F 614 - 447 8104
ideasare@aol.com

Psy/Ops
Rodrigo Cavazos
923 Folsom / #5
San Francisco, CA 94107, USA
P 415 - 896 5788
F 415 - 896 2290
rxc@psyops.com
www.psyops.com

Magnus Rakeng
Millimeter Design
Sagveien 23F
0458 Oslo, NORWAY
P +47 22 80 6900
F +47 22 80 6901

Darren Scott
Typographic Consultant
McCann-Erickson Manchester, UK
T+44 (0) 01625 822473
F +44 (0) 01625 822499
darren_scott@europe.mccann.com

Angus R. Shamal
ARS Design
Van Der Hoopstraat 39
1051 VB Amsterdam, THE NETHERLANDS
P / F +31 20 6864790
arsdsign@euronet.nl
www.euronet.nl/~arsdsign

David Shields
48 Montgomery Place
Brooklyn, NY 11215, USA
P 718 - 230 7131
dawash@aol.com

Spunk
Jeff Johnson
Sweet 507, 718 N.Washington Avenue
Minneapolis, MN 55401, USA
T 612 904 0541
spunk@bitstream.net
www.spunknation.com
www.handlines.com

[T-26] Digital Type Foundry
Carlos Segura
1110 North Milwaukee Avenue, 1st Fl.
Chicago, IL 60622, USA
P 773 - 862 1201
F 773 - 862 1214
t26font@aol.com
www.t26font.com

Greg Thompson
Mount Dora, FL, USA
greg@gregthompson.com
www.gregthompson.com

Dirk Uhlenbrock
Signalgrau Designbureau
Ladenspelderstr. 42
D-45147 Essen, GERMANY
P +49 201 730511
F +49 201 730521
post@signalgrau.com
www.signalgrau.com

Delve Withrington
Delve Media Arts
P.O. Box 641053
San Francisco, OH 94164-1053, USA
phone: 415.441.0743
fax: 415.474.0762
website: www.delvemediarts.com
email: delve@delvemediarts.com

Don Zinzell
art direction + graphic design
228 West Houston Street, 4th Fl.
New York, NY 10014, USA
T 212-243-9805
F 212-243-9806
zinzell@interport.net
www.zinzell.com